TRANSACTIONS

of the

American Philosophical Society

Held at Philadelphia for Promoting Useful Knowledge

VOLUME 77, Part 2, 1987

The Conseil Privé and the Parlements in the Age of Louis XIV: A Study in French Absolutism

ALBERT N. HAMSCHER

Kansas State University

THE AMERICAN PHILOSOPHICAL SOCIETY

Independence Square, Philadelphia

1987

Library of Congress Catalog
Card Number 86-72879
International Standard Book Number 0-87169-772-6
US ISSN 0065-9746

For Claire

First page of an *arrêt contradictoire* in a case of *évocation de justice*, 20 March 1685 (V⁶ 686, no. 38) (courtesy of Archives Nationales, Paris)

PREFACE

In several respects, this study is a sequel to one I published a decade ago, *The Parlement of Paris After the Fronde, 1653-1673* (Pittsburgh, 1976). In that book, I explored the nature of "royal absolutism"—its achievements as well as its limitations—by tracing the monarchy's relations with its leading court of law during the decades immediately following the civil wars of the mid-seventeenth century. Concentrating on a limited time period enabled me to examine in detail not only the family backgrounds, marriages, and official sources of income of Louis XIV's highest judges, but also their political activities, their response to judicial reform, and their methods of acquiring and transmitting offices. In one sense, this study is broader in scope, encompassing the entire reign of Louis XIV and all the parlements of the realm. But in another sense it is more narrowly focused: my intention here is to investigate the impact of royal policy on the judicial authority of the parlements as revealed in their relations with the king's councils, notably the one that specialized in judicial affairs, the Conseil Privé. This is above all a study of the evolution of conciliar jurisprudence and judicial procedure, as much an exercise in what the French call "l'histoire du droit" as an opportunity to observe in a novel way the resolution of some of the most pressing political problems in the Age of Louis XIV. But the overall aim of both projects is the same: to understand the practical consequences of royal absolutism for the kingdom's highest judicial institutions.

This study may be read on two levels. The text itself is tightly organized and argued, containing enough examples and technical information to illustrate and defend the major conclusions. For the interested specialist, however, I have included additional technical information—much of it pertaining to the details of conciliar procedures and the interpretation of archival sources—in the footnotes. I hope that this material will be as useful to future scholars as any interpretation of events and developments I can offer.

Over the years, many scholars have helped me in my research. I plan to thank them all in future work. For this particular project, however, I must single out some for special thanks. Richard Golden, Sarah Hanley, and John Hurt generously sacrificed some of their own valuable time in France to photocopy documents and even to consult for me some obscure works. Professor Hurt and William Beik were always willing to discuss with me subjects concerning the provinces they know best, Brittany and Languedoc respectively. Professor Hanley read the entire manuscript with a discerning eye. Friends and colleagues at Kansas State University—Burt Kaufman, John McCulloh, Don Nieman, Don Mrozek, Ken Jones, and Mike

Ossar—offered helpful suggestions on matters of organization and style. Most of all, I thank Michel Antoine for his interest in my work and his help on many occasions. I pestered this generous and brilliant scholar in every way—by letter, on the phone, in the corridors of the Bibliothèque Nationale, even at the dinner table. Always and without hesitation he shared with me his vast knowledge of council life in the Old Regime; never did he make me feel like a supplicant, although that is in fact what I was. I would never even have contemplated undertaking this study without the opportunity to tap his expertise. In return, I can only offer him my profound gratitude and respect. Finally, I dedicate this book to my companion since 1972, Claire Dehon. A busy scholar herself, she always found the time to give useful advice and to bring her exquisite knowledge of the French language to bear on difficult documents and texts. This book will occupy little shelf space. But that space, like my life itself, would be empty were it not for her.

Grants and fellowships from Kansas State University, the National Endowment for the Humanities, and the American Philosophical Society (Johnson Fund) made possible the research and writing of this volume.

A.N.H.   April 1986

CONTENTS

I. INTRODUCTION

Students of Louis XIV's France have increasingly recognized the need for balanced and nuanced interpretations of the domestic absolutism associated with the Sun King's personal rule, 1661–1715. The most traditional image of Louis in those years as the personification of Hobbes's Leviathan loses some of its luster when viewed from the vantage point of detailed studies of the reign. In many areas of national life, determined efforts by the king and his ministers to eradicate the disorder of the civil wars of mid-century and to provide the realm with a more efficient administration and regulated economy often ended in failure and frustration. A number of individual policies and broad programs of reform were abandoned or significantly modified under the impact of local opposition, foreign entanglements and war finance, and the inertia resulting from those large, "structural" forces of history that so limited the ability of any seventeenth-century government to accomplish fundamental change. Even the leading personalities at the center of power, the king included, approached the daily conduct of affairs in a more flexible and restrained way than historians several generations ago suspected. To acknowledge the various limitations of absolutism is not to deny its genuine achievements, which were many; it simply compels us to appreciate that both qualities were inherent in the process of expanding state power during the *grand siècle*.[1]

Recognizing the existence of these "two sides of absolutism" is especially important when considering the monarchy's relations with its judicial institutions. In the decades before Louis assumed direct responsibility for state affairs, judicial officials at every level—notably those in the most prestigious sovereign courts, the *parlements*—were among the most vocal opponents of a broad range of royal financial and administrative policies they perceived as jeopardizing their wealth, functions, and prestige.[2] During

---

[1] These generalizations emerge from the entire corpus of recent research on the reign of Louis XIV; the limits of absolutism have an important place even in recent synthetic and interpretive treatments of the reign in both French and English. See, for example, Robin Briggs, *Early Modern France, 1560–1715* (Oxford, 1977), 145–146, 160–161; P. J. Coveney, ed., *France in Crisis, 1620–1675* (London, 1977), 41–58; Pierre Goubert, *Louis XIV and Twenty Million Frenchmen*, trans. Anne Carter (New York, 1966), 137–144, 305–307; Andrew Lossky, "The Absolutism of Louis XIV: Reality or Myth?," *Canadian Journal of History* 19 (1984): 1–15; Robert Mandrou, *La France aux XVIIe et XVIIIe siècles* (Paris, 1970), 212–221; and David Parker, *The Making of French Absolutism* (London, 1983), chap. 4.

[2] See, for example: Richard Bonney, *Political Change in France Under Richelieu and Mazarin, 1624–1661* (Oxford, 1978); Albert N. Hamscher, *The Parlement of Paris After the Fronde, 1653–1673* (Pittsburgh, 1976); Sharon Kettering, *Judicial Politics and Urban Revolt in Seventeenth-Century France: The Parlement of Aix, 1629–1659* (Princeton, 1978); idem, "The Causes of the

the civil wars of the Fronde (1648–1653), many of the judges in the largest and most influential of these courts, the Parlement of Paris, had boldly asserted for their tribunal a legitimate constitutional role to approve and supervise royal actions and to participate with the king in the solution of national problems. But the defeat of the Fronde did not enable the monarchy to run roughshod over its former critics in the law courts. However much the king and his ministers aspired to silence judicial opposition in subsequent decades and to erode still further the traditional restraints on the exercise of royal power, they possessed neither the resources nor the assurance of widespread support to ignore completely the vested interests of the judges or to restructure judicial institutions in a fundamental way. As a result, royal control of the high judiciary in the second half of the seventeenth century depended as much upon compromise and skillful management as upon overt acts of discipline and administrative innovation.

For a number of reasons, however, themes other than conflict and confrontation in the crown's relations with the parlements are difficult to appreciate. The bitter controversies of the Richelieu and Mazarin years—indeed, the general orientation of much historical writing on the first half of the century around "crisis" themes—can easily obscure the role that accommodation, consensus, and good will played during Louis XIV's personal rule. Moreover, the imposing length of Louis's reign, the very number of parlements in *ancien régime* France (12 by 1715, in addition to three provincial "sovereign councils" that exercised parlementary authority in their areas of jurisdiction), and the abundance of documents available for study further complicate efforts to discern those features of royal policy toward established institutions that emerged only gradually and without great drama or contention.[3] Most important, historians have traditionally assessed the fate of the parlements after 1661 in terms of the waning political influence of these courts and their often ruthless exploitation as sources of revenue to finance France's foreign wars.[4] But one need not deny the sig-

---

Judicial Frondes," *Canadian Journal of History* 17 (1982): 275–306; and A. Lloyd Moote, *The Revolt of the Judges: The Parlement of Paris and the Fronde, 1643–1652* (Princeton, 1971). The historical literature on the Fronde rebellions often refers to the crown's conflicts with the parlements. See the bibliographies in Moote's study and in Albert N. Hamscher, "Ouvrages sur la Fronde parus en anglais depuis 1970," *XVIIe Siècle* no. 145 (1984): 380–383.

[3] The 12 parlements in order of their creation were: Paris (1254?), Toulouse (1443), Grenoble (1453), Bordeaux (1462), Dijon (1477), Rouen (1499), Aix-en-Provence (1501), Rennes (1554), Pau (1620), Metz (1633), Besançon (1676), and Tournai (1686; a *conseil souverain* since 1668; in Douai after 1713). The *conseils souverains* were those of Roussillon (1660), Artois (1677; technically, a *conseil provincial* enjoying parlementary powers in criminal matters only), and Alsace (1679). The other sovereign courts were the Parisian *Cour des Aides, Chambre des Comptes, Grand Conseil,* and *Cour des Monnaies* as well as their counterparts, if any, in the provinces.

[4] Despite the paucity of detailed scholarship on the parlements after 1661, their reduced political role is one of the most durable themes in the historiography of Louis XIV's reign. The theme certainly figures prominently in the pertinent sections of the standard and most widely consulted histories of these tribunals: C.-B.-F. Boscheron Des Portes, *Histoire du Parle-*

nificance of these developments to recognize that interpretations resting exclusively on the most striking examples of the resurgence of royal authority risk both exaggerating the decline of the parlements during Louis's reign and overemphasizing the degree of coercion in the monarchy's relations with its highest judges. After all, the parlements were first and foremost courts of law; their primary responsibility was to serve as the leading appellate tribunals of the realm, judging both civil and criminal litigation in last resort. So long as the monarchy's approach toward this aspect of the *parlementaires'* activities and interests remains unclear, our understanding of the nature of royal absolutism and its impact on the parlements will be incomplete and distorted.

Without question, a comprehensive view of the evolution of royal policies regarding the judicial authority of the parlements after 1661 must await the systematic study of a number of large and related issues: the origins, formulation, and enforcement of the celebrated "reformation of justice" of the 1660s and 1670s that produced, among other legislative acts, the famous codes of civil (1667) and criminal (1670) procedure; the way in which those who presided over the major domestic services of the state— chancellors, secretaries of state, and controllers general of finances—as well as provincial agents like the *intendants* dealt on a daily basis with matters of judicial importance and with the courts themselves; and the judicial activities of the various councils that together comprised the hub of royal administration, the *Conseil du Roi*.[5] But by focusing on one aspect of the problem—the relations between the parlements and a single royal council, the *Conseil Privé*—and this with attention to developments spanning the entire period of Louis's personal rule, we can observe how absolutism worked in practice regarding several issues of crucial importance to the kingdom's highest courts of law. This is true not simply because the Conseil Privé was the most specialized of all the royal councils in judicial affairs and thus dealt with the parlements on a regular basis. Equally im-

---

ment de Bordeaux depuis sa création jusqu'à sa chute (1451–1790) (2 vols.; Bordeaux, 1877); Jean-Baptiste Dubédat, *Histoire du Parlement de Toulouse* (2 vols.; Paris, 1885); Amable Floquet, *Histoire du Parlement de Normandie* (7 vols.; Rouen, 1840–1842); Ernest-Désiré Glasson, *Le Parlement de Paris, son rôle politique depuis le règne de Charles VII jusqu'à la Révolution* (2 vols.; Paris, 1901); E.-F. de Lacuisine, *Le Parlement de Bourgogne depuis son origine jusqu'à sa chute* (3 vols.; Dijon, 1864); Emmanuel Michel, *Histoire du Parlement de Metz* (Paris, 1845); and J. H. Shennan, *The Parlement of Paris* (Ithaca, 1968). The most recent and best work in the "absolutist" tradition is by John J. Hurt: "The Parlement of Brittany and the Crown, 1665–1675," *French Historical Studies* 4 (1966): 411–433; "La Politique du Parlement de Bretagne (1661–1675)," *Annales de Bretagne* 81 (1974): 105–130; and "Les Offices au Parlement de Bretagne sous le règne de Louis XIV: Aspects financiers," *Revue d'Histoire Moderne et Contemporaine* 23 (1976): 3–31. For the development of ceremonial issues of constitutional importance over a long time period, see Sarah Hanley, *The Lit de Justice of the Kings of France: Constitutional Ideology in Legend, Ritual, and Discourse* (Princeton, 1983).

[5] In a book dealing with Louis XIV's judicial reforms, I intend to explore each of these issues in detail.

portant, this council played a prominent role in the controversies that divided the parlements and the central administration in the years before and immediately following the Fronde. These controversies frequently centered on the judicial activities of the *parlementaires* and on the extent to which superior authorities were entitled to review their legal decisions and to interfere with their caseloads. Tracing the resolution of the conflicts between the parlements and the Conseil Privé will not only enhance our understanding of how judicial elites fared in the "Age of Absolutism," but it will reveal important patterns in the crown's administrative conduct that have received insufficient attention in the literature on the reign.

II. THE ADVERSARIES AND THE ISSUES OF CONTENTION

Despite the frequency of its sessions, the preservation of many of its records, and its status as the oldest of the permanent royal councils, the Conseil Privé has attracted little scholarly attention and no historian has investigated in depth its activities during the seventeenth century.[1] This neglect stems in large measure from the fact that by the era of the Bourbon kings, the Conseil Privé had become only a lesser or secondary council in the service of the monarchy. At the summit of conciliar organization stood the more illustrious *conseils de gouvernement*, so called

---

[1] For an overview of the king's councils in the seventeenth and eighteenth centuries, see: Noël Valois, ed., *Inventaire des arrêts du conseil d'état (règne de Henri IV)* (2 vols.; Paris, 1866–1893), 1: introduction; Roland Mousnier, "Le Conseil du roi de la mort de Henri IV au gouvernement personnel de Louis XIV," *Etudes d'Histoire Moderne et Contemporaine* 1 (1947): 29–67 (reprinted in his *La Plume, la faucille et le marteau* [Paris, 1970], 141–178); Arthur Michel de Boislisle, *Les Conseils du roi sous Louis XIV* (Paris, 1884); and Michel Antoine, *Le Conseil du roi sous le règne de Louis XV* (Genève, 1970). None of these works concentrates primarily on the Conseil Privé, but they all contain valuable factual information and interpretive insights about this and the other councils. Antoine's work is clearly the best: firmly rooted in archival sources, it provides a fine recapitulation of the major developments in council life during Louis XIV's reign (see pp. 43–77), and throughout it makes useful references to the seventeenth century. The studies by Mousnier and Boislisle rely heavily on published memoirs and the regulatory acts for the councils; whenever possible, the opinions of these authors should be verified in manuscript sources. Other useful studies of broad scope include: Julien Coudy, *Les Moyens d'action de l'ordre du clergé au conseil du roi (1561–1715)* (Paris, 1955); Christian Jouhaud, "Le Conseil du roi, Bordeaux et les Bordelais (1579–1610, 1630–1680)," *Annales du Midi* 93 (1981): 377–396; Roland Mousnier et al., *Le Conseil du roi de Louis XII à la Révolution* (Paris, 1970); and Roland Mousnier, *Les Institutions de la France sous la monarchie absolue* (2 vols.; Paris, 1974–1980), 2: 132–179. For the decades preceding Louis XIV's personal rule, see in particular: Ruth Kleinman, "Changing Interpretations of the Edict of Nantes: The Administrative Aspect, 1643–1661," *French Historical Studies* 10 (1978): 541–571; Georges Pagès, "Le Conseil du roi sous Louis XIII," in his *Etudes sur l'histoire administrative et sociale de l'ancien régime* (Paris, 1938), 7–38; and Orest Ranum, *Richelieu and the Councillors of Louis XIII: A Study of the Secretaries of State and Superintendents of Finance in the Ministry of Richelieu, 1635–1642* (Oxford, 1963). For the reign of Louis XIV, three useful studies are: Cynthia A. Dent, "The Council of State and the Clergy During the Reign of Louis XIV: An Aspect of the Growth of Royal Absolutism," *Journal of Ecclesiastical History* 24 (1973): 245–266; Gary Bruce McCollim, "The Formation of Fiscal Policy in the Reign of Louis XIV: The Example of Nicolas Desmaretz, Controller General of Finances (1708–1715)," (Unpublished Ph.D. dissertation, Ohio State University, 1979); and Thomas J. Schaeper, *The French Council of Commerce, 1700–1715* (Columbus, 1983). Two studies dealing with the eighteenth century that also contain useful information on developments during the seventeenth are Michel Antoine, *Le Conseil royal des finances au XVIIIe siècle et le registre E 3659 des Archives Nationales* (Genève, 1973), and Jacques Phytilis, *Justice administrative et justice déléguée au XVIIIe siècle: L'Exemple des commissions extraordinaires de jugement à la suite du conseil* (Paris, 1977). Still other works, narrower in focus, will be cited throughout this study.

5

because the king sat personally on these bodies with various combinations of his highest officials and other principal advisers.[2]

During the period of Louis XIV's personal rule, there were three of these high or governmental councils. The oldest and most prestigious was the *Conseil d'En haut*, which was composed of the king and those individuals who became "ministers" by virtue of his calling them to sit on this body. At any given time after 1661, there were between three and five such ministers, most of whom were chosen among the four secretaries of state (for war, foreign affairs, the king's household, and Protestant affairs). This council dealt primarily with foreign affairs and, during wartime, with military strategy. But it could also consider any domestic matter the king wished to discuss there. The secretary of state for foreign affairs normally reported business.[3]

The king and his ministers also sat in the *Conseil des Dépêches* along with the chancellor, the head (*chef*) of the *Conseil royal des Finances*, and the secretaries of state who were not ministers. This council, which enjoyed a stable existence only since the late 1640s, specialized in domestic affairs and administration. The four secretaries of state usually served as reporters, introducing affairs pertaining to the provinces that fell within their respective departments. The chancellor too could report matters concerning the administration of justice.[4]

The Conseil royal des Finances, the third of the *conseils de gouvernement*, was established in September 1661 shortly after Louis assumed personal rule upon Cardinal Mazarin's death in March of that year. As its name indicates, this council dealt with a broad range of financial affairs, from establishing policy and examining accounts to signing various orders for payment and judging important cases of a financial nature. It was composed of the king, the *chef* of this council, the chancellor (when invited), and three councillors of state (*conseillers d'état*), one of whom had to be an *intendant des finances* (this position being filled after 1665 by the controller general of finances, who served as reporter).[5]

---

[2] For the early parts of this section, which describe Louis XIV's councils in general terms, I have drawn on my own research in conciliar records as well as on the studies cited in the previous note, particularly those by Antoine, Mousnier, Boislisle, McCollim, and Kleinman.

[3] For a list of Louis XIV's ministers, see John C. Rule, ed., *Louis XIV and the Craft of Kingship* (Columbus, 1969), 27. Two published sources that provide valuable insights into the activity of this council at the very beginning and at the end of Louis's personal rule are Jean de Boislisle, ed., *Mémoriaux du conseil de 1661* (3 vols.; Paris, 1905–1907), and Frédéric Masson, ed., *Journal inédit de Jean-Baptiste Colbert, marquis de Torcy, ministre et secrétaire d'état des affaires étrangères pendant les années 1709, 1710 et 1711* (Paris, 1903).

[4] For accurate lists of the chancellors, controllers general of finances, and secretaries of state who served Louis XIV, see Hélion de Luçay, *Les Origines du pouvoir ministériel en France: Les Secrétaires d'état depuis leur institution jusqu'à la mort de Louis XV* (Paris, 1881), appendix. Luçay also reprints documents that describe the departments (including the provinces that fell within them) of the four secretaries of state in 1661, 1669, and 1715.

[5] The precise composition and authority of the *conseils de gouvernement* obviously experienced some changes throughout the seventeenth century. Before 1661, for example, the Conseil d'En haut was at times a larger body than it would become later, it tended to accomplish its

Together, these councils enjoyed a very broad competence, and practically any issue of local or national importance, be it a general statement of policy or the settlement of a specific dispute between individuals or corporate groups, was at least eligible for their consideration. With regard to the parlements in particular, the *conseils de gouvernement* routinely issued decisions, or *arrêts en commandement,* concerning such diverse matters as judicial finances, the internal functioning of the courts, disciplinary actions against individual judges, the resolution of quarrels over jurisdiction or precedence, and the enforcement of judicial legislation.

This is not to imply, however, that *arrêts en commandement* always emerged from formal council sessions. It is true that the Conseil d'En haut met regularly after 1661, as often as three or four times a week. But this council issued few *arrêts,* and in any case its concentration on foreign affairs limited the occasions when it considered matters concerning the parlements. The Conseil royal des Finances also assembled frequently, two or three times a week throughout the period of Louis XIV's personal rule. Nevertheless, the growing authority of the controller general of finances, the expansion of the bureaucratic apparatus at his disposal, and the king's practice of meeting privately with this official meant that the consultative role of this council diminished over time. Many decisions regarding the king's finances, expressed by *arrêts en commandement* and ostensibly coming from this council, were in fact taken elsewhere—in the various services that gravitated around the controller general or in the meetings that the king held with this official. The Conseil royal des Finances often simply ratified or lent its name to policies it had not formulated. As for the Conseil des Dépêches, the number of its formal sessions actually decreased as the reign progressed: meeting twice a week in the 1660s, it assembled only twice a month or less during Louis's final years. The reason for this development was the king's practice of meeting on an individual basis with the secretaries of state and the chancellor; *arrêts en commandement* could emerge from these encounters without consulting the entire council.

Whether *arrêts en commandement* resulted from formal council sessions or from more intimate meetings, however, they nevertheless expressed decisions taken at the highest levels of the central administration between the king and his principal advisers. The king's participation in the formulation of *arrêts en commandement* was in fact assured: in 1661, Louis instructed the secretaries of state, who dispatched these *arrêts* and conserved

---

work in smaller subcommittees, and there is reason to believe that it dealt more routinely with domestic and financial affairs. It and the Conseil des Dépêches also included personages who had no official existence after 1661, such as the first minister and the *surintendant des finances.* Even during Louis XIV's reign, persons who were not officially members of the *conseils de gouvernement* might be summoned to offer advice or to report on a specific matter. A full consideration of all the changes that swept these councils over time is beyond the scope of this study; the reader is referred to the literature cited in this chapter, n. 1, for details on major developments. I will deal with this subject only when it bears directly on the issues explored in this study.

them in their archives, to send off no *arrêt en commandement* without his prior consent. Given the extensive authority of the *conseils de gouvernement* and a predictable overlap of their activities and those of other council bodies, even research aimed specifically at understanding the conduct of the Conseil Privé must occasionally draw upon the *arrêts en commandement*.[6]

Details on the composition, duties, and procedures of the Conseil Privé will emerge throughout this study. Let it suffice to note at this point that compared to the three *conseils de gouvernement*, the Conseil Privé had a more modest membership and limited range of responsibilities. Presided over by the chancellor and composed of councillors of state and masters of requests (*maîtres des requêtes*), the Conseil Privé only very rarely enjoyed the presence of the king and his ministers. Indeed, the king's absence is reflected in the name of this council's decisions—*arrêts simples*. These *arrêts* had the same legal force as the *arrêts en commandement*, but they were dispatched and conserved by special secretaries of the council rather than by the secretaries of state.[7] The Conseil Privé met regularly throughout

---

[6] The *conseils de gouvernement* also used means other than *arrêts* to express their will, including written and oral orders, formal legislation, and administrative correspondence. But for the issues explored in this study, the *arrêts en commandement* are the most important source for tracing the activities of these councils. The *minutes* (original archival versions) of all but a few of these *arrêts* for the period of Louis XIV's personal rule are in Archives Nationales (hereafter AN), E 1712–1982. The *arrêts* are arranged chronologically in four parallel series, each corresponding to a secretary of state; a typical year, then, will have one or more volumes for each secretary of state, and each volume will contain *arrêts* arranged in chronological order. A useful descriptive index of these *arrêts*, 100 manuscript volumes in length and prepared in the eighteenth century, is *Répertoire chronologique et analytique des arrêts du conseil des dépêches des années 1611 à 1710* (hereafter cited as *Répertoire*). This index is currently available on 20 rolls of microfilm from the Service International de Microfilms in Paris; currently catalogued as *inventaire* 50 at the Archives Nationales, it is mentioned in Direction des Archives de France, *Etat des inventaires des Archives Nationales . . . au 1ᵉʳ janvier 1937* (Paris, 1938), 11, no. 35. While the title refers only to the Conseil des Dépêches, the entries in this index (31,685 for the years 1661–1710) actually give the volume reference and a brief description of every *arrêt en commandement* located in *série* E for the years 1611–1710 (thus *all* the *conseils de gouvernement* are represented in the index). As I shall demonstrate in the seventh chapter of this study, this index, whose entries are arranged in chronological order, enables the historian to discern broad patterns in the conduct of the *conseils de gouvernement* and it provides easy access to the original *arrêts*. For other studies that have utilized the index, see Kleinman, "Changing Interpretations of the Edict of Nantes," and Jouhaud, "Le Conseil du roi, Bordeaux et les Bordelais." Note that a careful reading of Michel Antoine, *Le Fonds du conseil d'état du roi aux Archives Nationales* (Paris, 1955), should precede research in all manner of conciliar *arrêts*. This guide reviews the organization of the councils, indicates the location of conciliar documents and their inventories, and describes the different kinds of *arrêts* and their formats. Less informative but still useful is Edmond Esmonin, "Les Arrêts du conseil sous l'ancien régime," in his *Etudes sur la France des XVIIe et XVIIIe siècles* (Paris, 1964), 183–199.

[7] The *minutes* of the *arrêts* of the Conseil Privé for the personal rule of Louis XIV are arranged chronologically in cartons: AN, V⁶ 422–836. Details on these *arrêts* and information about how to interpret them will appear throughout this study. Unfortunately, there is no descriptive index of these documents for the reign of Louis XIV. A modern inventory of this council's *arrêts* from an earlier period is François Dumont, ed., *Inventaire des arrêts du conseil privé (règnes de Henri III et Henri IV)* (2 vols.; Paris, 1969–1971). Note that judgments rendered by the "Conseil de Chancellerie," a *bureau* of the councils created in July 1699 to decide cases

Louis's reign, either once or twice a week, and even a cursory examination of its *arrêts* and the various regulations (*règlements*) guiding its conduct reveals that it accomplished a number of important tasks pertaining to the administration of justice: judging appeals from the sentences and rulings (*ordonnances*) of the provincial intendants in civil matters; resolving disputes concerning provisions for royal offices; settling conflicts over competence or precedence within or between lesser tribunals, and so on. Both before and after 1661, however, its primary responsibility was the adjudication of three matters of judicial procedure and supervision, each of which directly concerned the parlements.

The first entailed ruling on requests for *évocations de justice*, which were changes in venue from one sovereign court to another, or between lesser tribunals subordinate to different sovereign courts, when parties proved that their adversaries had a prohibitive number of relatives sitting as judges in the court of pending litigation. The second involved resolving, by *règlements de juges*, jurisdictional disputes that arose when identical litigation was pending simultaneously either in several sovereign courts or in lesser tribunals subordinate to different sovereign courts.[8] Third, the Conseil Privé was empowered to nullify the civil and criminal judgments that various courts of the realm rendered in last resort. In practice, such *cassation* often pertained to the sentences, or *arrêts*, of the parlements when these courts could be shown to have exceeded their jurisdiction or to have violated royal legislation or private law in judging litigation.[9] Owing to the nature of its work, the Conseil Privé has been referred to variously as "l'organe de la justice retenue" (Mousnier), "la juridiction suprême en matière civile" (Boislisle), and that council which was "spécialisé dans le contentieux ju-

---

pertaining to the *chancelleries*, *librairies*, and *imprimeries* of the realm, could take the form of *arrêts* of the Conseil Privé and thus often can be found in *série V*[6].

[8] When *évocations de justice* and *règlements de juges* pertained to lesser tribunals subordinate to the same sovereign court, this court decided these matters. Note also that the Grand Conseil— a Parisian sovereign court not to be confused with the king's councils—adjudicated certain kinds of *règlements de juges* (between the parlements and the *présidiaux*, for example) and *cassations* (such as those pertaining to judgments of criminal competence rendered in favor of the *présidiaux* and the *prévôts des maréchaux*). Because the activities of the Grand Conseil do not bear directly on the issue of the parlements' relations with the royal councils, they do not figure in this study.

[9] Tribunals that were not sovereign courts but which nevertheless judged certain kinds of cases in last resort included the *présidiaux*, the *prévôtés des maréchaussées*, the *tables de marbre*, and urban courts of commerce (*juridictions consulaires*). The interested reader will find some *cassations* pertaining to these tribunals among the *arrêts* of the Conseil Privé, but not many: *cassations* almost always concerned the sovereign courts (especially the parlements), which routinely judged litigation in last resort. The Conseil Privé also had the authority to rescind its own *arrêts* as well as the judgments rendered by the councils' own *commissions extraordinaires*. Note that in order to avoid confusion in this study, I will use the word *arrêt* to apply only to the decisions of the royal councils. As regards the *arrêts* of the parlements, I will use the words "judgment" and "sentence"; I intend these words to be synonymous (as they are in the broadest sense), applying to both civil and criminal affairs.

diciaire et formait par excellence le domaine des juristes" (Antoine). That contemporaries also called it the *Conseil des Parties* (roughly, the "council of litigants") further indicates that its functions were predominantly judicial rather than executive in nature.

Even the companion council of the Conseil Privé, the *Conseil d'Etat et des Finances,* enjoyed a greater participation in the general administration of the realm. Composed of the same men as the Conseil Privé (with the addition of certain financial officials) but meeting on different days, this council considered a broad range of domestic affairs, notably royal finances (thus its *arrêts* are known as *arrêts simples* "en finance"). This council was an active and important institution in the first half of the seventeenth century, but it gradually ceased functioning during the course of Louis XIV's personal rule. Already meeting infrequently in the 1660s, it disappeared altogether sometime before the mid-1690s. The emergence of the Conseil des Dépêches with its specialization in domestic administration was in part responsible for this development, and the creation of the Conseil royal des Finances in 1661 further reduced the jurisdiction of the Conseil d'Etat et des Finances. The fact that the controller general of finances and the officials who worked under his direction could decide among themselves many issues of a financial nature also eliminated the necessity to convene this council.

But the public was never officially notified of this change, and *arrêts simples* "en finance" continued to be issued in great quantity throughout Louis's reign. Both before and after the disappearance of the Conseil d'Etat et des Finances, these *arrêts* emanated from other council bodies that participated in the administration of the king's revenues: the Conseil royal des Finances, which issued *arrêts simples* "en finance" as well as *arrêts en commandement;* and two subcommittees of the Conseil d'Etat et des Finances that survived its demise—the *Grande* and *Petite Directions.*[10] Another important source of these *arrêts* became the meetings that the king held with the controller general and that this official held in turn with his principal collaborators, notably the *intendants des finances* and, after 1708, the *intendants de commerce.* Although as a general rule the *arrêts simples* "en finance" issued during the period of Louis XIV's personal rule did not decide cases pertaining to the judicial activities of the parlements, they

---

[10] During Louis XIV's personal rule, the Grande Direction was composed of the chancellor, the members of the Conseil royal des Finances (except for the king), the *intendants des finances,* the masters of requests, and the councillors of state who sat on the financial *bureaux* of the councils. Smaller in size, the Petite Direction comprised the *chef* of the Conseil royal, the controller general, the *intendants des finances,* the *gardes* of the *Trésor Royal,* and certain masters of requests and councillors of state. Known as *commissions ordinaires* of the councils, the two Directions judged certain cases of a financial nature and accomplished technical duties involving financial administration. According to Antoine, however, these bodies played only a "rôle effacé" after the disappearance of the Conseil d'Etat et des Finances: *Le Conseil du roi sous le règne de Louis XV,* 386. For the origins and early history of the Directions, see Mousnier, "Le Conseil du roi," 46–48.

occasionally did so owing to the important place that financial matters occupied in the overall administration of the realm.[11] For this reason, we will have cause to return to these *arrêts*.[12]

If the Conseil Privé was the most specialized of all the royal councils in judicial affairs, it did not act alone in accomplishing even the duties specifically assigned to it. The Conseil Privé certainly decided the great majority of *évocations de justice*, *règlements de juges*, and *cassations* pertaining to the parlements. But all the other council bodies mentioned above considered these matters under certain circumstances. This underscores the need to complement a study of the *arrêts* issued by the Conseil Privé with an examination of the other types of conciliar *arrêts*. When parlementary sentences dealt with royal finances and other public affairs, for example, procedures for *cassation* almost always unfolded at the *conseils de gouvernement*, the Conseil d'Etat et des Finances, and even before this latter body disappeared, at the various services attached to the controller general of finances. Even when the parlements judged strictly private litigation between contesting parties, requests for *cassation* that administrative logic would dictate belonged before the Conseil Privé occasionally came instead before other council bodies. Nothing prevented the king, a minister, or the Conseil Privé itself from sending noteworthy cases of *cassation* of whatever nature to other sections of the king's council for resolution.

Cases of *évocation de justice* and *règlement de juges* concerning the parlements were almost exclusively decided by the Conseil Privé. But other councils dealt with these subjects from time to time because a degree of fluidity in administrative responsibility characterized most aspects of royal government at the highest levels. Far more important, the Conseil Privé rarely granted the most controversial *évocations*, those that withdrew cases from the courts either as a favor to influential persons or because a particular case or entire category of litigation was deemed to be sufficiently important

---

[11] The *minutes* of the *arrêts simples* "en finance" issued between September 1661 and September 1715 are arranged chronologically in AN, E 348^B–879. A descriptive index for these *arrêts* (whose entries are also arranged chronologically)—AN, E 1683$^{29-187}$—is less complete and much less detailed than the *Répertoire* for the *arrêts en commandement* discussed above in this chapter, n. 6. For a recent discussion of these *arrêts* and their index, see Gary Bruce McCollim, "Council Versus Minister: The Controller General of Finances, 1661–1715," *Proceedings of the Annual Meeting of the Western Society for French History* 6 (1978): 67–75, as well as his "The Formation of Fiscal Policy," 92–101. For a remarkable use of these *arrêts* to explore royal financial policies in the first half of the seventeenth century, see Richard Bonney, *The King's Debts: Finance and Politics in France, 1589–1661* (Oxford, 1981), as well as his *Political Change in France*. Daniel Dessert has made an exhaustive examination of these *arrêts* in order to investigate the activities of financiers during Louis XIV's reign: *Argent, pouvoir et société au grand siècle* (Paris, 1984). In the seventh chapter of this study, I shall give the results of some sampling of these *arrêts*.

[12] In addition to the principal councils discussed above, a variety of assemblies, *bureaux*, *commissions ordinaires* and *extraordinaires*, and temporary councils were an integral part of conciliar organization in the seventeenth and eighteenth centuries. The literature cited above in this chapter, n. 7, provides details on these "satellite" bodies serving the various councils, and I shall return to them as the need arises.

or politically sensitive to warrant a change of judges. These *évocations*, which were granted either on the request of parties (*évocations de grâce*) or on the king's own initiative (*évocations de propre mouvement*), were in fact executive acts of pure royal will having little or nothing to do with the family ties between litigants and their judges (the basis for *évocations de justice*). As a result, they are normally found among the *arrêts en commandement* and the *arrêts simples* ''en finance'' rather than among the *arrêts* of the Conseil Privé.

The action of the Conseil Privé was restricted in still other ways. At all times during the *ancien régime*, the parlements exercised considerable judicial powers within their areas of jurisdiction. They routinely regulated the conduct of lesser magistrates, revised civil and criminal sentences on appeal, and settled jurisdictional conflicts in the lesser courts—and all this normally with little interference from central authorities. Indeed, the Conseil Privé seldom acted on its own initiative. Unless litigants (and, on occasion, the king or royal officials) solicited proceedings, the Conseil Privé did not concern itself with the judicial business of the kingdom's many tribunals. Moreover, at least in theory the Conseil Privé was not a rival of the parlements and other sovereign courts, competing with them as an ordinary court of law. Its principal responsibility was to supplement their activities by resolving certain procedural matters that the judges simply lacked the authority to settle on their own. This role was most evident in cases of *évocation de justice* and *règlement de juges:* only a superior authority could resolve jurisdictional disputes arising at the highest level of the ordinary judiciary or in lesser tribunals subordinate to different sovereign courts. With regard to *cassations*, which were instead acts of discipline, we shall see that few legal grounds justified contesting the validity of a sovereign court's sentences before any of the king's councils. There even existed a judicial procedure, known as *requête civile*, that enabled the sovereign courts in certain well defined circumstances to rescind their own judgments in last resort without conciliar intervention.

Given the various limits of its jurisdiction in relation to that of the other councils and of the courts themselves, the Conseil Privé might have become a candidate for historical obscurity had not the legal actions in which it specialized offered numerous possibilities for conflict with the sovereign courts. This potential for conflict was especially clear in the decades before Louis XIV assumed personal rule, when the parlements and the governments of Cardinals Richelieu and Mazarin clashed frequently over judicial issues. For as the *parlementaires* of those years drew upon all their powers— including the judgment of litigation—to block the implementation of a broad range of royal financial and administrative policies, the councils naturally responded to this opposition by changing the venue of sensitive litigation, by resolving jurisdictional disputes in favor of more compliant judges, and by nullifying the judicial sentences and administrative acts of the parlements. The Conseil Privé participated with the other councils in these activities. As its role of adversary in the judicial life of the parlements expanded, its conduct became an important part of a larger controversy concerning the proper spheres of authority of the king's leading institutions. The general contours of the disputes between the parlements and the councils before 1661 are now known.[13] But a brief review of the principal issues of contention will provide the context necessary for understanding later developments.

Confronted with the judicial opposition of the parlements, the councils considered *évocations* to be a convenient way to remove controversial litigation from potentially recalcitrant judges.[14] When changes in venue resulted from the family ties between litigants and magistrates, and when a case once withdrawn from one parlement was then sent to another, the judges rarely complained because these arrangements were firmly rooted in the great ordinances of the sixteenth century and in the *règlements* of the councils themselves. But the *parlementaires* perceived a threat to their jurisdiction and to established law when *évocations de justice* seemed to lack sound legal justification. Moreover, the parlements were almost certain to protest when any council, for whatever reason, removed cases from the parlements only to retain final jurisdiction over the litigation in question or to transfer it to more docile instruments of the royal will, such as specially constituted commissions, the provincial intendants, or the tribunal of the councils' own masters of requests—the *Requêtes de l'Hôtel*.[15] As regards

---

[13] For an overview of these conflicts, see: Mousnier, "Le Conseil du roi," 60–67; idem, *Les Institutions de la France*, 2: bk. 8, chaps. 1–3; Moote, *The Revolt of the Judges*, 33, 85–86, 120–121; and Hamscher, *The Parlement of Paris After the Fronde*, 98–107. These works concentrate on the Parlement of Paris, but we shall see that opposition to the councils was not confined to that court alone. The standard histories of the parlements (see above, chap. I, n. 4) all provide examples of disputes between the parlements and the councils before 1661, but usually in an anecdotal fashion. Only additional research on the provincial parlements before 1661 will place these conflicts within the broader context of the judges' other grievances, which often reflected diverse local circumstances. Such has been done well, for example, in three studies by Sharon Kettering: "The Causes of the Judicial Frondes"; *Judicial Politics and Urban Revolt*, 97–99, 274; and "A Provincial Parlement During the Fronde: The Reform Proposals of the Aix Magistrates," *European Studies Review* 11 (1981): 151–169. See also Paul Logié, *La Fronde en Normandie* (3 vols.; Amiens, 1951–1952), 1: 37–38, and William Beik, *Absolutism and Society in Seventeenth-Century France: State Power and Provincial Aristocracy in Languedoc* (Cambridge, 1985), 77–85, 163–166, 193–194. I thank Professor Beik for allowing me to consult portions of this study before its publication.

[14] The following paragraphs are based on the works cited in the previous note as well as on memoranda in which the judges themselves expressed their grievances: in the papers of Chancellor Pierre Séguier—Bibliothèque Nationale (hereafter BN), *manuscrits français* (hereafter MSS. Fr.) 18467, fols. 212–213, 214–216v (1651: Aix); 17315, fols. 167–173v (1656: Bordeaux); in the "registres civils, conseil secret" of the Parlement of Paris—AN, X^1A 8391, fols. 207v–217v (1658: Paris). Equally informative are extracts from the registers of the Parlement of Paris for 1645 and 1647: AN, U 2098, fols. 335v–352, 453–457v; 2100, fols. 157–159v, 181v–182.

[15] In August 1656, the Parlement of Paris published a compendium of legislation it accused the councils of violating, including the ordinances of 1539 (arts. 34, 109, 170–171), Orléans (1560: arts. 38, 53), Blois (1579: arts. 91–93, 97–99, 109, 117, 121, 135), and the declaration of 22 October 1648: "Articles, édits et déclarations touchant la jurisdiction du Parlement et la connoissance du conseil privé," BN, Joly de Fleury MS. 1051 (collection on "évocations"), fols. 19–23v. Even *règlements* for the councils recognized the existence of a problem. Those

specifically those instances whereby the councils transferred cases or brought them before a particular council as an expression of the king's sovereign authority—the *évocations de grâce* and *de propre mouvement*—royal legislation actually discouraged the practice.[16] When used sparingly, however, the judges were willing to tolerate it because in theory the king could dispose of important litigation as he saw fit. But the judges asserted that a legitimate right became an abuse of arbitrary power when such *évocations* occurred frequently or when they were granted by lesser councils that the king rarely attended. The parlements were especially hostile toward *évocations générales*, a type of *évocation de grâce* that transferred from one jurisdiction to another *all* litigation, both pending and future, that the concerned parties might have during a specified time period.

The *parlementaires* expressed similar views about *règlements de juges* and *cassations*. If identical litigation was pending simultaneously at several sovereign courts, a council should confine itself to designating one of these courts to hear the case; it should not retain final jurisdiction over the litigation in question or transfer it to judges outside the ordinary judiciary. The same principle applied to *cassations:* if a parlement's judgment warranted nullification, any retrial should occur only at another parlement. On the matter of *cassations* in particular, the parlements also resented the nullification of their sentences solely on the basis of a petitioner's request. In their opinion, nullification should occur only after all the litigants involved in a disputed sentence had received the opportunity to present evidence to the councils. In addition, the parlements objected when a council suspended the enforcement of judgments rendered after full instruction in the courts while it considered the merits of a request for *cassation*. Finally, as a deterrent against chicanery, the judges called for fines against parties who initiated and then lost legal actions at the councils.

Disputes over all these issues formed an important dimension of the conflict between the crown and the parlements in the decades preceding the Fronde. On the eve of civil war, the government of Cardinal Mazarin, under considerable pressure from the law courts, pledged in a declaration of 22 October 1648 to curtail the attacks of the councils on the judicial authority and traditional jurisdiction of the sovereign courts.[17] But the rapid reappearance during the 1650s of many royal programs the parlements had opposed in the past, such as the monarchy's reliance on extraordinary

---

of 21 May 1615 and 18 January 1630 called for the return to the ordinary courts of cases pending before the lesser councils and for the enforcement of existing legislation on *cassations:* Roland Mousnier, ed., "Les Règlements du conseil du roi sous Louis XIII," *Annuaire-Bulletin de la Société de l'Histoire de France* (1946–1947): 93–211 (see pp. 146–148, 150, 184–185, 187).

[16] The judges were fond of citing art. 97 of the ordinance of Blois: "Nous avons déclaré et déclarons, que nous n'entendons d'oresnavant bailler aucunes lettres d'évocation, soient générales ou particulières, de nostre propre mouvement. . . ."

[17] François-André Isambert et al., eds., *Recueil général des anciennes lois françaises depuis l'an 400 jusqu'à la révolution de 1789* (29 vols.; Paris, 1822–1833), 17: 80–81, 92.

financial policies to support the war against Spain, ensured that the quarrels between the parlements and the councils continued unabated. The Parlement of Paris remained the councils' most persistent and vocal critic, at times countermanding conciliar *arrêts* with its own, attempting to bring the masters of requests before the court to explain their conduct in the councils, and forbidding *avocats* and *procureurs* to handle disputed litigation. The number of cases involved was significant: in five memoranda prepared between 1656 and 1660, for example, the Parisian *parlementaires* listed over 200 instances of the various councils ignoring past legislation and encroaching upon their court's rightful jurisdiction since the mid-1640s, a number that even Chancellor Pierre Séguier did not dispute.[18] Nor was this court alone in its protests: fully documented charges of conciliar impropriety came also from the Parlements of Aix, Bordeaux, and Toulouse as well as from the leading financial court of the realm, the *Cour des Aides* of Paris.[19] All the councils were targets of criticism, but the Conseil Privé was especially vulnerable to the courts' hostility because of its close identification with *évocations*, *règlements de juges*, and *cassations*.[20] Louis XIV

---

[18] In Chancellor Séguier's papers: BN, MSS. Fr. 17288, fols. 523–537v; 17315, fols. 104–105v, 106–107, 139–152v (the memorandum on fols. 139–152v is virtually identical to the one in 17288). In a collection dealing with the Parlement of Paris: BN, *manuscrits nouvelles acquisitions françaises* (hereafter n.a.f.) 7982, fol. 334^A–H. For Séguier's comment (I believe the handwriting is his; if not, we are dealing with a report to him), see MSS. Fr. 17288, fol. 445: "Of 200 cases the *gens du roi* have claimed to be in the parlement's jurisdiction, and not in the council's, only 80 have been returned to them, the others having been judged in the council; only 12 or 15 [cases] remain to be adjudicated, and these are being instructed according to the ordinary forms for *évocations* and *règlements de juges*. . . ." The titles of these memoranda are revealing. The one on fols. 104–105v is entitled, "Extrait des principaux arrests cassés par arrest du conseil contre les ordonnances et des procès évoqués et retenus aud. conseil." The one on fols. 139–152v is "Mémoire des principaux arrests du conseil qui ont sursis et cassé plusieurs arrests du Parlement, évoqué, renvoyé et rettenu divers procès contre la teneur et disposition des ordonnances ès années 1651, 52, 53, 54, 55 et présente 1656."

[19] For Aix and Bordeaux, see above, this chapter, n. 14. For Toulouse, see the allusion to difficulties over *évocations générales* in the Bordeaux memorandum, as well as in letters to Séguier by First President Fieubet and by the *parlementaires*, 28 July 1656, in British Library (hereafter BL), Harleian MS. 4490 (part of a collection of Séguier's papers), fols. 38, 40. For the Cour des Aides, see BN, MSS. Fr. 17315, non fol., and Bibliothèque du Sénat (hereafter BS), MS. 904 ("Mémoires de ce qui s'est passé en la Cour des Aydes"), fols. 589 (August 1658) and 635–638 (January 1660).

[20] Mousnier, "Le Conseil du roi," 50, perhaps exaggerates when he refers to the Conseil Privé as "un instrument essentiel de réalisation du pouvoir absolu" (see the comment of Bonney, *Political Change in France*, 21, n. 1), but this council did play an important role in the conflicts with the parlements. While the lists and memoranda prepared by the parlements do not often distinguish between the different councils, they do show by the nature of the cases cited the activity of the Conseil Privé; practices the judges protested can also be found among this council's *arrêts* of the 1640s and 1650s—for example, AN, V^6 215, 319, 325–326 (I shall return to these cartons later in this study). See also the administrative correspondence and working papers of the era, such as Séguier to Le Tellier, 8 August 1656 (BN, MSS. Fr. 6893 [part of a collection of Michel Le Tellier's papers], fols. 240–244) and the anonymous "Discours sur l'authorité des parlemens et du conseil privé du roi" in Séguier's papers (ibid., 17315, fols. 96–103v). When the Parlement of Paris complained about frequent *évocations* in 1645 (see ibid., 18467, fols. 157–160v), Séguier reported the matter to the Conseil Privé: Olivier Lefèvre d'Ormesson, *Journal*, ed. Adolphe Chéruel (2 vols.; Paris, 1860–1861), 1: 245–246.

himself referred specifically to its conduct when he reflected upon this controversy in his memoirs.[21]

The judges certainly defended their vested interests in these quarrels: each case lost to some form of conciliar intervention translated into missing fees and, less tangibly, wounded pride. But constitutional principles were also involved.[22] While acknowledging that the councils legitimately exercised a broad range of executive and administrative functions, the parlements also maintained that these bodies possessed only a limited number of regulatory powers in the daily administration of justice. They enjoyed the status of courts of law only occasionally and incidentally, such as when the king judged sovereignly in a *conseil de gouvernement* or when he made a special delegation of authority with full cognizance of cause. On all other occasions, the resolution of disputes between the king's subjects should occur before their natural and traditional judges, even when controversial royal policies were involved. For their part, defenders of the councils like Chancellor Séguier asserted that the *parlementaires* too frequently used their positions as judges, as they often did their administrative duties and their privilege of registering royal legislation to give it the force of law, to undermine the implementation of policies they opposed and to assume an active and unsolicited participation in the vaguely defined realm of "affairs of state." When this occurred, all the councils possessed full authority to censure such conduct and to deny the courts specific litigation either as a disciplinary or as a preventive measure. Such debates, of course, reflected a larger and more fundamental problem of a "confusion of powers" among the principal organs of royal government. For if the kings of France had historically amplified the jurisdictions of their highest officials according to particular circumstances, one legacy of this eclectic delegation of authority was to bequeath to all the councils and sovereign courts ample precedents to exercise functions the others considered to be part of their own competence. At those times when fundamental disagreements about the direction of royal policy divided the central administration and the law courts, the perennial problem of defining institutional authority gained particularly sharp focus.

In their conflicts with the councils, the parlements raised some persuasive legal arguments in their own defense, an important point for understanding

---

[21] *Mémoires for the Instruction of the Dauphin,* ed. and trans. Paul Sonnino (New York, 1970), 40–41. After briefly reviewing the duties of the Conseil Privé, Louis noted how in the years before he assumed personal rule the parlements "deferred to it only when they saw fit and proceeded every day in all sorts of cases in spite of its prohibitions. . . ."

[22] Constitutional issues appear throughout the documents related to these controversies. They are especially clear in *Avocat Général* Denis Talon's speech before the Parlement of Paris on 6 August 1658 (AN, X[1A] 8391, fols. 207v–217v), in letters of Séguier to Le Tellier and to Mazarin in August 1656 (BN, MSS. Fr. 6893, fols. 264–265v; BL, Harleian MS. 4489, fols. 42–43v), in a remonstrance the masters of requests made to the king in August 1656 (Bibliothèque de l'Institut de France [hereafter BI], Godefroy MS. 182 ["Mélanges sur les parlements"], fols. 123–124), and in an *arrêt* of the Conseil d'En haut, 19 October 1656 (AN, E 1704).

the resolution of the controversy in later years. The judges couched their opposition in moderate terms, never denying any of the councils their traditional regulatory powers or the king his right to intervene in important cases. Rather, they protested what they perceived to be a persistent disregard for procedural formalities and an excessive and seemingly random interference in their judicial business. They then substantiated these claims with citations from past legislation and with references to specific violations. The councils themselves lent support to these grievances because their actions against the courts were not nearly as well planned or as warranted as one might suppose. The principal justification for the councils ignoring procedural rules or modifying the order of jurisdictions was to protect controversial royal policies from a type of judicial review before hostile or undependable judges. It comes as no surprise, then, that many *évocations*, *règlements de juges,* and *cassations* about which the parlements complained concerned such politically sensitive matters as royal taxation, Jansenism, municipal elections, the activity of the provincial intendants, and favors to influential persons in civil and criminal cases. Yet many other instances of arbitrary action by the councils were far less defensible, involving instead either strictly private or minor litigation in which the king's interests even broadly defined were not crucial.

One need not rely upon the historian's intuition or even the parlements' memoranda to draw this distinction. Throughout the 1650s, leading figures in Mazarin's administration acknowledged the legitimacy of many of the judges' complaints. *Surintendant des finances* Nicolas Fouquet and Minister of War Michel Le Tellier favored accommodation with the judges, and even Jean-Baptiste Colbert, at that time the cardinal's personal intendant, conceded the accuracy of the Parlement of Paris's citations from past legislation while at the same time defending the councils' freedom of action.[23] Mazarin himself, who firmly supported the councils in principle, was nevertheless reportedly angry with Séguier on several occasions for allowing matters to get out of hand in the councils over which he presided—the Conseil Privé and the Conseil d'Etat et des Finances.[24] The chancellor, no partisan of the parlements, admitted that errors had occurred in the processing of certain cases, and he even held conferences with the Parisian *parlementaires* to arrange the return of some litigation pending at the coun-

---

[23] BN, Morel de Thoisy MS. 394 (collection on *évocations*), fols. 20–43v (Talon's account of events at the Parlement of Paris between August 1656 and January 1657); Jean-Baptiste Colbert, *Lettres, instructions et mémoires,* ed. Pierre Clément (7 vols.; Paris, 1861–1882), 1: 252–258 (memorandum on *évocations*).

[24] See Talon's account cited in the previous note as well as Jacques Dupuy to Achille II de Harlay, 23 September 1656, BI, Godefroy MS. 274 (miscellaneous letters), fol. 386. In a letter to Mazarin dated 3 January 1659, Colbert recalls the cardinal's opposition to the councils retaining evoked cases for final judgment: Archives du Ministère des Affaires Etrangères (hereafter AAE), *mémoires et documents, France* (hereafter *France*) 907, fol. 1. All citations in this chapter from this series pertain to the collection of correspondence received and dispatched by Cardinal Mazarin.

cils.[25] Several courts benefited from formal orders of remand (*arrêts de renvoi*) to this effect.[26]

Such attempts at compromise did not stem entirely from altruistic motives. They also resulted from a recognition in the highest circles of royal government that whenever the councils acted against the parlements with insufficient regard for legal forms and without a clear rationale of urgency or *raison d'état,* they not only exposed themselves to continuous and bitter quarrels over individual cases, but they jeopardized political stability in general by providing the judges with legitimate grievances on which they could base a more extensive critique of the councils and crown policy.[27] Although the parlements differed in the fervor with which they pressed their grievances against the councils and showed little inclination to co-ordinate their protests, the risks inherent in unnecessarily provoking them were widely appreciated in Mazarin's administration. Surveying the tense Parisian scene in the 1650s, such luminaries as *surintendant des finances* Abel Servien, Séguier, and the cardinal himself feared that deteriorating relations between the councils and the Parlement of Paris might give that court a pretext to incite a new judicial Fronde and to renew old claims for a greater participation in state affairs; this spirit of opposition might then easily spread to other sovereign courts.[28] But efforts to pacify the parlements were far too sporadic and grudging to produce a lasting accommodation. Instead, they had the opposite effect of encouraging the judges to urge for greater concessions, with the result that the controversy remained unresolved when Louis assumed personal rule upon Mazarin's death in March 1661.[29]

Confusion in establishing priorities for conciliar intervention was not, of course, unique to the Conseil Privé, but disorder in that body was con-

---

[25] Séguier to Mazarin, 23 August 1656 and 21 August 1658: AAE, *France* 900, fols. 324–326v; 905, fols. 405–407v.

[26] For example: the Parlement of Paris, 11 January 1657 and 18 August 1658 (AN, X^{1A} 8660 [part of the "registres civils, lettres patentes et ordonnances"], fols. 7–8, 15–17; 8661, fols. 235v–236); the Parlement of Toulouse, 18 May 1656 (a partial repeal of *évocations générales*—AN, E 1706); and the Parisian Cour des Aides, 6 March 1656 and August 1658 (AN, Z^{1A} 164 [part of a collection of copies of "registres secrets"], fol. 179; BS, MS. 904, fol. 590).

[27] The provincial parlements seem to have joined their grievances against the councils to protests about the activity of the provincial intendants and the crown's intervention in matters of local concern, such as municipal elections. In Paris, the judges protested conciliar activity at times when other delicate matters—royal taxes and the renewal of the *droit annuel,* for example—were topics of heated discussion and when, conveniently, royal armies were faring poorly in the field.

[28] See the letters of Séguier to Mazarin and to Le Tellier, Servien to Mazarin, and Mazarin to Tambonneau in August–October 1656: BL, Harleian MS. 4489, fols. 39v, 42–43v; BN, MSS. Fr. 6893, fol. 308; AAE, *France* 274, fol. 162, *France* 291, fols. 260–263v, and *France* 900, fols. 324–326v. See also the letters of Séguier and of Servien to Mazarin, and Mazarin to Séguier in August 1658: AAE, *France* 279, fols. 129–130v; 905, fols. 405–407v, 408–409.

[29] The Parlement of Bordeaux, for example, submitted its memorandum of 1656 after learning that the *parlementaires* of Toulouse had won concessions; the Parlement of Paris pressed for a formal declaration against frequent *évocations* in 1658 after having received the return of several cases pending at the councils.

siderable. The very involvement of this council in conflict with the parlements and other sovereign courts was in itself an ominous development because the bulk of its caseload consisted of matters that by their nature should not have generated serious controversy. After all, many of the more obvious targets for judicial opposition—*cassations* regarding royal finances and *évocations de grâce* and *de propre mouvement*—were normally, even if not always, decided by other councils. The sources of disorder in the Conseil Privé were several. Certainly, years of conflict with the judges had created an atmosphere in this council conducive to indiscriminate action against the parlements. Chancellor Séguier had a long record of hostility toward the pretensions of the sovereign courts, and the masters of requests, who served as reporting magistrates in the Conseil Privé, had quarrelled for decades with the ordinary judiciary about their conduct in the council and about their activities as provincial intendants and as judges in their own tribunal, the Requêtes de l'Hôtel.[30] Indeed, recent research has confirmed the judges' allegation that the masters of requests used their duties as reporters at the Conseil Privé to syphon lucrative litigation from the parlements to the Requêtes de l'Hôtel.[31] As for the councillors of state, many of these men had served as masters of requests, and some of them had undoubtedly felt the sting of parlementary opposition during their own tours as provincial intendants; as a group they seemed willing to tolerate the more questionable actions of their junior colleagues.[32] That certain ministers might have used *arrêts* of the Conseil Privé to help their supporters, and this without consulting the council as a whole, only heightened the perception that this body acted in a capricious fashion.[33]

The size of the Conseil Privé also presented a serious problem. Between June 1624 and May 1657, for example, the number of councillors of state grew from 31 to 144, and the corps of masters of requests expanded from 56 in 1623 to 72 in 1642.[34] Of course, the king had no intention of calling all those with *brevets* of councillor of state to the council, and even those councillors and masters eligible to attend the Conseil Privé did not do so at the same time: the masters of requests served in *quartiers* of three months each, and the councillors of state sat for three, six, or twelve months depending upon their rank of *quadrimestre, semestre,* or *ordinaire*. Nevertheless, the rapid growth of the Conseil Privé generated disputes over precedence

---

[30] On the relations between the *parlementaires* and the masters of requests, see Bonney, *Political Change in France,* passim and especially chap. 11, and C. R. E. Kaiser, "The Masters of Requests: An Extraordinary Judicial Company in an Age of Centralization (1589–1648)," (Unpublished Ph.D. dissertation, University of London, 1977), especially pt. 3, chaps. 1–3. I thank Dr. Kaiser for allowing me to consult and cite his study.

[31] Kaiser, "The Masters of Requests," 326, 376–377, and appendix, graph 2, which shows the increase in the number of judgments in last resort the Requêtes de l'Hôtel rendered between 1618 and 1638.

[32] Such is Kaiser's view: ibid., 330, 343.

[33] Ormesson raises this issue in his *Journal,* 1: 245–247.

[34] Bonney, *Political Change in France,* 21–22, 101.

and made supervision of its activities difficult: in 1644, Séguier complained about the "great confusion and disorder" stemming from the fact that "each day produced a new councillor of state."[35]

Finally, although progress had been made in all the councils during the first half of the century in defining responsibilities and refining methods of work, important points of judicial procedure in the Conseil Privé remained undecided, or at best existing rules lacked rigorous enforcement. Such was the case not only for matters of obvious importance to the parlements—whether the enforcement of their judgments should be suspended during *cassation* proceedings, for example—but also for more routine subjects like assigning reporters, setting firm time limits for initiating various legal actions, and determining the type of preliminary examination that different kinds of cases should receive after their introduction in the council.[36] Confusion about these and other matters not only hindered the council's efficiency, but it offered an open invitation to litigants to fish in troubled waters, and this in an era that witnessed a two-fold increase in this council's business.[37] When added to an inconsistent jurisprudence on such crucial issues as whether the Conseil Privé should itself retain litigation for final judgment, problems in the council's internal operation further undermined the parlements' confidence in this body's ability to render carefully prepared and impartial decisions.

---

[35] Ibid., 22. For examples of this confusion, see Ormesson, *Journal*, 1: 76–80, 175–179, 246–247.

[36] The best first-hand discussions of problems in the Conseil Privé can be found in the lengthy memoranda that several councillors of state submitted to Colbert and the king in 1665 on the eve of Louis's judicial reforms. See in particular BN, Clairambault MS. 613, pp. 13–14, 40–46, 92–93, 134–139, 147–148, 289, 331–333, 372–374, 475–476, 563–567. I shall return to these memoranda in the next chapter of this study. Information in several anonymous memoranda is also informative: ibid., pp. 495–500, 519–520, 529–531, 588–590, 619–625, and BN, Mélanges Colbert MS. 33, fols. 113–141v, 186–190v, 200–214. See also Antoine, *Le Conseil du roi sous le règne de Louis XV*, 63–64.

[37] Kaiser, "The Masters of Requests," appendix, graph 4, plots the number of *arrêts* the Conseil Privé issued during its three-month January *quartier* between 1623 and 1673. The graph reveals that between 1623 and 1640, the January *quartier* issued an annual average of 677 *arrêts*; during the years 1641–1660, this figure rose to 1174 (and this includes two years during the Fronde that witnessed few *arrêts*—1648 [200] and 1649 [160]).

III. FORCES FOR ACCOMMODATION

Louis XIV appreciated the dangers to royal authority posed by acrimonious debates between his councils and the parlements, and shortly after assuming personal rule he established the broad outline for a settlement. On 8 July 1661, the Conseil d'En haut issued an important *arrêt* aimed at rectifying the problem of confusion of powers and clarifying the relationship between the sovereign courts and the councils.[1] It ordered that in the future all the sovereign courts would "defer to the *arrêts* of his councils, forbidding them [the courts] to take cognizance of affairs and proceedings His Majesty reserves to himself and his councils." If at any time the judges had complaints about the conduct of the councils, they were to deliver these directly to the king rather than take independent action. In theory, of course, this *arrêt* threatened both the political aspirations and the judicial authority of the parlements. But assessing its practical consequences requires drawing a distinction, as the king clearly did, between these two spheres of the judges' interests.

By firmly establishing the supremacy of conciliar *arrêts*, Louis wished to assert his sovereignty—and by extension that of his councils—over the judges and to limit their capacity to subject royal policies to judicial review. In this sense, the *arrêt* was part of a broader offensive along these lines after 1661 that included such actions as restricting the right of judicial remonstrance in 1667 and 1673, and referring to the "sovereign" courts as simply "superior" ones after 1665. But the king did not intend the *arrêt* to establish a virtual *carte blanche* for the councils to continue indiscriminately the practices that had so distressed the parlements in previous decades. Louis had no illusions that the parlements' conflicts with the councils had been solely the fault of the former. "Even my council," he asserted bluntly in his memoirs for 1661, "instead of regulating the other jurisdictions, all too often confused them through an incredible number of conflicting decisions given in my name as if coming from me, which made the disorder even more shameful."[2] Just two weeks after issuing the famous *arrêt* of July, he informed a group of his highest advisers that he desired that "nothing occurs in the council that will give the sovereign courts reason to remonstrate to him about the execution of the *arrêt* prohibiting them from making enterprises against his authority or the *arrêts* of the council.

---

[1] Isambert et al., eds., *Recueil général des anciennes lois*, 17: 403–405.
[2] Louis XIV, *Mémoires*, 26 (Louis refers to all the councils when he speaks of "the council" in the singular).

. . . [The king intends] that no *arrêt* emerges from his council that is contrary to past ordinances, and he will discipline reporting magistrates responsible for any contraventions."[3] On several occasions in the 1660s, the king also assured the Parlement of Paris and reminded his own advisers that the judicial reforms he contemplated would apply to the councils as well as the ordinary judiciary.[4]

The king's agenda was therefore clear: while it called for trimming the parlements' political pretensions and giving the councils freedom to act in important occasions, it also entailed a fundamental respect for the judges' judicial functions and a more restrained exercise of conciliar authority. For the monarchy, such a policy had the advantage of providing the flexibility necessary for the conduct of state affairs while at the same time defusing a number of potentially explosive grievances on the part of the parlements. For the judges, there was the consolation that a renewed consideration for their traditional authority in the daily administration of justice would accompany any reduction of their political activities.

In the Conseil Privé, the approach toward the parlements favored by Louis XIV emerged throughout his personal rule. It was most evident in this council's jurisprudence after 1661 on issues of crucial concern to the parlements and in the evolution of certain judicial procedures that increased efficiency and smoothed points of friction with the judges. The lack of basic research on these subjects compels our attention to them, but such an investigation must be placed within the context of still other important developments both within and outside the Conseil Privé that facilitated an accommodation with the *parlementaires*. One cannot review here all the changes that swept the councils after 1661 or evaluate the many forces that in some way influenced the conduct of the Conseil Privé. But the most significant developments warrant at least brief mention.

On the matter of the council's composition, for example, progress had been made even before Louis assumed personal rule. A *règlement* of May 1657 abolished the rank of councillor of state *quadrimestre* and reduced the number of councillors to 32: 18 *ordinaires* (12 robe, three ecclesiastical, three sword) and 14 *semestres* (all robe); this number was reduced to 30 in 1673 with elimination of two *semestre* posts and was modified only slightly and occasionally thereafter.[5] As regards the masters of requests, their number grew from 72 in 1661 to 88 in 1689. But we shall see that a greater

---

[3] Boislisle, ed., *Mémoriaux du conseil de 1661,* 2: 233.

[4] For example: AN, X¹ᴬ 8392, fol. 431 (2 September 1661); Colbert, *Lettres,* 6: 371 (first session of the *Conseil de Justice* established to accomplish judicial reform, 25 September 1665).

[5] For details on changes in the council's composition over time, see Boislisle, *Les Conseils du roi sous Louis XIV,* 9–38, and Antoine, *Le Conseil du roi sous le règne de Louis XV,* bk. 1, chap. 3. The conciliar *règlement* of 3 January 1673 noted that the secretaries of state, the ministers, the controller general of finances, and the *intendants des finances* were entitled to attend the Conseil Privé, but I have uncovered no evidence that they did so on a regular basis: this council remained the preserve of the chancellor, the councillors of state, and the masters of requests.

attention to procedural formalities in the council and an expansion of the permanent committees (*bureaux*) that served it considerably reduced the ability of these officials to promote arbitrary decisions. Among the councillors of state, the distinction between *ordinaires* and *semestres* gradually disappeared except for salary considerations, and in 1674 the masters of requests gained the right to participate in the council's deliberations irrespective of their *quartier*; together, these developments reduced delays in reporting cases and ensured that the inevitable absence of certain councillors and masters on other duties (intendancies and ambassadorships, for example) did not leave the Conseil Privé understaffed.

In terms of their professional backgrounds, the masters of requests and councillors of state who served Louis XIV were also well suited to handle complex legal matters and to deal with the parlements on a daily basis.[6] All the masters of requests were *avocats*, and the overwhelming majority of them had previous experience in the sovereign courts: of the 78 masters received between 1661 and 1677, for example, information exists on the previous careers of 66, and 63 of these men had served in a sovereign court (44 in a parlement) before assuming the office of master of requests; of the 100 masters received between 1688 and 1704, 62 of the 69 for whom such information exists shared the same experience (51 in a parlement). As for the councillors of state, three-quarters of those sitting in 1658 and 1663 had exercised previously both the office of master of requests and a judgeship in a sovereign court, a pattern that would continue into the next reign, when nine-tenths of the councillors of state were former masters of requests. In addition, neither group lacked maturity or experience in governmental affairs. The average age of the masters in place in 1714 was 43, of the councillors, 61. Councillors of state normally achieved their rank only after many years of service in a variety of administrative positions, and while many masters of requests were destined to take a similar path (especially in the intendancies), a substantial group of them passed their entire careers serving the councils and gaining invaluable experience in the conciliar routine (and the proportion of these "demeurés" among the masters of requests increased over time). To be sure, one must not overstate the significance of figures pointing to professional experience in the council. Broad familiarity with judicial affairs had also characterized the membership of the Conseil Privé in the first half of the century, and this had not prevented serious quarrels with the *parlementaires*.[7] During Louis XIV's personal rule,

---

[6] The information in this paragraph is drawn principally from Mousnier et al., *Le Conseil du roi de Louis XII à la Révolution*, bk. 1. But the interested reader will find a wealth of information on the social and professional composition of the councils in other studies as well, for example: Antoine, *Le Conseil du roi sous le règne de Louis XV*, bk. 1, chap. 3; Bonney, *Political Change in France*, chap. 5; Hamscher, *The Parlement of Paris After the Fronde*, 47–48; and Kaiser, "The Masters of Requests," pt. 2, chaps. 3 and 5.

[7] For information on the professional backgrounds of the masters of requests received between 1620 and 1659, see Bonney, *Political Change in France*, 93–98, which shows that the sovereign courts were the source of 93.6 percent of the 205 masters received in those years:

a more streamlined council, ably staffed, was certainly an important pre-
requisite for reduced tensions with the parlements. But in itself it did not
guarantee harmony. Other aspects of council life were equally important.

One of the most noteworthy of these was a sustained effort throughout
the reign to establish broad principles guiding the council's conduct and
to define clearly the procedural formalities for resolving legal actions. One
must not exaggerate the novelty of this enterprise. Professor Mousnier has
published 28 *règlements* for the various councils from Louis XIII's reign
alone, and several of these—notably the ones of May 1615 and January
1630—included articles applying to the Conseil Privé in particular.[8] Just a
few months before Mazarin's death, a substantial (85 articles) *règlement* of
27 February 1660 defined procedures for a limited number of technical
issues—acquiring and contesting default judgments, for example, and exchanging documents between parties—and regulated the activities of the
avocats and lesser officials who served the council.[9] But neither these *règlements* nor even the great ordinances of the previous century exhibited
the detail and the comprehensive quality of the three legislative acts of
Louis's personal rule that dealt primarily with the Conseil Privé: the ordinance of August 1669, three of whose six titles concerned *évocations de
justice* and *règlements de juges* in civil and criminal matters, establishing
the conditions of eligibility for initiating these actions and explaining the
methods for introducing them in the council; the *règlement* of 3 January
1673, whose 91 articles not only defined the council's membership and
considered such internal matters as the distribution of cases and the signing
of *arrêts*, but also specified the form for requests in *cassation;* and, most
impressive of all, the *règlement* of 17 June 1687, whose 164 articles grouped
in 15 titles drew upon, supplemented, and occasionally modified all previous
regulations in order to establish the council's judicial procedures for the
next half century on the broad spectrum from the initial summons to the
liquidation of court costs.[10] Still other *arrêts* and *règlements*, briefer and
narrower in focus, resolved particular problems as they arose.[11]

---

105 from the Parlement of Paris, 54 from the Grand Conseil, 31 from the provincial sovereign
courts, and so on. Throughout the seventeenth century, the Parlement of Paris remained the
primary recruiting ground: 49.8 percent of the 205 masters received in 1620–1659; 54.7 percent
of the 245 masters received in 1660–1715. Kaiser, "The Masters of Requests," 244–247, shows
that between 40 and 66 percent of the councillors of state in 1632, 1644, and 1657 were
former masters of requests.

[8] Mousnier, ed., "Les Règlements du conseil du roi sous Louis XIII," 148–150, 152, 185–
189. Of course, one could argue that this plethora of regulations indicated disorder in the
councils.

[9] AN, V⁶ 400; abbreviated version in Isambert et al., eds., *Recueil général des anciennes lois*,
17: 375–379.

[10] Isambert et al., eds., *Recueil général des anciennes lois*, 18: 341–352 (1669); AN, E 1770,
fols. 3–21 (1673); ibid., 1840, fols. 201–229 (1687). The next major legislation dealing primarily
with the Conseil Privé was the ordinance of August 1737 (on *évocations de justice* and *règlements
de juges*) and the *règlement* of 28 June 1738 (on judicial procedure and *cassations*): Isambert
et al., eds., *Recueil général des anciennes lois*, 22: 33–40, 42–106. This legislation drew heavily
upon that of Louis XIV.

[11] The most readily accessible collection of regulatory acts pertaining to Louis XIV's Conseil
Privé through 1698—including the *règlements* of 1660, 1673, and 1687 as well as ten others—

To acknowledge the importance of this activity is not to imply that an institution's formal regulations constitute an infallible guide to its daily conduct. Like all such administrative texts, the legislation pertaining to the Conseil Privé did not discuss every practice in that body, nor did the official mention of a procedural rule for the first time necessarily mean that it was not in force previously. Moreover, what matters is the utility of various procedures and the extent to which they were implemented, issues that merit consideration in view of the parlements' experience. But even if we put aside for a moment the practical effects of all these regulations, they remain significant for two reasons. First, they show that pronouncements about conciliar supremacy did not preclude serious, indeed unprecedented efforts not only to improve the internal operation of the Conseil Privé, but also to make its actions more predictable to litigants and judges alike, an indispensable step in restoring confidence in this council's decisions. Second, the cumulative nature of this legislation—with each act building carefully upon previous ones, consolidating some practices and modifying others in the light of experience—indicates that efforts to reform the Conseil Privé did not result from a short lived flurry of regulatory zeal, soon to be forgotten. Several generations of administrators addressed problems in the council in a methodical fashion, and each chancellor contributed to the enterprise as a whole.

Reduced tensions between the Conseil Privé and the parlements also required the active collaboration of the chancellor of France, and not simply for the preparation of formal regulations. In certain respects, one can hardly speak of the continuing vitality of this venerable post during Louis's personal rule because one of the most striking developments of that era was a dramatic decline in the chancellor's responsibilities in the general administration of the realm. Virtually excluded from all aspects of financial administration after the rise of Colbert, denied automatic ministerial status after 1661, and often relegated to only a secondary role in preparing the great codification projects of the reign, the chancellor was increasingly confined to duties pertaining almost exclusively to the daily administration of justice.[12] But his influence in this area remained considerable. As presiding magistrate in the Conseil Privé, he participated in each major stage of its operation, from determining the membership of its permanent *bureaux* and assigning reporting magistrates to establishing the agenda for deliberations and breaking tie votes in formal session. Meeting on a regular basis with the masters of requests and councillors of state, he was in an excellent position to supervise their activities and to encourage adherence to the council's regulations. As chief of the entire judiciary, he continued to correspond extensively with judicial officials at every level, not only on issues

---

is in Philippe Bornier, *Conférences des ordonnances de Louis XIV* (2 vols.; Paris, 1729), 2: 808–864. I will cite some of these acts below and indicate the location of still others that Bornier did not include.

[12] The plight of Louis XIV's chancellors is well summarized in Antoine, *Le Conseil du roi sous le règne de Louis XV*, 46–53.

of great moment, but also on a host of undramatic and routine matters regarding discipline, the interpretation of procedural rules, and the current status of certain cases in the courts and in the councils. The chancellor was the crucial link between the Conseil Privé and the parlements, and his general approach toward the judges' judicial authority and interests helped to shape this council's own position on these matters.

In this respect, the parlements were fortunate throughout Louis's personal rule, and especially after Séguier's death in 1672, to deal with chancellors who pursued a common policy of reconciliation with the judges on issues related to the administration of justice. Existing historical literature unfortunately provides little information about the attitudes and judicial activities of Louis's chancellors after 1661: the deterioration of their status as general administrators after that date has directed attention to the more dynamic aspects of institutional change.[13] Generalizations offered at this point are subject to refinement, but several observations can be made with assurance based on the surviving correspondence of three of the five chancellors who served Louis after Séguier's death and who enjoyed long tenures in office: Michel Le Tellier (1677–1685), Louis Boucherat (1685–1699), and Louis Phélypeaux de Pontchartrain (1699–1714).[14]

Each of these men accepted the reduced responsibilities of his position, but as if in compensation they all devoted considerable effort to their remaining duties, and this in ways that frequently benefited the parlements. They shared a willingness, for example, to consult the *parlementaires* about pending legislation of a judicial nature and to incorporate useful suggestions for revision.[15] They also considered seriously and acted upon proposals

---

[13] Two exceptions worthy of note are Louis André, *Michel Le Tellier et Louvois* (Paris, 1943), chap. 13, and Charles Frostin, "Le Chancelier de France Louis de Pontchartrain, 'ses' premiers présidents, et la discipline des cours souveraines (1699–1714)," *Cahiers d'Histoire* 27 (1982): 9–34. Neither author, however, makes much use of available manuscript sources.

[14] The following two paragraphs are based on a broad range of sources pertaining to the judicial activities of Louis's chancellors, especially the major collections of their correspondence (consisting of letters dispatched): BN, MSS. Fr. 5267 and 21118 (Le Tellier; these volumes are nearly identical in content); AN, V¹ 577–585 (Boucherat, for the years 1685–1691 only); BN, MSS. Fr. 21119–21142 (Pontchartrain). Letters written by the chancellors also exist in the papers of other notable persons, including prominent judicial officials like Achille III de Harlay (BN, MSS. Fr. 16485, 16579, 17413–17439, 19582, etc.) and Nicolas Brûlart (Bibliothèque Municipale [hereafter BM] de Dijon, MSS. 541–542), as well as provincial intendants like Henri d'Aguesseau (AN, H¹ 1688–1713) and Pierre Cardin Le Bret (BN, MSS. Fr. 8821–8905). In future work, I will discuss in greater detail the judicial activity of Louis's chancellors and the pertinent sources. The notes below are intended only to provide a few examples of their work. In excluding Séguier from the following remarks, I do not wish to deny that he had his better moments with the judges, although in general terms his often bitter relations with the parlements stand in sharp contrast to the experience of later chancellors. His surviving correspondence received after 1661 (BN, MSS. Fr. 17396–17412) indicates that he could cooperate with the *parlementaires*, and certainly the preparation of the *règlements* of 1657 and 1660 required his participation and good will. But the paucity of extant letters written by him in the 1660s cautions against making broad statements about his daily approach toward parlementary affairs in that decade. Few letters written by Chancellors Etienne d'Aligre (1674–1677; *garde des sceaux* since 1672) and Daniel Voisin (1714–1717) have survived, but the few that remain are in accord with the generalizations offered here.

[15] For example: Le Tellier to Harlay (Paris), 30 November 1679, BN, MSS. Fr. 17415, fol. 92; Boucherat to Le Mazuyer (Toulouse), 28 April 1686, AN, V¹ 578, pp. 16–17; and Pontchartrain to Jobelot (Besançon), 16 November 1702, BN, MSS. Fr. 21121, fols. 518–519v.

from the parlements to modify existing royal legislation on law and judicial procedure when such change seemed to be reasonable and in the interest of orderly judicial administration; each of them occasionally tolerated particular usages in the courts when these conformed to the spirit if not always to the letter of the crown's judicial ordinances.[16] The chancellors also corresponded regularly with the parlements, responding promptly and at length to queries about both the general intent of royal acts and procedural difficulties in specific cases, often urging the judges to resolve even thorny questions on their own initiative.[17] In similar fashion, the chancellors encouraged the *parlementaires* to exercise their supervisory powers over lesser judges, and upon receiving reports about questionable conduct in the parlements, the chancellors generally declined to resolve problems personally, preferring instead to advise concerned parties either to follow ordinary channels within the judicial hierarchy or, better still, to persist in efforts for a settlement on the local level without involving central authorities.[18] Not without irony, former Controller General of Finances Pontchartrain especially liked to portray himself as an ally of the judges in the king's councils, shielding the courts whenever possible from the adverse consequences of royal financial policies of expediency.[19] Even on matters regarding the parlements' judicial functions over which the chancellors enjoyed only limited authority, they could still make their influence felt to the judges' advantage. Provincial intendants, for example, periodically requested and received jurisdiction over certain cases of a financial, administrative, or criminal nature that fell within the competence of the ordinary courts. While the intendants normally obtained this delegation of judicial power from the controller general or a secretary of state and thus reported directly to these officials, they sometimes worked through the chancellor. When this occurred, the chancellors screened such requests with care, approving some while rejecting others, and they consistently admonished intendants who exceeded the limits of their authority having once received it.[20]

It is true, of course, that such considerate treatment of the parlements was not without precedent even in the recent past, and it would also be a

---

[16] For example: Le Tellier to Harlay (Paris), 14 February 1680, BN, MSS. Fr. 21118, pp. 178–179; Pontchartrain to Barale (Tournai), September–December 1704, ibid., 21123, fols. 483v–484, 543v–544, 625–626; Pontchartrain to Fenoyl (Pau), 26 June 1712, ibid., 21135, fols. 548v–549.

[17] For example: Le Tellier to Brûlart (Dijon), 16 February and 10 April 1680, BM, Dijon, MS. 542, fols. 100, 166; Pontchartrain to Doroz (Besançon), 23 June 1704, BN, MSS. Fr. 21141, fols. 423v–428; Pontchartrain to Parisot (Dijon), 28 March 1708, ibid., 21127, fols. 273v–276.

[18] For example: Le Tellier to Le Mazuyer (Toulouse), 11 July 1679, BN, MSS. Fr. 5267, pp. 67–68; Boucherat to Le Bret (Aix), 26 August 1692, ibid., 8844, fols. 83, 92–93v; Pontchartrain to Chauflessat (Chaumont-en-Bassigny), 14 December 1705, ibid., 21124, fols. 714v–715.

[19] See, for example, his letters to Harouys (Besançon; 2 November 1702) and La Porte (Metz; 27 August 1707) in: BN, MSS. Fr. 21121, fol. 510; 21126, fols. 716v–718.

[20] For example: Boucherat to Bérulle (Auvergne, Lyon), 28 January 1686, 1 and 17 May 1689, and 5 June 1689, AN, V¹ 577, pp. 141–142; 582, pp. 391–392; 583, pp. 13–14, 44–45; Pontchartrain to Nointel (Brittany), 13 December 1702, BN, MSS. Fr. 21121, fols. 591v–592; Pontchartrain to Barillon (Roussillon), 16 September 1710, ibid., 21132, fols. 948–949.

mistake to paint too rosy a picture of Louis's personal rule: the correspondence of the chancellors contains numerous examples of harsh words and reprimands directed at the parlements when lapses in internal discipline or non-compliance with royal judicial legislation were simply too serious to ignore.[21] One might also reasonably argue that the chancellors' generally prudent behavior was consistent with changing conditions during the reign. In an era following an already intense period of judicial reform during the 1660s and early 1670s, and at a time when the pressures of war and financial difficulties increasingly influenced the direction of the crown's domestic policies, the chancellors no doubt lacked both the authority and the inclination to promote major changes in judicial administration that might well have antagonized the judges. Nevertheless, for *parlementaires* accustomed to prolonged and bitter conflicts about their judicial authority, a series of chancellors acting in a spirit of compromise and cooperation augured well for improved relations with the Conseil Privé.

Nor did these efforts to improve relations with the parlements strike an unresponsive chord within the Conseil Privé itself. Unfortunately, few sources exist that reveal how individual councillors of state and masters of requests viewed their work in this council. Secrecy characterized the sessions of the Conseil Privé and no minutes were kept of its deliberations.[22] Only when its members performed duties outside the council, as provincial intendants for example, did they generate a substantial administrative correspondence.[23] Nevertheless, the activity that surrounded the famous "reformation of justice" of the 1660s and early 1670s did result in a number of documents that provide valuable insights into opinion within the Conseil Privé during the early years of Louis XIV's personal rule. In 1665, on the eve of reform, the king and Colbert solicited memoranda on the subject of judicial abuse from royal officials (and an occasional *avocat* and professor of law) throughout France. Over 70 of these reports have survived, and no fewer than 15 were submitted by councillors of state.[24] These memo-

---

[21] For example: Le Tellier to Daulède (Bordeaux), 17 September 1681, BN, MSS. Fr. 5267, pp. 403–405; Boucherat to Saint André (Grenoble), 31 July 1687, AN, V^1 580, p. 71; Pontchartrain to the Parlement of Bordeaux, 10 March 1702, BN, MSS. Fr. 21121, fols. 126v–128.

[22] *Plumitifs* recording who attended a formal session of the Conseil Privé and how they voted do exist, but only for some years in the period 1730–1790: AN, V^6 1155–1160. In his *Journal*, Ormesson occasionally reports what transpired in sessions of the Conseil Privé, but only during the 1640s (for example, 1: 12–13, 183–185, 245–246; 2: 813–814). The bulk of the surviving documents of the Conseil Privé are the *minutes*—in the sense of the original archival versions—of this council's decisions (*arrêts*).

[23] Thus the great value, for Louis XIV's reign, of archival collections like AN, G^7 (*contrôle général des finances*), cartons 71–571, and such published collections as Arthur Michel de Boislisle, ed., *Correspondance des contrôleurs généraux des finances avec les intendants des provinces* (3 vols.; Paris, 1874–1897).

[24] Most of the memoranda are located in BN, Mélanges Colbert MS. 33. All but a few of these reports are anonymous, but I have determined in related research that many were submitted by judicial officials, including *parlementaires*. I will discuss this issue and indicate the location of still other memoranda in future work. The reports of the councillors of state that interest us here are located in BN, Clairambault MS. 613 (for Colbert's abstract of them,

randa provided a detailed description of problems in the administration of justice, analyzed their causes, and offered suggestions for reform. Like most of the respondents, the councillors of state did not confine their remarks to a single subject. Instead, they surveyed every level of the judiciary and discussed a broad range of issues concerning the nature of the law, the utility of various jurisdictional rules, and the intricacies of judicial procedure. In casting wide nets, however, few councillors failed to comment on the conduct and practices of the Conseil Privé.

What is perhaps most striking is that these officials, many of whom had quarrelled with the parlements in the past, echoed many of the opinions the *parlementaires* themselves had expressed in the era of the Fronde. There was general agreement, for example, that existing regulations concerning *évocations de justice* and *règlements de juges* warranted more careful observation in the council, and some councillors even suggested modifications favorable to the judges' interests. Thus Louis Le Maistre de Bellejambe and Jean d'Estampes urged that litigants be prohibited from seeking a change in venue once a court had begun to deliberate on the substantive legal issues in a given case.[25] Michel de Marillac and François de Verthamon called for an increase in the number of relatives a litigant had to have in a parlement before his adversaries could request an *évocation*.[26] On the matter of the more politically sensitive *évocations*, those *de grâce* and *de propre mouvement*, several councillors recognized that special circumstances might prompt the king and his ministers to remove litigation from the sovereign courts in the interest of public utility or in favor of "powerful persons." But like the judges, the councillors of state believed that such "cas singuliers"—to use the words of a future chancellor of France, Etienne d'Aligre—should arise infrequently; as a general rule, litigants belonged before their natural judges in the ordinary judiciary.[27] The councillors also took a dim view of *évocations générales*, suggesting that these too be granted rarely. To Louis Laisné de La Marguerie, such blanket removals of litigation "cause great prejudices to the parties concerned," and Estampes urged that all *évocations générales* currently in force be revoked.[28]

The councillors also used such phrases as "for important considerations" and "only important occasions" when they discussed the council's practice

---

see his *Lettres*, 6:18–22). The most recent examination of these documents is in Hamscher, *The Parlement of Paris After the Fronde*, 157–164. Other historians who have used them include Adhémar Esmein, *Histoire de la procédure criminelle en France* (Paris, 1882), 180–192, and Josef van Kan, *Les Efforts de codification en France: Etude historique et psychologique* (Paris, 1929), 67–76. For a recent overview of Louis XIV's "reformation of justice," see Hamscher, *The Parlement of Paris After the Fronde*, chap. 6, as well as the older study by Francis Monnier, *Guillaume de Lamoignon et Colbert: Essai sur la législation française au XVIIe siècle* (Paris, 1862).

[25] BN, Clairambault MS. 613, pp. 46, 136. For similar suggestions, see the memoranda by Claude Gobelin (p. 148), Alexandre de Sève (p. 498), and an anonymous author (p. 588). For a call to obey existing regulations by future Chancellor Boucherat, see pp. 91–93.

[26] Ibid., 331–332, 563–564.

[27] Ibid., 14. See the related comments by Estampes, 136.

[28] Ibid., 136, 289–290. See also the comments of Antoine Barillon de Morangis, 43.

of occasionally retaining final jurisdiction over the litigation involved in the legal disputes it resolved. "No case should be retained at the council which can be judged elsewhere," noted Le Maistre de Bellejambe, and according to Antoine Barillon de Morangis, "it is necessary to remand all cases involving contentious jurisdiction to the judges who should know them."[29] Aligre was quite blunt in denouncing the practice. While reviewing the reasons why he believed litigation was so time consuming in French courts, he asserted that "the procedure of the council is in part responsible . . . owing to the cognizance that one takes or wishes to take [in the council] of all sorts of affairs, either because of the credit or because of the artifice of litigants who find protection there. . . ."[30] On a related matter, Le Maistre de Bellejambe and Estampes encouraged the adoption of severe restrictions on the types of cases that the Requêtes de l'Hôtel could judge in last resort.[31]

When the councillors turned to *cassation*, they expressed views that would have pleased the *parlementaires.* Aligre spoke of his "deference to the parlements on the issue of *cassations*," and other councillors emphasized that few legal grounds justified the council nullifying parlementary judgments rendered in last resort: *cassation* "ought to be accorded with great difficulty," stated Alexandre de Sève; "for the blatant [*formelle*] contravention of [royal] ordinances and conciliar *arrêts,* and not otherwise," in the words of Verthamon.[32] Aligre and Sève also criticized the practice of suspending the enforcement of parlementary judgments while cases of *cassation* were pending at the council; Sève went so far as to condemn the procedure as "the greatest vexation that arises in the distribution of justice."[33] There was even some support for the parlements' position that the council should not pronounce *cassation* solely on the basis of a petitioner's request without allowing the other litigants involved in a disputed sentence to present evidence.[34]

The memoranda contained still other suggestions for reform. Believing that the *avocats* who served the council often increased the length and cost of litigation (as well as their own fees) by manipulating judicial procedures and by generating paperwork of dubious value, several councillors recommended a reduction in the number of these officials and a closer supervision of their activities.[35] Other councillors agreed with the parlements that parties who initiated and then lost legal actions at the council should

---

[29] Ibid., 41, 46. See also the related comments by Estampes, 137.

[30] Ibid., 14.

[31] Ibid., 46, 137.

[32] Ibid., 13, 478–479, 565. Aligre would allow *cassation* only for "the notorious contravention of ordinances," the "lack of [parlementary] jurisdiction," and regarding "a fact whose cognizance does not belong to the parlements."

[33] Ibid., 13, 478.

[34] Noted an anonymous memorandum (but whose author knew conciliar procedures well): "*Cassations* should never be pronounced, nor summonses [to the council] voided, nor anything judged definitively *sur requête*." Ibid., 589.

[35] Ibid., 45 (Le Maistre de Bellejambe), 374 (Jean de Mesgrigny), 500 (anonymous).

be fined.[36] Verthamon advocated improvements in the system by which groups of council members reviewed cases before their introduction to the full council, and Le Maistre de Bellejambe counseled reducing the role that litigants played in selecting reporting magistrates.[37]

We shall see that these proposals as well as many of the other suggestions for reform offered by the councillors of state eventually became permanent features of the council's jurisprudence and judicial procedure. Of course, not every recommendation set forth in the memoranda found a receptive audience. Pleas for the king to attend meetings of the Conseil Privé on a regular basis fell on deaf ears, as did a suggestion that the councillors of state rather than the masters of requests report cases to the council.[38] An intriguing proposal that *évocations* be abolished altogether, or at least that a special tribunal (*chambre des évocations*) be established in Paris to decide them, also came to nothing.[39] What warrants emphasis at this point, however, is that influential members of the Conseil Privé both acknowledged the existence of serious problems in the operation of this body and suggested reforms analogous to those advocated by the parlements. In so doing, the councillors of state not only complemented the chancellors' efforts to seek a reconciliation with the judges, but they confirmed the king's belief that the council itself had been partly to blame for its conflicts with the parlements in previous years. A common thread running through all the memoranda was the assumption that judicial reform, to be truly effective, must begin at the very heart of the royal administration. As Barillon de Morangis succinctly put the matter: "[I am] obliged to inform Your Majesty with profound respect that the first reformation of justice ought to begin in your council, which gives movement to all the other courts [*compagnies*] of the realm, [and] which ought to serve them as a model, an example, and a law. . . ."[40]

If important developments at the highest levels of the royal administration paved the way for an accommodation between the parlements and the Conseil Privé, a durable settlement of differences would have been inconceivable had not the judges themselves contributed substantially to the enterprise by curtailing their political ambitions and by considerably reducing their opposition to royal policies throughout Louis's personal rule. This important change in the magistrates' conduct was well underway in Paris during the 1660s and was firmly established in the provinces by the mid-1670s with few notable exceptions thereafter. To be sure, many aspects of this change remain unclear despite the numerous references to the "do-

---

[36] For various suggestions on fines, see ibid., 45 (Le Maistre de Bellejambe), 498 (anonymous), 567 (Verthamon), and 588–589 (anonymous).

[37] Ibid., 46, 565.

[38] Ibid., 42 (Barillon de Morangis), 495 (anonymous), 571 (Verthamon).

[39] Ibid., 619–625 (anonymous).

[40] Ibid., 40. Le Maistre de Bellejambe (p. 45) noted that reform should begin in the king's council, "so that it serves as an example to the courts of the realm for the care and the vigilance that one is obliged to bring to the administration of justice."

mestication" of the parlements found in many accounts of the reign. On the one hand, the full range of national and local forces responsible for a more docile judiciary are only imperfectly understood owing to the paucity of detailed scholarship on Louis's parlements after 1661: the standard histories of these tribunals—most of which were written in the nineteenth century—made only limited use of pertinent archival sources, and more recent and sophisticated studies have examined just a few courts within restricted chronological or topical frameworks.[41] On the other hand, historians have only begun to investigate and to evaluate the consequences of the various other pressures that seem to have weighed heavily upon the *parlementaires* as the reign progressed, such as declining office prices and official income, a decrease in the volume of litigation coming before the courts, and the monarchy's seemingly endless recourse to expedients like office creations and forced loans to help finance France's foreign wars.[42] To complicate matters further, even the most generous assessment of Louis's control of the parlements must recognize that these courts retained considerable authority on the local level and continued to lobby effectively for at least some of their interests with central authorities who never completely abandoned the traditional inclination to compromise; the very themes elaborated upon in this study illustrate that the reign of Louis XIV offered the parlements far more than a dreary succession of coercive acts.

However much all these subjects require additional research, the fact remains that the decline of the parlements' political activities was both genuine and widespread by the second decade of Louis's personal rule, and this influenced the magistrates' relations with the Conseil Privé in two significant ways. First, if the parlements' opposition to a broad range of royal policies had originally prompted the Conseil Privé and the other councils to increase their intervention in the courts' judicial business before 1661—and to do so in an often indiscriminate way—the necessity and the justification for this infringement diminished as new patterns of judicial conduct emerged in subsequent years. During the 1660s and early 1670s, greater consideration for the parlements' interests in the Conseil Privé was certainly in part a defensive act: in years marked by great judicial and financial reform, and at a time when memories of the Fronde were fresh

---

[41] In addition to the scholarship cited above in chap. I, n. 4 and the works by Hamscher and by Beik cited in chap. I, n. 2 and chap. II, n. 13, see Maurice Gresset, *Gens de justice à Besançon, de la conquête par Louis XIV à la Révolution française, 1674–1789* (2 vols.; Paris, 1978), and Jean-Claude Paulhet, "Les Parlementaires toulousains à la fin du dix-septième siècle," *Annales du Midi* 76 (1964): 189–204.

[42] Of course, the timing, extent, and particular combination of these problems in each parlement need to be explored fully in future research. For an introduction to the question, see: Colin Kaiser, "The Deflation in the Volume of Litigation at Paris in the Eighteenth Century and the Waning of the Old Judicial Order," *European Studies Review* 10 (1980): 309–336; John J. Hurt, "Forced Loans and the Wealth of the Magistrates of the Parlement of Brittany Under Louis XIV," (unpublished paper presented to the American Historical Association, 1979; I thank Professor Hurt for allowing me to consult this work); idem, "Les Offices au Parlement de Bretagne."

and some courts still engaged in obstructionist tactics, it simply made little political sense to provoke the judges on issues the king himself considered worthy of compromise. But in later decades the general quiescence of the parlements coupled with their growing financial difficulties provided a far more positive incentive to protect the integrity of their traditional judicial functions. One must of course take care not to view this process in too mechanistic a way: the submission of the parlements to the royal will might have conceivably offered the councils an open invitation to increase their inroads into the *parlementaires'* judicial authority. That this did not occur, however, underscores the qualities of restraint and moderation that formed a vital part of Louis XIV's policy toward the parlements.

Second, and here we must speculate, the declining political role of the parlements might have had what can be called a generational impact. Over the course of Louis's long personal rule, the Conseil Privé was continually replenished with men who had not experienced the heated controversies of mid-century. Accustomed by their own professional backgrounds to a more compliant high judiciary, new generations of masters of requests and councillors of state not only had fewer reasons to act in a spirit of animosity once they arrived at the Conseil Privé, but a less highly charged political atmosphere might well have made them more amenable to working within this council's increasingly regulated and orderly routine.

IV. THE JURISPRUDENCE OF THE CONSEIL PRIVÉ: *CASSATIONS*

The best evidence for a greater attentiveness to the parlements' interests in the Conseil Privé comes from this council's own *arrêts*, documents that have never been studied systematically for any period of French history.[1] The large quantity of these *arrêts*, as many as 100,000 for Louis XIV's personal rule alone, necessitates sampling only a portion of them. To this end, I have examined over 1,500 *arrêts* from nine years between 1668 and 1715, years chosen both to include *arrêts* from the tenure of each of Louis's chancellors and to take into account the appearance over time of the major regulatory acts guiding the council's conduct.[2] My intention here is neither to provide a detailed profile of all the council's activities nor to consider every matter that in some way brought the parlements into contact with the Conseil Privé: such is beyond the scope of this study, and I suspect that only a team of researchers could accomplish this task given the lack of an adequate descriptive index for this council's *arrêts* from the seventeenth century. Rather, my aim is to trace the fate of those issues that had proven to be so divisive before 1661. In this respect, because the adjudication of *cassations, évocations de justice,* and *règlements de juges* constituted the principal and ongoing business of the Conseil Privé, a sample of 1,500 *arrêts* includes for analysis several hundred *arrêts* concerning the parlements in each of these categories.

As one might expect from an institution whose procedures closely resembled those of a court of law, the Conseil Privé issued various kinds of *arrêts* with different juridical purposes. The two most common varieties, and those that will be of greatest interest to us in the following pages, were *arrêts sur requête* and *arrêts contradictoires*. As their name implies, *arrêts sur*

---

[1] Even Antoine, whose *Le Conseil du roi sous le règne de Louis XV* frequently cites *arrêts* of the Conseil Privé to illustrate this body's conduct and procedures, did not isolate a specific sample of *arrêts* for analysis in depth. See, for example, his discussion of *cassation, évocation de justice,* and *règlement de juges* on pp. 289–291, 523–536.

[2] AN, V⁶ 544 (dossiers for 13, 18, 22, 24, and 28 [nos. 56–66 only] September 1668: 119 *arrêts*); 554 (dossiers for 3, 6, 9, and 10 [nos. 54–69 only] July 1669: 165 *arrêts*); 626 (dossiers for 7, 16, 20, 21, and 28 May, and 14 and 23 April 1676: 240 *arrêts*); 686 (dossiers for 13, 20, and 27 February, and 9, 13, 20, and 27 March 1685: 246 *arrêts*); 755 (dossiers for 9, 23, 24, 26, 28, and 30 September, and 19, 21, and 25 October 1695: 252 *arrêts*); 802 (all dossiers, September–December 1705: 218 *arrêts*); 805 (dossier for 5 July 1706: 23 *arrêts*); 831 (dossier for 19 March 1714: 27 *arrêts*); and 834 (all dossiers, December 1714–March 1715: 221 *arrêts*). For certain issues regarding the council's judicial procedures, I also gleaned V⁶ 577 (18 March–14 April 1671), 666 (February–March 1682), and 790 (September–November 1702). All these *arrêts* were chosen at random.

requête were issued pursuant to requests filed by parties, and the council used these *arrêts* to express a broad range of legal decisions: to grant or reject a petitioner's demands outright without calling for further procedures; to summon parties to the council to engage in additional proceedings prior to a final judgment; to solicit the advice of outside authorities; and to make a variety of interlocutory judgments. *Arrêts contradictoires,* which for the sake of convenience may be called *arrêts* "between parties," resolved cases after both sides in a dispute had been given the opportunity to present evidence. There were other kinds of *arrêts* as well, such as those *d'instruction* that assembled the results of certain proof proceedings, but these will figure less prominently in this study.[3]

I have supplemented this primary sample of *arrêts* in four ways. First, a summary examination of nearly 600 *arrêts* from the years 1647 and 1656,

---

[3] I offer the following technical observations for scholars interested in consulting this council's *arrêts.* First, unlike many judicial courts, the Conseil Privé did not catalogue different kinds of *arrêts* separately in its archives. Instead, all *arrêts* issued on a given date are grouped together without particular order in a dossier bearing that date. Second, historical literature on the king's councils often distinguishes between *arrêts sur requête* and *arrêts de propre mouvement,* the former having been issued pursuant to requests filed by parties, the latter having been issued on a council's own initiative (such as executive orders). Both kinds of *arrêts* could be either *simple* or *en commandement.* But this distinction between *arrêts sur requête* and *arrêts de propre mouvement* is not particularly helpful when dealing with the Conseil Privé, not only because it ignores other kinds of *arrêts* issued by this body (*contradictoires, d'instruction,* etc.), but also because in practice the Conseil Privé issued few *arrêts de propre mouvement* (most of these *arrêts* will be found instead among the *arrêts en commandement* and the *arrêts simples* "en finance"). When considering the activities of the Conseil Privé, therefore, it is best to think in terms of *arrêts sur requête, contradictoires, d'instruction,* and so on. Third, recognizing by their official wording the different kinds of *arrêts* the Conseil Privé issued is a subject too complex to address here in detail: scholars interested in working with all manner of conciliar *arrêts* should first consult two works by Antoine for general guidance on this matter: *Le Conseil du roi sous le règne de Louis XV,* 343–361; *Le Fonds du conseil d'état du roi aux Archives Nationales,* 33–43. In general terms, and concentrating on the *arrêts* cited most often in this study, *arrêts sur requête* begin with the words, "Sur la requête . . . ," (or a similar phrase); *arrêts* between parties begin, "Veu au conseil du roi . . . ," often preceded by the word "entre" and a listing of the parties in a case. Bear in mind, however, that all kinds of legal actions—*cassations, évocations de justice, règlements de juges,* and others—could involve both kinds of *arrêts* and thus this wording; some *arrêts* that were not between parties also employed the protocol, "Veu au conseil du roi. . . ." In short, only a careful reading of the *arrêts* themselves will reveal the nature of the legal action in question. Fourth, although most cases at the Conseil Privé were resolved by *arrêts sur requête* and by *arrêts* between parties, there were some exceptions to this general rule: I will discuss the most important ones as the need arises (see below, this chapter, n. 15 and chap. V, n. 18). Finally, whether *arrêts* of the Conseil Privé were *sur requête* or between parties, they shared a common basic structure of two elements: the *exposé* and the *dispositif.* In fact, the same can be said of all manner of conciliar *arrêts,* whether *simples* or *en commandement.* Depending upon the nature of the case and the status of procedures, the *exposé*—or introduction—could explain the *desiderata* of petitioners, cite reasons for royal intervention in a case, set forth proof to be added to a pending action, or review the procedures and documents serving as the basis for a decision. The *exposé* concludes by noting the intervention of a reporter and often by mentioning any preliminary examination given the case by permanent *bureaux* of the council or by delegated *commissaires.* The *dispositif* gives the council's decision, beginning with the words, "Le Roi en son conseil . . . ," (for all *arrêts simples,* including those "en finance"; the phrase, "Le Roi étant en son conseil . . . ," was reserved for the *arrêts en commandement* issued by the *conseils de gouvernement*).

while certainly no substitute for a detailed study of *arrêts* issued prior to Louis XIV's personal rule, at least permits direct observation of the practices the parlements had protested in their memoranda of mid-century and provides some informative contrasts to developments in later years.[4] Second, because the council's *arrêts* between parties cited any previous *arrêts* issued in a given case, it is often possible to consult a number of documents related to the same legal action. This method is useful for following the flow of the council's judicial procedures, and I employed it several dozen times for this purpose.[5] Third, the chancellors occasionally wrote to the parlements either to discuss specific cases pending at the council or to explain the council's rationale for a particular judgment; working from the dates of these letters, one can frequently locate the pertinent *arrêts* in the council's archives.[6] Because the *arrêts* of the Conseil Privé did not mention the judicial reasoning (*motifs*) behind decisions, these letters offer valuable information about the council's jurisprudence that does not appear in the *arrêts* themselves. Equally important, the chancellors sometimes discussed informal methods of work in the council not to be found in official regulations. Although these letters are not numerous—perhaps some 60 exist for the entire period of Louis XIV's personal rule, primarily from Pontchartrain's administration and dealing mostly with *cassations*—their qualitative significance compensates for their small number. Finally, the archives of the parlements have left some traces of the judges' contact with the Conseil Privé.[7]

Together, all these sources reveal the evolution of the council's jurisprudence and judicial procedures on matters of crucial concern to the

---

[4] AN, V⁶ 215 (303 *arrêts* from various dossiers, 12 February–15 March 1647); 319 (268 *arrêts* from various dossiers, 11–28 February 1656). For certain procedural issues, I also gleaned V⁶ 325 (30 May–9 June 1656) and 326 (13–27 June 1656). These *arrêts* were chosen at random.

[5] For example: an *arrêt* between parties of 12 October 1705 in a case of *règlement de juges* (AN, V⁶ 802, no. 8) cites an *arrêt sur requête* of 18 August 1704 introducing this case at the council; this earlier *arrêt* is catalogued under this date in V⁶ 797 (no. 9). As another example, an *arrêt* between parties in a case regarding *cassation* of 19 March 1714 (V⁶ 831, no. 23) refers to two previous *arrêts sur requête* issued in this case, both of which exist in the council's archives: 29 May 1713 (V⁶ 828, no. 26), and 20 November 1713 (V⁶ 830, no. 13).

[6] For example, on 22 July 1710, Pontchartrain notified the Parlement of Bordeaux that one of its judgments had recently been nullified because it violated the ordinance of August 1669, tit. 1, art. 17 (BN, MSS. Fr. 21142, fols. 1145v–1148). A search in the council's archives leads to the pertinent *arrêt*, one between parties dated 21 July (AN, V⁶ 819, no. 24); this *arrêt* in turn mentions an *arrêt sur requête* dated 27 March 1708 that originally introduced this case at the council, and it is located in V⁶ 811 (no. 18). The chancellors' correspondence consulted for this study is listed above in chap. III, n. 14.

[7] To my knowledge, no parlement established a special collection of any appreciable size for preserving its correspondence with central authorities. But a sampling in a variety of records—civil and criminal judgments as well as the various types of *registres secrets* for public affairs (where these have survived)—occasionally yields examples of the ways in which the parlements and the Conseil Privé dealt with one another. In the course of this and other research, I sampled the records of seven parlements, and four (Aix, Grenoble, Paris, and Rennes) contained references to the Conseil Privé. My sampling was done randomly, however, so I suspect that a thorough search in the records of all the parlements would uncover additional traces of the judges' relations with this council.

parlements. The number and variety of *arrêts* as well as the need to combine different research strategies to answer particular questions mean that statistical accuracy is difficult to achieve for all the conclusions that follow. However, I have attempted to give a quantitative dimension to my findings when this proves to be especially enlightening.

Of all the powers the Conseil Privé exercised, none tested the legal expertise and political acumen of its members more than the nullification, or *cassation*, of the civil and criminal judgments the parlements and other sovereign courts rendered in last resort.[8] In this respect, the contrast between *cassations* on the one hand and *règlements de juges* and *évocations de justice* on the other is instructive. These latter actions were ordinary and necessary features of the daily administration of justice, settling as they did jurisdictional disputes the sovereign courts simply lacked the authority to resolve on their own. To pursue these matters at council was the undisputed right of all parties who satisfied requirements that could be set forth clearly and publicly in formal legislation like the ordinance of August 1669. Of course, the council had to abide by established rules if it were to avoid conflict with the judges, and certainly no court relished the possibility of losing litigation because of a contest over jurisdiction. But at least the magistrates found nothing inherent in these legal actions that undermined their authority or challenged the validity of their judicial work.

The same cannot be said of *cassations*. To seek the nullification of a parlement's judicial sentences before the Conseil Privé was to have extraordinary recourse to the king's sovereign power against judgments that in normal circumstances were nonappealable. A petitioner pursuing this course both questioned the conduct of magistrates in specific litigation and called into play the council's disciplinary powers over even the highest levels of the ordinary judicary. Neither prospect pleased the *parlementaires*, with the result that each time the Conseil Privé examined requests for *cassation*, it had to take into account not only the interest of parties and the need to uphold respect for the law, but also the dignity of the high magistracy and the controversy that too liberal a policy of granting *cassations* might generate. To complicate matters further, although recourse to *cassation* was not an ordinary right of litigants but a privilege to be used sparingly, the monarchy never defined explicitly the grounds (*ouvertures*) for this legal action for fear of setting limits that were too precise on the

---

[8] As noted above in chap. II, n. 9, the Conseil Privé could also nullify the sentences issued by lesser tribunals when they judged in last resort. I am not concerned with these *cassations* in this study. The best introduction to *cassation* is Antoine, *Le Conseil du roi sous le règne de Louis XV*, 289–291, 446–447, 525–536. See also: R. Martinage-Baranger, "Les Idées sur la cassation au XVIIIe siècle," *Revue Historique de Droit Français et Etranger* 47 (1969): 244–290; Emile Chénon, *Origines, conditions et effets de la cassation* (Paris, 1882); and Jean Plassard, *Des Ouvertures communes à cassation et à requête civile* (Paris, 1924). All these works focus primarily on the eighteenth century (Chénon and Plassard considering later eras as well), and only Antoine has consulted manuscript sources, the others relying instead on the writings of jurists.

discretionary authority of its central institutions. Only by acting with restraint and consistency in this matter and by developing procedures aimed at discouraging frivolous attacks on the parlements' sentences could the Conseil Privé hope to accomplish its mission efficiently and with a minimum of political risk. Finally, while the Conseil Privé dealt only with *cassations* of a judicial nature—those arising from the judgment of civil and criminal cases in tribunals judging in last resort—these *cassations* were by far the most numerous and they most directly concerned the *parlementaires'* exercise of their judicial duties. The keen interest the parlements showed in these *cassations* is thus understandable.

The pressures on the Conseil Privé are particularly well illustrated by the problems associated with defining the grounds for *cassation*. At all times during the *ancien régime,* the lack of royal legislation on this matter gave the council considerable freedom of action. But this freedom also entailed a responsibility to act prudently. For if the council confused *cassation* with ordinary appeals, it not only would have taken on a caseload beyond its material means to handle, but it would have profoundly disturbed the order of jurisdictions, threatening both the security of victorious litigants and the authority of superior magistrates by raising doubts about the ability of the parlements to judge cases in last resort. The clearest statement we have on the grounds for *cassation* is a memorandum that Councillor of State Pierre Gilbert de Voisins prepared for Louis XV in 1767. Reflecting upon the conciliar practice of his day, Gilbert noted that these grounds arose in only a limited number of circumstances: (1) when a court in entering judgment exceeded its jurisdiction; (2) when a judgment contravened royal legislation or the fundamental laws of the realm; (3) when a judgment violated well established private law, either customary or Roman; (4) when serious errors occurred in judicial procedure or in the redaction of the judgment itself; (5) when obvious inequity ("iniquité évidente") characterized a judgment. He added that as a general rule claimed mistakes in a court's opinion on the merits of litigation ("mal jugé au fond") were not grounds for nullification; otherwise, *cassation* would assume the character of an ordinary appeal.[9]

This refined view of *cassation* was not unique to the mid-eighteenth century. Although jurists writing in previous years did not discuss the grounds for *cassation* in such precise terms, we shall see that criteria identical

---

[9] The memorandum is published in full in Michel Antoine, "Le Mémoire de Gilbert de Voisins sur les cassations: Un Episode des querelles entre Louis XV et les parlements (1767)," *Revue Historique de Droit Français et Etranger* 36 (1958): 1–33. See also the same author's *Le Conseil du roi sous le règne de Louis XV,* 527–529. Gilbert actually lists six grounds, considering the contravention of the fundamental laws of the realm as a separate category; having not found this ground in my sample of *arrêts,* I have combined it here with violations of royal ordinances. Note that one can make a case for subdividing certain grounds: for example, Martinage-Baranger divides jurisdictional violations into "l'excès de pouvoir" and "l'incompétence." Following Gilbert, however, I will consider all manner of jurisdictional violations as a single ground for *cassation.*

to those set forth by Gilbert guided the conduct of Louis XIV's Conseil Privé.[10] Even in the tumultuous years before 1661, the parlements might well have objected to certain of the council's practices in *cassation*—suspending the enforcement of parlementary judgments during conciliar proceedings, for example, or pronouncing *cassation* solely on the basis of a petitioner's request—but the magistrates never accused the council of nullifying their sentences for all manner of infractions. If the grounds for *cassation* were few in number, however, they were sufficiently broad and ambiguous to require a high degree of interpretation in individual cases. A petitioner's allegation of inequity, for example, might simply express dissatisfaction with a court's ruling on the substantive issues in a case. Claimed breaches of law, royal legislation, and judicial procedure might not only lack solid foundation, but they might also be either too minor to warrant the council's attention or perfectly within a court's own power to correct. And what skilled *avocat* of the *ancien régime* could not at least attempt to turn the perennial confusion about proper jurisdiction to his client's advantage? For good reason, then, Gilbert repeatedly emphasized in his memorandum that violations had to be both serious and well proven to warrant the council's intervention.

Indeed, the need for a judicious approach to *cassation* was especially necessary during Louis XIV's personal rule, and this for two reasons. First, by virtue of their broad scope and great detail, the codes of civil and criminal procedure issued in April 1667 and August 1670 gave litigants an unprecedented opportunity to detect procedural errors in the parlements and to protest these before the council.[11] Charged as it was with defending the integrity of royal legislation in the judgment of litigation by the sovereign courts, the Conseil Privé faced the delicate task of enforcing compliance with the two codes while at the same time protecting the parlements from potential harassment by disgruntled litigants.

---

[10] Jurists of the seventeenth and eighteenth centuries differed among themselves in defining the grounds for *cassation*. For example, Jean Domat, a celebrated jurist during Louis XIV's reign, mentioned only violations of royal legislation as grounds; a contemporary, the *avocat* J. Gauret, refers to additional grounds but does not include violations of judicial procedure. Earlier, the *avocat* Lazare du Crot in his *Style* of the Conseil Privé published in 1645 mentions as grounds the contravention of royal ordinances, conciliar *arrêts*, and customary law; writing in 1662, another *avocat*, François du Chesne, does not even discuss *cassation* in his *Style*. For more information on this issue, see Martinage-Baranger, "Les Idées sur la cassation," 259–264, and Tony Sauvel, "Les Demandes de motifs adressées par le conseil du roi aux cours souveraines," *Revue Historique de Droit Français et Etranger* 35 (1957): 529–548 (especially pp. 533–534). In his *Histoire du conseil du roy depuis le commencement de la monarchie jusqu'à la fin du règne de Louis le grand* (Paris, 1718), 81, the *avocat* René Guillard speaks only of the violation of royal legislation and inequity as grounds for *cassation*. Differences such as these underscore the utility of Gilbert's memorandum: he alone among the jurists sat in the council itself. My contention that the grounds in force during Louis XIV's reign were identical to those stated by Gilbert is based on my own examination of conciliar *arrêts* and not on the works of the jurists, who on this matter were not particularly well informed.

[11] For the two codes, see Isambert et al., eds., *Recueil général des anciennes lois*, 18: 103–180, 371–423.

Second, the council's mission in this respect was complicated by the fact that it alone did not enjoy sole responsibility for enforcing the two codes. There existed in French law a legal action known as *requête civile* that enabled the parlements themselves in certain circumstances to retract their own judgments in last resort and to rehear litigation. A litigant interested in pursuing this remedy against a parlement's judgment requested the chancery affiliated with the parlement in question to issue a writ directing the judges to reconsider their decision. If the chancery agreed to issue the writ, the parlement held a formal hearing to weigh the merits of the petitioner's contentions. The judges then either rejected the writ, which had the effect of keeping their original judgment in force, or they confirmed the writ, thereby rescinding their original judgment and ordering a new trial. Either way, a parlement retained ultimate control over both the proceedings and the fate of its original judgment.[12] The ordinance of April 1667 defined the grounds for *requête civile* with precision, and for the most part these grounds were quite distinct from those for *cassation*. But in one important instance—the violation of the procedural rules set forth in the two codes—an aggrieved party had the option to pursue either a *requête civile* or *cassation*.[13] Clarifying this overlap of conciliar and parlementary authority provided yet another test of the council's ability to act with circumspection.[14]

Determining how the Conseil Privé responded to all these considerations requires a basic familiarity with the *arrêts* it issued in cases of *cassation* and the information one can find in them. With few exceptions, procedures for *cassation* resulted in two kinds of *arrêts*. A petitioner seeking the nullification of a parlement's judgment submitted to the council a request (*requête*) that summarized the attacked judgment and explained the reasons (*moyens*) for challenging it. The council replied with an *arrêt sur requête* that either

---

[12] For clear descriptions of this legal action and its procedures, see: Bornier, *Conférences des ordonnances de Louis XIV*, 1: 337–372; Marc-Antoine Rodier, *Questions sur l'ordonnance de Louis XIV du mois d'avril 1667* (Toulouse, 1777), 638–690; and François Serpillon, *Code civile, ou commentaire sur l'ordonnance du mois d'avril 1667* (Paris, 1776), 671–724.

[13] Grounds for *requête civile*, which were set forth in the ordinance of 1667, tit. 35, arts. 34–36, included such issues as fraud on the part of a litigant's opposite party, the issuance of a judgment based on forged documentary evidence, inconsistent provisions in a given judgment, and most important for our purposes, "si la procédure par nous ordonnée n'a point été suivie."

[14] Were still other grounds for *requête civile* also grounds for *cassation*? In his *Ouvertures communes*, chap. 2, Plassard raises the possibility for such grounds for *requête civile* as the failure of a judgment to pass on the head (*chef*) of a demand, the conflict between two judgments issued by the same court between the same parties, the failure of a court to consult the *gens du roi* in cases requiring their participation, and the fault of a judgment in passing on something that was not demanded or in granting more than was demanded. One can indeed find these grounds for *requête civile* mentioned in the *arrêts* that the Conseil Privé issued in *cassation*. But these grounds appear infrequently and always in combination with the better established grounds for *cassation* listed by Gilbert de Voisins. I thus tend to agree with Martinage-Baranger's hypothesis ("Les Idées sur la cassation," 272) that, except for violations of judicial procedure, grounds that were common to both *requête civile* and *cassation* were not well developed in the *ancien régime*.

granted or rejected the petitioner's demands outright or, more often, summoned all the litigants involved in the disputed judgment to contest the complaint fully in writing. In this latter instance, a second *arrêt*—a definitive one between parties—eventually resolved the action.[15] Because the council did not give the judicial reasoning for its decisions, the *arrêts* do not indicate which circumstances in a given case led the council to find as it did, nor do they contain explicit statements by the council defining its policies on *cassation.* The letters of the chancellors fill in some of these gaps, but only for a relatively small number of cases. For many other questions regarding the council's jurisprudence, however, the *arrêts* are very instructive. For example, although the original *requêtes* submitted by petitioners are rarely found in the council's archives, the *arrêts sur requête* repeated their contents in detail.[16] We thus have a record of the grievances the council was at least willing to consider as grounds for *cassation,* information that is indispensable for understanding how broadly the council conceived its authority to nullify parlementary judgments. As regards the *arrêts* between parties, in addition to giving the council's decision, these provide only a chronology of procedures followed in a case and a list of the documents submitted in evidence; the *moyens* of parties are either absent or described only briefly. But these *arrêts* can lead one to *arrêts sur requête* issued earlier in an action.[17] More-

---

[15] The researcher working with the council's *arrêts* will discover some variations in this basic pattern. For example, if a request for *cassation* concerned a case that was already pending at the council between the same parties (an *évocation de justice,* for example), the *arrêt sur requête* usually joined the request to the pending action for final resolution later in a single decision. Another possibility: upon receiving a request for *cassation,* the council could use an *arrêt sur requête* to instruct the public minister (*procureur général*) of the parlement in question to submit a written explanation of his court's judicial reasoning (*motifs*) behind the contested sentence. Upon receiving these *motifs,* the council could then resolve the action either for or against the petitioner without ever having summoned his opposite parties. Yet another variation: if an action in *cassation* concerned a parlement's judgment of a serious criminal offense prosecuted solely at the request of the public minister, this official was rarely summoned to contest a complaint as private parties often were. Instead, if the council did not use an *arrêt sur requête* to resolve the action immediately, it could pursue other procedural options before deciding the case, such as consulting the Requêtes de l'Hôtel for a preliminary opinion about the petitioner's complaint or requesting the public minister to submit the *motifs* for the contested sentence. In all these examples, however, the council still expressed its decisions in two basic kinds of *arrêts*—those *sur requête* that either resolved an action immediately or called for additional procedures; and final decisions rendered after additional proceedings had occurred (although, as just indicated, these final decisions might not have been strictly speaking "between parties"). The only exception to this general rule were cases that the council decided on the basis of *requêtes respectives.* In such cases, both sides in a dispute submitted requests, and the council then settled the matter in a single *arrêt* "sur les requêtes respectives" (this phrase appearing in the opening sentence of the *arrêt*), in effect combining an *arrêt sur requête* and an *arrêt* between parties in a single document. But the council abolished this method of resolving cases by an *arrêt* of 14 October 1684: Isambert et al., eds., *Recueil général des anciennes lois,* 19: 463–464.

[16] *Règlement* of 27 February 1660, art. 10. Sometimes a *requête* was transformed into a formal *arrêt sur requête* with the simple addition of official wording: for example, AN, V^6 834, 31 December 1714, no. 18. For rare original *requêtes* in the council's records, see V^6 831, 19 March 1714, no. 9.

[17] Almost always, however, the *arrêts sur requête* traced from *arrêts* between parties pertain to a petitioner's original request for *cassation.* As a general rule, the surviving documents of

over, when combined with those *arrêts sur requête* that do give a final decision, the *arrêts* between parties indicate how often attempts to secure *cassation* succeeded. The decisions as well as the textual notations in both kinds of *arrêts* in *cassation* also indicate noteworthy changes in the council's judicial procedures.

Although no parlement appreciated a challenge to its judicial work before a superior authority, the *arrêts* of Louis XIV's Conseil Privé reveal a jurisprudence favorable to the parlements' interests in many respects. The most general indication of this is that the grievances of petitioners as set forth in the council's own *arrêts sur requête* fall easily within the few categories outlined by Gilbert de Voisins: no less than their counterparts in the next reign, the councillors of state and masters of requests who served Louis XIV restricted the grounds for *cassation* to questions of equity and to violations of law, royal legislation, judicial procedure, and jurisdictional rules. But to appreciate fully the council's efforts to accommodate the parlements, one must distinguish actions in *cassation* that were relatively routine and minor from those that posed a greater threat to the judges' reputations and authority. For in fact if not in theory, some complaints about the magistrates' judicial activity were far more serious than others. The manner in which the Conseil Privé handled these more serious cases provides the best evidence for a sense of restraint and moderation in the council's exercise of its disciplinary power.

Both before and after 1661, in fact, the majority of actions in *cassation* at the Conseil Privé transpired smoothly and generated little interest in the parlements.[18] These cases involved purely jurisdictional issues in which

---

the Conseil Privé—the bulk of which are *minutes* of *arrêts*—provide more information about the legal arguments made by petitioners than by their opposite parties. After all, it was petitioners who initiated proceedings in *cassation* by filing requests, and the *arrêts sur requête* that ruled on these requests repeated in full the petitioners' complaints. For the opposite parties of petitioners, however, the situation was different. If the Conseil Privé did not use an *arrêt sur requête* to resolve a case but instead called a petitioner's opposite parties to contest his complaint, these litigants then followed procedures leading to an *arrêt* between parties. But most of the paperwork associated with these procedures has not survived in the council's archives and, as just noted, *arrêts* between parties did not normally recount the legal arguments made by either side in a dispute. Moreover, the opposite parties of petitioners did not often solicit *arrêts sur requête* in their own behalf, preferring instead to follow procedures leading to *arrêts* between parties. This tendency of the council's *arrêts* to illuminate the legal arguments of petitioners, but not those of their opposite parties, holds true for other legal actions at the council as well, including *évocations de justice* and *règlements de juges*. To be sure, the legal arguments made by a petitioner's opposite parties do sometimes surface in the council's records: see the procedure of *requêtes respectives* mentioned above in this chapter, n. 15 as well as the procedure of *opposition* referred to below on p. 67. Moreover, the particular circumstances in a case might have prompted a petitioner's opposite parties to solicit an *arrêt sur requête*. But this was exceptional, not ordinary conduct.

[18] In the remainder of this study, I have included in the term "parlement" not only the *chambres de l'édit* that were attached to several parlements to judge litigation involving Protestants, but also the three provincial conseils souverains of Alsace, Artois, and Roussillon. But this inclusion, which is justified on the grounds that these courts exercised a civil and criminal jurisdiction analogous to that of the parlements, adds only a handful of cases to the various samples and in no way distorts any of the interpretations offered. Focusing on the

neither the conduct of the magistrates in judging litigation nor the legitimate right of the parlements to decide certain kinds of legal questions were in dispute. Rather, it was the timing or the inappropriateness of parlementary judgments in very special circumstances that prompted complaints.

For example, when cases of *évocation de justice* and *règlement de juges* in civil matters were pending at the council, all procedures in the courts pertaining to these cases were suspended until the council determined proper jurisdiction; in criminal cases, the judges could continue procedures but not render final judgments. Any procedures undertaken or judgments rendered in violation of these rules were obviously premature and thus subject to nullification.[19] The same fate awaited a judgment rendered by one court after the council had already transferred jurisdiction in a case to another tribunal. This situation arose most often in the aftermath of the council's adjudication of *évocations de justice* and *règlements de juges*.[20] Moreover, a parlement risked *cassation* if it judged litigation even though one or more of the parties held letters patent (such as those of *état, répit,* or *committimus*) that either postponed litigation for a specified time period or awarded special jurisdiction in a case.[21] Finally, the ordinances of April 1667 and August 1670 placed restrictions on the right of the parlements to remove and judge litigation that was pending in lesser tribunals. The *parlementaires* were entitled, for example, to evoke cases from lesser courts if they then judged these cases after oral pleading had occurred in open session (*à l'audience, sur-le-champ*); if, on the other hand, they removed cases only to channel them through more expensive and lengthy written procedures (*procès par écrit, appointements*), the ensuing judgments were susceptible to nullification.[22]

---

parlements, this study does not discuss in detail the relations between the councils and the other sovereign courts mentioned above in chap. I, n. 3.

[19] See the ordinance of August 1669, tit. 1, arts. 39 and 41; tit. 2, art. 7; tit. 3, art. 2. See also Bornier's commentary in *Conférences des ordonnances de Louis XIV*, 1: 415–418, 428–429, 433. For illustrative examples, see the *arrêts sur requête* of 19 October 1695 (AN, V⁶ 755, no. 12) and 11 February 1715 (V⁶ 834, no. 2).

[20] In such cases, the council acted to defend the integrity of its own previous decisions. For illustrative examples, see the *arrêts* between parties of 7 May 1676 (AN, V⁶ 626, no. 44) and 14 September 1705 (V⁶ 802, no. 17; see with the related *arrêt sur requête* of 20 November 1702 in V⁶ 790). Note that in this type of action in *cassation* one can occasionally find allegations that the parlements had ignored the *règlements de juges* that another sovereign court, the Grand Conseil, adjudicated between the parlements and the présidiaux. See, for example, two *arrêts sur requête* of 17 December 1714 (V⁶ 834, no. 18) and 28 January 1715 (V⁶ 834, no. 2).

[21] On these letters patent, see the ordinance of August 1669, tit. 4–6, and Bornier's commentary in *Conférences des ordonnances de Louis XIV*, 1: 438–517. For an illustrative example involving *lettres de répit*, see the *arrêt sur requête* of 23 April 1676 in AN, V⁶ 626, no. 8.

[22] For details on the parlements' rights of *évocation*, see the ordinances of April 1667 (tit. 6, art. 2) and August 1670 (tit. 25, art. 5), as well as the commentaries in Rodier, *Questions sur l'ordonnance de Louis XIV*, 84–87, and François Serpillon, *Code criminel, ou commentaire sur l'ordonnance de 1670* (2 vols.; Lyon, 1767), 2: 1149–1179. For illustrative cases, see the *arrêts sur requête* of 19 March 1714 (AN, V⁶ 831, no. 17) and 4 February 1715 (V⁶ 834, no. 2).

Together, these kinds of actions in *cassation* outnumbered all other varieties that came before the Conseil Privé, resulting in over a hundred *arrêts* pertaining to the parlements in the primary sample. But the lack of tension these cases occasioned between the parlements and the Conseil Privé reduces their importance for our purposes. A smaller sample of 32 *arrêts* (27 *sur requête*, including four traced from five *arrêts* between parties) will suffice to illustrate the reasons for this absence of controversy.[23]

In the first place, the jurisdictional rules involved in these cases were well established: all the complaints of parties had solid statutory foundation, often in such recent legislation as the ordinances of April 1667, August 1669, and August 1670. Given the uncertainties about proper jurisdiction that characterized judicial administration in this era, the parlements could well anticipate encountering occasional difficulties on this score. But they had no quarrel with the Conseil Privé so long as it considered nullifying only those judgments that were in clear violation of well known principles, a policy to which the council adhered rigorously throughout Louis XIV's personal rule.[24]

Second, it bears repeating that the complaining parties in these jurisdictional disputes challenged neither the professional competence nor the general judicial authority of the *parlementaires*. In this connection, it is noteworthy that the parlementary sentences under attack in these cases were often default judgments.[25] By having refused to contest their grievances before the parlements, parties had avoided acquiescing, however indirectly, in a court's jurisdiction. In his memorandum of 1665, Councillor of State Aligre noted how litigants sometimes "allow themselves to be judged by default . . . in the hope of recommencing their cases in the councils of Your Majesty."[26] But this strategy, which made sense from the vantage point of parties who suspected the parlements of having exceeded their jurisdiction, also increased the chances that the judges had decided a case without full knowledge of all the pertinent facts.

Third, if we set aside those cases in which the parlements were accused of having improperly removed litigation from lesser courts, the complaining parties themselves often indicated that the parlements had been unwitting accomplices to jurisdictional errors. The *arrêts sur requête* bristle with charges

---

[23] This smaller sample was taken randomly. Note that the Conseil Privé occasionally considered nullifying simple procedures (for example, summonses) in the parlements for violations of the principles set forth in the preceding paragraph. Because I am concerned with parlementary judgments (*arrêts*), I have not included these *cassations* in this smaller sample. For an example, however, see the *arrêt sur requête* of 18 September 1668 in AN, V⁶ 544, no. 41.

[24] Even in the decades immediately preceding the Fronde, when the Parlement of Paris protested in principle against most types of *cassations*, it did not object to them for the kinds of jurisdictional issues raised in the paragraphs above. See, for example, AN, U 2098, fols. 453v–457v (17 August 1645).

[25] For example, see the *arrêts sur requête* of 10 July 1669 (AN, V⁶ 554, no. 57), 20 February 1685 (V⁶ 686, no. 33), and 19 October 1695 (V⁶ 755, no. 24).

[26] BN, Clairambault MS. 613, p. 14.

of improper conduct levelled by petitioners against their adversaries. Thus Alexandre Petau asserted that his opposite party, Dame Aubry de Roussy, won a judgment at the Parlement of Paris within hours of his having formally notified her that he had initiated proceedings at the council for an *évocation de justice,* a passive response on her part that now compelled Petau to request nullification of the parlement's sentence.[27] Pierre d'Auvetay sought *cassation* of a judgment the Parlement of Rennes had rendered before his *lettres de répit* postponing litigation had expired, noting however that his opposite party had acted "surreptitiously" in securing this judgment.[28] And Thierry Bignon claimed that one L'Orée, "whose chicanery knows no limits," had initiated several actions at the council and introduced litigation at the Parlement of Paris under the names of his son and a friend in order to prevent the judgment of a case the council had already sent to the Parlement of Rouen, a series of ruses that now placed a sentence of the Parisian judges in danger of *cassation.*[29]

The omission of harsh words about the parlements in these and similar cases is significant because it was not simply a sign of deference to the *parlementaires:* we shall see that in other types of actions in *cassation* parties were frequently less hesitant to criticize their judges in strong terms. Clearly, the magistrates could be caught off guard as litigants maneuvered in the thorny fields of jurisdiction. The council itself was not immune to the chicanery of those who came before it. Its archives contain numerous examples of petitioners requesting the council to withdraw or modify its decisions on the grounds that the other parties in a case had violated procedural rules, withheld crucial evidence, or, to use a favorite expression of the era, otherwise "surprised the religion of messieurs du conseil."[30] Few members of the Conseil Privé or of the parlements themselves would not have nodded in agreement when one of these petitioners, Mathurin Goeslin, complained about "the surprises and the chicanery of those who always find new ways to attack judgments rendered in last resort [*les choses jugées*]."[31]

Finally, despite the routine nature of these jurisdictional cases, the Conseil Privé proceeded with great care in adjudicating them. Of the 23 *arrêts sur requête* drawn from the primary sample on this matter, only seven gave a final decision at this stage, the other 16 calling instead for additional procedures; and because the members of the Conseil Privé did not assess

---

[27] *Arrêt sur requête* of 18 September 1705, AN, V⁶ 802, no. 18.

[28] *Arrêt sur requête* of 23 April 1676, AN, V⁶ 626, no. 8.

[29] *Arrêt sur requête* of 31 May 1683 (in AN, V⁶ 674) traced from an *arrêt* between parties of 20 March 1685 (V⁶ 686, no. 23).

[30] For examples, see the *arrêts sur requête* of 10 July 1669 (AN, V⁶ 554, no. 54), 7 May 1676 (V⁶ 626, no. 37), and 20 February 1685 (V⁶ 686, no. 17).

[31] *Arrêt sur requête* of 18 September 1668, AN, V⁶ 544, no. 33. In this case, Goeslin complained that the council, acting on a request filed by his opposite party, had suspended the enforcement of a judgment in last resort even though this person had failed to observe the council's own procedural rules. In nullifying its original decision, the council actually noted in the *arrêt* that the reporting magistrate, Master of Requests L'Avocat, "a esté surpris en sursoyant des arrests contradictoires, il a signé la cassation."

personal fees, or *épices*, for their work, one cannot assume a motive of financial gain in the order for further proceedings. The council especially exhibited caution in resolving those cases in which the parlements were suspected of having improperly removed cases from lesser tribunals. Of the nine *arrêts sur requête* that exist on this matter in the entire primary sample, only two ventured a decision at this stage of the proceedings. Nor did the simple allegation of parlementary misconduct guarantee ultimate success, even in these purely jurisdictional disputes for which proof was in theory relatively easy to assemble. The smaller sample of 32 *arrêts* includes 12 *arrêts* (seven *sur requête* and five between parties) that gave a final decision: seven parties won their bid for *cassation*, but five lost.

Far more crucial to the parlements' relations with the Conseil Privé were the more serious cases of *cassation*, those in which the complaining parties drew upon the full range of grounds for nullification and in the process raised fundamental questions about the judges' conduct and authority. For whenever a disgruntled litigant asserted that a parlement had violated law, royal legislation, or procedural rules in rendering a judgment, by definition he disputed the magistrates' professional abilities. An allegation that a sentence lacked equity raised doubts about a court's integrity and sense of fairness. Nor were all complaints about jurisdiction benign: it was one thing to claim that a parlement had shown poor timing in entering a judgment, but quite another to maintain that certain kinds of legal issues lay completely outside its legitimate competence. Moreover, it was cases such as these that not only prompted correspondence between the parlements and the chancellor, but also produced bitter remarks on the part of parties. When François Auvil complained that the Parlement of Rennes had decided an inheritance case without a sufficient number of judges, for example, he spoke of the "little attention and exactitude with which this sentence was rendered"; and when the Parlement of Dijon issued a warrant for the arrest of Augustin Forestier on the request of his creditors, he not only claimed that the *parlementaires* had usurped the jurisdiction of lesser judges, but he added that the warrant itself was "the pure work of intrigue or of the credit those who obtained it [enjoy with the judges]."[32] A few bold petitioners came close to using openly disrespectful language when accusing the parlements of incompetence or blatant favoritism. In 1675, the Parlement of Rouen ordered several judicial officials at the *vicomté* of Valognes to stand trial on charges that they had stolen court records. These officials complained to the council that the *parlementaires* had made over a dozen procedural errors in arriving at this decision, remarking caustically that "it appears that the parlement had no other design than to spare the truly guilty persons who committed this crime."[33]

---

[32] *Arrêts sur requête* of 11 March 1715 (AN, V⁶ 834, no. 1) and 7 May 1676 (V⁶ 626, no. 29).

[33] *Arrêt* on *requêtes respectives* of 20 May 1676, AN, V⁶ 626, no. 25. For equally bitter remarks on the part of petitioners, see also the *arrêt sur requête* of 27 February 1685 (V⁶ 686,

The importance of the more serious cases of *cassation* requires that we isolate them with greater precision, an operation accomplished by setting aside the routine disputes over jurisdiction discussed in the preceding paragraphs. The primary sample then yields a total of 67 *arrêts sur requête* pertaining to the parlements in the matter of *cassation*. I have supplemented these *arrêts* with ten *arrêts* between parties drawn from the primary sample and with an additional seven *arrêts sur requête* traced from these ten.[34] If one bears in mind that for most of Louis XIV's personal rule a sample of some 1,500 *arrêts* is the equivalent of between six months and two years of the Conseil Privé's work, it is readily apparent that these serious cases of *cassation* not only constituted a small portion of the council's overall caseload, but they also represented only a very small percentage of the thousands of civil and criminal judgments the parlements together rendered each year.[35] But the relative rarity of complaints that the parlements had committed grave errors in judging litigation gave little consolation to the magistrates affected. Neither the Conseil Privé nor the parlements took such charges lightly.

At first glance, these *arrêts* offer a confusing variety of grievances and legal issues that seem to defy systematic analysis. Very few complaints to the council were as simple and straightforward as the one of Jean Benet, who based his request for the nullification of a judgment rendered by the Parlement of Aix solely on a claimed violation of a single article in the marine ordinance of August 1681.[36] More typical were petitioners who, like Joseph de Belloc, presented several distinct grounds for *cassation:* Belloc asserted that in the course of judging an inheritance contest involving the attachment and sale of real property for debt, the Parlement of Toulouse had not only exceeded its jurisdiction by deciding several issues belonging before local judges, but it had also violated two procedural rules set forth in the ordinance of April 1667; he added that the sentence itself contravened principles of Roman law as embodied in specific royal legislation.[37] Indeed, 31 of the 74 *arrêts sur requête* mention two grounds for *cassation* while

---

no. 6) as well as two *arrêts sur requête* traced from an *arrêt* between parties of 19 March 1714 (V⁶ 831, no. 23): 29 May 1713 (V⁶ 828, no. 26) and 20 November 1713 (V⁶ 830, no. 13).

[34] By court, the 67 *arrêts sur requête* break down as follows: Parlements of Paris (22), Bordeaux (10), Toulouse (8), Rennes (8), Aix (5), Rouen (5), Dijon (4), Grenoble (3), Pau (1), and the Conseil Souverain of Alsace (1). For the *arrêts* between parties, which were chosen randomly and include two *arrêts* on *requêtes respectives* also counted among the 67 *arrêts* above: Parlements of Rouen (4), Besançon (1), Bordeaux (1), Grenoble (1), Rennes (1), Paris (1), and the Conseil Souverain of Artois (1). In short, all the pertinent courts appear in the sample save for the Parlements of Metz and Tournai and the Conseil Souverain of Roussillon.

[35] I shall return to the size of the council's caseload later in this study. Unfortunately, we lack detailed studies of the number of judgments the various parlements rendered each year in the seventeenth century. For an idea of the magnitude, see Hurt, "Les Offices au Parlement de Bretagne," 19, and the graphs in Kaiser, "The Deflation in the Volume of Litigation at Paris," 331–332. Clearly, fewer than one percent of a given parlement's judgments ever became the subject of a request for *cassation* at the Conseil Privé.

[36] *Arrêt sur requête* of 3 December 1714, AN, V⁶ 834, no. 17.

[37] *Arrêt sur requête* of 3 December 1714, AN, V⁶ 834, no. 5.

eight *arrêts* refer to three. Thirty-five *arrêts* indicate only one ground, such as the violation of procedural rules, but within this single category petitioners normally cited many individual infractions to substantiate their complaints. Félicien Calliat, for example, invoked only procedural errors when he protested his conviction for forgery at the Parlement of Grenoble, but he listed seven such errors, including four different violations of the ordinance of August 1670.[38]

When coupled with the absence of the council's judicial reasoning in its decisions, the tendency of petitioners to submit elaborate requests for *cassation* frustrates attempts to determine precisely which circumstances in a given case led the council to rule as it did. Despite this problem, the *arrêts* can be examined in ways intended to reveal broad patterns in the council's jurisprudence. On one level, a simple overview of the final decisions in the *arrêts* is informative, suggesting as it does that most serious challenges to parlementary judgments were unsuccessful. Among the 67 *arrêts sur requête* and the ten *arrêts* between parties drawn from the primary sample, 26 gave a final decision, and 14 of these (or 54 percent) rejected the request for *cassation*. But the best method for gaining insights into both the nature of the grievances that parties raised and the council's response to different kinds of complaints is to examine the *arrêts* from the vantage point of the grounds for *cassation* they mention.

If we review the principal grounds for *cassation*, the paucity of complaints about a lack of equity in parlementary judgments is among the most striking features of the council's *arrêts*. Gilbert de Voisins noted that in the eighteenth century questions of equity were "the most delicate and certainly the most rarely considered" grounds for *cassation* because litigants must never be encouraged to confuse simple dissatisfaction with a judicial opinion with more serious charges of injustice.[39] A similar situation prevailed during Louis XIV's personal rule: only 12 of the 74 *arrêts sur requête* contain allegations that the *parlementaires* had unfairly decided the substantive issues involved in the litigation that came before them, and not a single petitioner expressed this grievance as the sole reason for seeking nullification of a parlement's sentence. Given the proclivity of losing litigants then as now to doubt the fairness of judgments against them, the reluctance of petitioners to base their cases at the Conseil Privé exclusively on this complaint illustrates the council's basic respect for both the legal decisions that the parlements made in last resort and the great freedom that French magistrates traditionally enjoyed in weighing evidence in individual cases.

Petitioners themselves testified to the council's unwillingness to allow *cassation* to assume the character of an ordinary appeal on the merits of litigation. Bernard de Genevois, who sought the nullification of a judgment the Parlement of Paris had rendered against him in a contest over land

---

[38] *Arrêt sur requête* of 7 December 1705, AN, V⁶ 802, no. 4.
[39] Antoine, "Le Mémoire de Gilbert de Voisins," 24.

possession, acknowledged that "the supplicant well knows that claims of injustice are not capable of destroying [parlementary] sentences if there are no other grounds for nullity and *cassation*," and Isaac Marchays, who believed that the Parlement of Bordeaux had shown excessive leniency toward his opposite party in a prosecution for theft, granted that "even the most crying injustice does not alone constitute grounds for *cassation*, although it always determines His Majesty in favor of those who [also] draw on [royal] ordinances [to justify their complaints]."[40] Jean-Baptiste Nivet, an *avocat* at the Parlement of Paris who maintained that this court erred in finding against him in litigation he had initiated to secure the payment of debts, also recognized that "there is no more solid ground for *cassation* than the contravention of [royal] ordinances and conciliar *arrêts*. . . ."[41] Like all the other parties who appealed to the council's sense of fairness, these petitioners did so only to supplement additional, fully documented claims of judicial error. Thus both Genevois and Marchays alleged that their judges had violated the crown's codes of judicial procedure (eight separate infractions in Marchay's case), while Nivet argued that the Parisian *parlementaires* had misinterpreted important provisions in a royal declaration of February 1683 that regulated the distribution to creditors of sums arising from the attachment and sale of royal offices.[42]

But even this tactic of combining claims of inequity with other grounds for *cassation* was not particularly effective. Of the 12 *arrêts sur requête* that raised questions of equity, four gave a final decision at this stage, and only one of these ordered *cassation* (none of the *arrêts* between parties in the sample dealt with this issue). Nor is it likely in this single case that the issue of equity influenced the council. The petitioner, Jean La Roque, alleged that the Parlement of Paris had not only violated judicial procedure while judging a *requête civile* in which he was a party, but that the judges had unfairly awarded an excessively high sum to his adversary. Although the council rescinded the parlement's sentence, it nevertheless returned the parties to the same court for a rehearing and final decision on the *requête civile*. The council rarely remanded cases to the judges whose sentences it had just nullified, and it is highly improbable that it would have done so in this instance had it suspected that the Parisian *parlementaires* were incapable of judging fairly the merits of La Roque's litigation.[43] Moreover,

---

[40] *Arrêts sur requête* of 9 March 1685 (AN, V⁶ 686, no. 17) and 25 February 1714 (V⁶ 834, no. 3).

[41] *Arrêt sur requête* of 12 October 1705, AN, V⁶ 802, no. 12.

[42] For additional examples of cases in which claims of inequity supplemented other grounds for *cassation*, see the *arrêts sur requête* of 18 September 1668 (AN, V⁶ 544, no. 36), 3 July 1669 (V⁶ 554, no. 23), and 16 October 1705 (V⁶ 802, no. 6). In one case, a petitioner was so reluctant to mention "injustice" as a formal ground that he referred to it only in passing, "par manière de remonstrance." *Arrêt sur requête* of 27 March 1685 (V⁶ 686, no. 22).

[43] *Arrêt sur requête* of 18 September 1668, AN, V⁶ 544, no. 35. Indeed, of the 12 *cassations* that appear in the primary sample, only two returned parties to the parlement whose judgment was rescinded. In the other cases, the council either sent the parties to another parlement or made no jurisdictional determination at all.

when the council did consider questions of equity, it could do so to the advantage of the judges. Chancellor Pontchartrain's correspondence indicates that the council occasionally rejected requests for *cassation*, even when petitioners had fully proven their contentions, if the "merits of the case" or "principles of equity" dictated that a parlement's judgment should stand.[44] As both Genevois and Marchays assumed, there is no evidence to suggest that the council showed similar consideration for litigants by ordering *cassation* for reasons of inequity if other grounds for nullification were not well founded.

The *parlementaires* also endured few complaints regarding another important aspect of their discretionary authority: their right to interpret and to apply in individual cases the private law of the realm, whether this be embodied in the customary laws (*coutumiers*) of northern and central France or in the Roman law (*droit écrit*) of the south. To be sure, parties rightly considered a violation of private law to be a legitimate cause for complaint before the Conseil Privé. Eleven of the 74 *arrêts sur requête* mention this issue, eight petitioners feeling sufficiently confident to designate it as the sole ground for *cassation*. Upon close scrutiny, however, these cases appear to have been less onerous to the judges' interests than one might imagine. On the one hand, the council seems to have been no more liberal in pronouncing *cassation* in cases raising this grievance than in those involving allegations of inequity: of the four final decisions we have on these 11 actions (three *sur requête* and one between parties), three rejected the request for nullification.[45] On the other hand, the issues in contention in these 11 cases were generally not of a nature either to undermine the magistrates' authority or to tarnish their reputations in a serious way.

In five cases, petitioners claimed that parlements had violated laws that, in fact, the judges had only limited experience in applying. This situation could arise, for example, when an *évocation de justice* sent a case from a tribunal in a region of Roman law, like the Parlement of Aix, to a court that normally decided cases on the basis of customary laws, such as the Parlement of Paris. Because any act of transfer required the parlement receiving litigation to apply the law of the case's origin, occasional and honest mistakes were bound to occur.[46] "I would not presume [to imply]

---

[44] For example, see Pontchartrain to Montholon and Bermonville, both at the Parlement of Rouen, 6 March 1701, BN, MSS. Fr. 21120, pp. 266–270. We shall see later in this study that Pontchartrain occasionally wrote to the parlements to discuss errors the *parlementaires* had committed in judging a case even though requests for *cassation* had failed.

[45] In the single case in which *cassation* was ordered, it is impossible to determine the weight the council gave to the claimed violation of law because the petitioner, an abbess from Aix, also offered other grounds for nullification, including alleged violations of judicial procedure: *arrêt sur requête* of 14 September 1705, AN, V⁶ 802, no. 1.

[46] For the legal principle, see the ordinance of August 1669, tit. 1, art. 46. For the pertinent cases, see the *arrêts sur requête* of 18 September 1668 (AN, V⁶ 544, no. 1) and 7 September 1705 (V⁶ 802, no. 4). Of course, a similar situation could arise when a court in one area of customary law (e.g., the Parlement of Rennes) received a case from a court in a region with a different custom (e.g., the Parlement of Rouen): *arrêt sur requête* of 27 February 1685 (V⁶ 686, no. 17).

that if the [legal] issues had been understood, the parlement would have wished to judge against the custom of the region," noted Jacques Charpentier, who claimed that the Parlement of Paris had violated the custom of Normandy in the course of judging litigation between him and his creditors.[47] Yet another case concerned the problem of "contrariété des arrêts," which arose when two sovereign courts rendered contradictory judgments between the same parties on the same substantive issues; that a petitioner would seek nullification of the judgment against him was understandable.[48]

Three other cases involved clerics who maintained that parlementary sentences had violated either the constitutions of religious orders or canonical regulations on the possession of benefices, documents that enjoyed the force of law in France. Thus in 1714 a *clerc tonsuré* in the diocese of Grenoble, Pierre Joubert, asserted that the Parlement of Grenoble had contravened the canons of the Church (backed by royal "precautions" against abuses in distributing benefices) when it awarded the possession of a priory to another individual.[49] The clergy of France was notoriously jealous of its privileges, and it traditionally looked to the king and his councils to safeguard them.[50] The parlements might have resented such challenges to their legal decisions, but at least they could view quarrels with the clergy as an ordinary feature of judicial life. Moreover, the three cases in question concerned strictly private litigation that did not raise larger and more sensitive questions about the parlements' general authority in religious affairs.[51]

Only in the two remaining cases were the parlements alleged to have violated laws with which they should have been perfectly familiar, as in the case of Jean de La Care, who claimed that the Parlement of Paris had disregarded key provisions in the custom of Bourges when it called for a "useless" ordering of creditors in litigation involving an inheritance burdened with debt.[52] Citing what he believed to be the general jurisprudence of the realm and the opinions of "the most respected jurists," Joseph de Calmeilh maintained that when the Parlement of Bordeaux ordered his

---

[47] *Arrêt sur requête* of May 1676, AN, V⁶ 626, no. 9. This and one other case in the primary sample (*arrêt sur requête* of 19 March 1714, V⁶ 831, no. 1) did not arise from the formal transfer of litigation from one court to another, but rather from the principle that even in the ordinary course of judging litigation the parlements must apply the custom of the region where the objects of litigation are located.

[48] *Arrêt sur requête* of 3 July 1669, AN, V⁶ 554, no. 5. The Grand Conseil could also judge these disputes, but in this case it was one of the courts involved (along with the Parlement of Rouen). Note that some jurists in the *ancien régime* considered *contrariété des arrêts* to be a distinct ground for *cassation:* Martinage-Baranger, "Les Idées sur la cassation," 262. Because I found only one example of it in the primary sample, I have included it in this discussion of violations of law.

[49] *Arrêt sur requête* of 3 December 1714, AN, V⁶ 834, no. 16.

[50] For general studies of the relations between the clergy and the king's councils, see Coudy, *Les Moyens d'action de l'ordre du clergé*, and Dent, "The Council of State and the Clergy."

[51] In addition to the case cited in this chapter, n. 49, see also the *arrêt sur requête* cited in this chapter, n. 45 and the one of 20 May 1676 in AN, V⁶ 626, no. 17. The former concerns several nuns acting as creditors in a private civil suit; the latter, the transfer of a nun from one religious house to another.

[52] *Arrêt sur requête* of 9 September 1695, AN, V⁶ 755, no. 11.

arrest in 1690 on charges stemming from a homicide that had occurred in 1657, the judges ignored the time limits after which criminal offenses could not be punished.[53] But neither of these attempts to secure *cassation* succeeded.

It is worth noting at this point that the relative infrequency of requests for *cassation* on the grounds of inequity or violation of law in no way means that the parlements did not commit more errors along these lines than those brought to the attention of the Conseil Privé. As a general comment pertaining to all cases of *cassation* at council, we shall never know how many litigants believed they had legitimate grievances against the parlements but who, for one reason or another, decided against soliciting conciliar intervention. What merits underscoring, however, is that the parlements were most vulnerable to attack on the issues of equity and the interpretation of law precisely because the judges exercised their broadest discretion and independence of judgment in these matters. Had Louis XIV's Conseil Privé aspired to review the parlements' legal decisions in a systematic way, these subjects offered the clearest path, and surely many unhappy litigants would have jumped at the opportunity to raise cries of injustice or to exploit to their own advantage the complexity, not to mention the many ambiguities, inherent in private law. That few parties did so, and then with only limited success, shows how cautiously the council proceeded in these important areas of the parlements' authority.[54]

The same prudence can be observed as well in those cases of *cassation* that raised fundamental questions about the limits of parlementary jurisdiction in judicial affairs. In one respect, the parlements were spared numerous challenges of this sort because their right to hear a broad range of civil and criminal cases was well established and widely recognized. But the lines of jurisdictional authority in early modern France overlapped sufficiently to leave ample room for heated disagreements even at the highest levels of the judiciary. Twenty-three of the 74 *arrêts sur requête* under consideration contain complaints that a parlement had exceeded its legitimate power in the course of judging litigation. We may set aside 12 of

---

[53] *Arrêt sur requête* of 31 January 1691 (AN, V⁶ 726, no. 3), traced from the *arrêt* between parties of 26 September 1695 (V⁶ 755, no. 22). The parlement wanted Calmeilh in jail while it decided whether to register letters of mercy (*grâce*) he had received; Calmeilh believed this was unnecessary because over 20 years had elapsed since the commission of the crime in question (and, indeed, Calmeilh's prior conviction for it *in absentia*). Strictly speaking, of course, this case did not concern a parlement's interpretation of private law. But I have included it in this category because Calmeilh in effect claimed that a customary statute of limitations existed for the prosecution of crime.

[54] According to Antoine, *Le Conseil du roi sous le règne de Louis XV*, 531, when Louis XV's Conseil Privé retained jurisdiction over litigation after pronouncing *cassation*—something that occurred an average of three times a year between 1721 and 1767—this was because the council believed that a sovereign court had erred in judging the merits, or *fond*, of litigation. An error in *fond*, of course, usually raises questions about equity or the interpretation of law. If Louis XIV's Conseil Privé operated in a similar fashion, it was even less inclined to order *cassation* for these reasons: we shall see shortly that not a single *cassation* in the primary sample resulted in the council retaining litigation for final judgment.

these cases because they involved the routine and minor grievances discussed previously, the only difference being that in these dozen actions such grievances were joined to other grounds for *cassation*.[55] Far more noteworthy were the 11 remaining actions, in which petitioners went beyond criticizing simply the timing of a judgment, maintaining instead that certain legal issues fell completely outside a parlement's competence. Although the petitioners in all but one of these cases also presented other grounds for *cassation*, the issue of jurisdiction clearly predominated. In some of these complaints, parties granted that a parlement could hear a particular case, but they asserted that in entering judgment the magistrates had ruled on some matters that properly belonged before other authorities. The *grand vicaire* of the bishop of Langres, for example, did not deny that the Parlement of Besançon could receive appeals from church courts, in this instance the case of a priest who had been suspended from his functions. But the *grand vicaire* insisted that when the judges summarily reinstated this priest to his cure, they decided a purely spiritual matter over which the bishop alone had jurisdiction.[56] Other complaints were bolder still, asserting that a parlement lacked the power to judge entire categories of litigation. Thus the syndic of the clergy in the diocese of Quimper contended that when the Parlement of Rennes decided a case concerning a clergyman's *capitation* tax, it violated a contract between the king and the clergy of France that had awarded jurisdiction in such matters to local ecclesiastical institutions.[57] As another example, a judge in the town of Saint-Union in the Limousin, Etienne Lamy, contested the right of the Parlement of Bordeaux to hear appeals from the rulings (*ordonnances*) that the provincial intendants issued in police matters.[58]

Without underestimating the threats that such challenges posed to the parlements' authority and pretensions, it is also important to recognize that recourse to *cassation* for serious jurisdictional reasons was a remedy pursued most often by a well defined and privileged group, namely clerics and lesser royal officials anxious to defend their jurisdictional rights from parlementary encroachments. Seven of the 11 cases fall into this category (six being initiated by clergymen), and the high rate of success in these actions (three of the four final decisions we possess pronounced *cassation*) indicates that when called upon the Conseil Privé acted to maintain an equilibrium between the various public authorities of the realm, especially when com-

---

[55] For example, see the *arrêts sur requête* of 27 February 1685 (AN, V⁶ 686, no. 6) and 9 September 1695 (V⁶ 755, no. 41).

[56] *Arrêt* between parties of 28 January 1715 (AN, V⁶ 834, no. 8) and the related *arrêt sur requête* of 15 June 1711 (V⁶ 822, no. 8).

[57] *Arrêt sur requête* of 14 January 1715, AN, V⁶ 834, no. 2.

[58] *Arrêt sur requête* of 14 September 1705, AN, V⁶ 802, no. 3. The intendant of Limousin, Jean Rouillé, had issued an *ordonnance* empowering Lamy to investigate the conduct of a merchant suspected of tampering with weights and measures. The merchant appealed to the parlement and won a judgment, thus prompting Lamy to assert that only the king's councils could overturn an intendant's rulings.

plaining parties cited recent royal legislation to justify their jurisdictional claims (as was done in five cases).[59] But the quashing of some of their judgments in individual cases did not jeopardize the parlements' general authority in religious affairs, which remained substantial throughout Louis's reign.[60] Moreover, the council was apparently less receptive to ordinary litigants questioning the limits of parlementary jurisdiction in a fundamental way. The presence of only four such attempts in the entire primary sample reveals the reluctance of petitioners to follow this course, a reluctance that stands in sharp contrast to their willingness to seek *cassation* for more routine and less controversial jurisdictional reasons. Thus very few petitioners filed complaints like the one of the merchants of Provence who, acting through their syndic, alleged in 1669 that the Parlement of Aix had exceeded its jurisdiction and introduced a "novelty" into the law by prohibiting the sale of goods to minors without their fathers' consent.[61] And in only one of these four cases did the complaining party raise a major point about jurisdiction as his only ground, and this involved a clear-cut instance of a parlement having issued an order in a case that another sovereign court had already judged in last resort.[62]

The Conseil Privé proved to be equally circumspect when considering *cassation* for the two grounds that petitioners cited most often in their complaints: errors in judicial procedure and violations of royal legislation. Strictly speaking, drawing a sharp distinction between these two issues might seem to be artificial because throughout Louis XIV's personal rule the procedures that the kingdom's courts were to follow in judging civil and criminal cases were codified by a series of important legislative acts— the great ordinances of April 1667 and August 1670, as well as a host of supplementary measures dealing with such diverse matters as the organization of court dockets, the assessment of judicial fees, and the judgment of litigation by special court sessions known as *commissaires*.[63] In practice,

---

[59] In addition to the *arrêts* cited in the previous three notes, see the *arrêts sur requête* of 13 September 1668 (AN, V⁶ 544, no. 16), 3 July 1669 (V⁶ 554, no. 13), and 31 December 1714 (V⁶ 834, no. 11) as well as the *arrêt* between parties of 7 September 1705 (V⁶ 802, no. 13). Petitioners cited such legislation as the edict of April 1695 on ecclesiastical jurisdiction and the declaration of December 1700 on the functions of the *lieutenants généraux de police*.

[60] For concise reviews of this issue, see Dent, "The Council of State and the Clergy," 256–258, and Hamscher, *The Parlement of Paris After the Fronde*, 146–152.

[61] *Arrêt sur requête* of 10 July 1669, AN, V⁶ 554, no. 58.

[62] In this case, a woman imprisoned as a result of a forgery case judged at the Requêtes de l'Hôtel had then initiated proceedings at the Parlement of Paris, an inappropriate action that her opposite party, Guillaume Thomin, successfully protested at the council. *Arrêt sur requête* of 16 May 1676, AN, V⁶ 626, no. 42. For the other two cases, see the *arrêt* between parties of 21 May 1676 (V⁶ 626, no. 10; see with the related *arrêt sur requête* of 16 October 1675 in V⁶ 622) and the *arrêt sur requête* of 14 January 1714 (V⁶ 834, no. 3). In these four cases, the council pronounced *cassation* in one, refused the request in another, and ordered additional proceedings in the remaining two.

[63] There exists no published compendium of all the legislation issued during Louis XIV's reign dealing with judicial procedure, but the collection edited by Daniel Jousse contains many important acts: *Recueil chronologique des ordonnances, édits et arrêts de règlement cités dans les nouveaux commentaires sur les ordonnances des mois d'avril 1667, août 1669, août 1670, et mars 1673* (3 vols.; Paris, 1757).

however, this royal legislation on judicial procedure occupied such an important place in the contacts between the Conseil Privé and the parlements that the policies the council adopted regarding its enforcement warrant separate attention.

There can be no doubt that the appearance of the two procedural codes and their supplementary legislation provided litigants with an unprecedented opportunity to protest the conduct of the *parlementaires* before a superior authority and thereby increased the council's ability to subject parlementary sentences to judicial review. In the decades prior to the 1660s, complaints of a procedural nature at the Conseil Privé were rare, no doubt because the paucity of existing royal legislation that set forth judicial procedures in a comprehensive fashion had given all the parlements wide latitude to develop their own particular usages.[64] This situation changed during Louis's personal rule, however, when complaints that the parlements had violated procedural rules became the most frequently cited ground for *cassation*. Of the 74 *arrêts sur requête* under consideration, 50 (or 68 percent) raised this issue, and 20 of these *arrêts* mentioned it as the sole reason for a party seeking relief from a parlementary judgment. All but five of these 50 *arrêts* referred specifically to alleged violations of the codes of April 1667 and August 1670. Moreover, the council's willingness to receive such complaints was not limited to the early decades of Louis's reign, when most of the procedural legislation appeared: as with the other grounds for *cassation*, complaints of a procedural nature run uniformly through the nine years represented in the primary sample.

But if the Conseil Privé exhibited a general commitment to enforcing compliance with the new legislation in the parlements, there were sound political and legal reasons to temper this commitment with restraint and moderation. On the one hand, we have noted that the legal action of *requête civile* allowed the parlements to rectify errors stemming from the application of the two procedural codes, and this without conciliar interference. Any attempt by the council to substitute actions in *cassation* for those in *requête civile* would have eroded the parlements' powers of self-regulation and undoubtedly provoked spirited opposition. On the other hand, the very nature of the crown's procedural legislation counseled caution in its enforcement. Together, the two codes and their related acts contained literally hundreds of procedural rules, and some of these were obviously more important than others. In addition, these rules were not immutable: throughout Louis's reign and after, many provisions in the original legislation were modified either on the initiative of the central administration or in response to requests by individual parlements, and the judges never completely abandoned their traditional practices.[65] In these complex cir-

---

[64] My summary examination of *arrêts* from 1647 and 1656 (see above, this chapter, n. 4) uncovered only one case in which the petitioner's principal complaint dealt with a claimed violation of judicial procedure: *arrêt sur requête* of 18 February 1656, AN, V^6 319, no. 127.

[65] In future work, I will explore this issue in depth from the vantage point of both local and central archives. For a general idea of the major changes in Louis XIV's procedural leg-

cumstances, a rigorously literal interpretation of procedural rules would have invited disgruntled litigants to besiege the council with all manner of complaints, be they serious or minor in nature. What was called for instead was a conciliar policy of flexibility and discrimination, a policy that would permit the council to censure major errors in judicial procedure while at the same time respecting the dignity of superior magistrates and their ability to supervise their own conduct.

Louis XIV's Conseil Privé attempted to strike just such a delicate balance. It is clear, for example, that the council had no intention of undermining the use of *requêtes civiles* as a remedy for errors in judicial procedure. Evidence for this comes from the 20 cases in which petitioners raised only procedural grounds for *cassation*, that is, precisely those cases that one would think these parties could have resolved at the parlements by means of *requêtes civiles*. In fact, the recourse of petitioners to the council in these cases accorded perfectly with established legal principles and in no way signified attempts to diminish the authority of the parlements to reform their own conduct. In seven of the 20 cases, petitioners alleged that the parlements had either violated the rules for judging *requêtes civiles* as set forth in the ordinance of April 1667 or had revised one of their judgments by a legal action other than *requête civile*, something the same code prohibited.[66] Either way, the petitioners were well aware of the legitimacy of *requêtes civiles* and some had already resorted to them prior to coming to the council. But because a *requête civile* was the final remedy a litigant could pursue before a parlement, any complaint that the judges had in some way erred in adjudicating this legal action by definition had to be aired before a superior authority—the Conseil Privé.

In nine other cases, petitioners claimed that a parlement had violated not only provisions in one of the two procedural codes, but other royal legislation on judicial procedure as well. In 1714, for example, Cécile de Davasse alleged that in the course of judging litigation pertaining to a disputed inheritance, the Parlement of Toulouse had ignored several procedural rules in the ordinance of April 1667, especially those dealing with the reception of testimonial evidence in civil cases. But she also maintained that the judges had violated two other legislative acts concerning judicial procedure—an edict of August 1669 that required appellants to deposit an

---

islation over time, see Jousse's collection of acts cited above in n. 63 as well as the eighteenth-century commentaries on Louis's codes cited earlier in this chapter, in nn. 12 and 22, and below in n. 70.

[66] For example, Suzanne Jaussande claimed that the Parlement of Paris violated at least eight provisions in the code of 1667 for judging *requêtes civiles*, including the prohibition (tit. 35, art. 37) against deciding the merits of litigation (*rescisoire*) at the same time as ruling on the grounds for the *requête civile* itself (*rescindant*): *arrêt sur requête* of 9 March 1685, AN, V⁶ 686, no. 22. Antoine Bonhomme alleged that this court violated the same code (tit. 35, art. 1) by retracting one of its judgments without even having heard a *requête civile*: *arrêt sur requête* of 21 October 1705, V⁶ 802, no. 7. For similar cases, see the *arrêts sur requête* of 27 February 1685 (V⁶ 686, no. 5), 22 December 1705 (V⁶ 802, no. 12), and 31 December 1714 (V⁶ 834, no. 21).

appeal fine with a court before initiating proceedings, and a declaration of February 1691 that determined the order in which cases should be called for oral pleading at the Parlement of Toulouse.[67] Certainly, a *requête civile* was an appropriate way for a party to protest a parlement's errors in applying either of the two procedural codes. But the Conseil Privé retained legal jurisdiction over claimed violations of all other royal legislation, including that dealing with judicial procedure. The presence of cases like Davasse's at the council thus is no surprise.[68]

Only in the four remaining cases, in which petitioners referred solely to alleged violations of the ordinances of April 1667 and August 1670, could the council even be suspected of denying a parlement the opportunity to emend its mistakes. Yet a careful reading of these cases indicates that the council's interest in them was justified and reasonable. An example is the case of Julien de La Gonnière, who maintained that the Parlement of Rouen had violated provisions in both procedural codes not only when it permitted a lesser tribunal, the *bailliage* of Coutances, to judge a case of verbal injury according to procedures intended for more serious criminal offenses, but also when it failed during appellate proceedings to correct an important error committed by the judges at Coutances (La Gonnière claiming that one of these judges had been ineligible to participate in his trial).[69] It so happens that this party lost his bid for *cassation*, but the fact remains that his case raised sufficiently serious charges of procedural irregularity to warrant the council's allowing him to bypass a *requête civile*. But the existence of only four such cases in the entire primary sample indicates how rarely the Conseil Privé chose to exercise this option.[70]

The council's basic respect for *requêtes civiles* was no secret to its clientele. In their requests for *cassation*, some petitioners took great pains to explain that although several of their complaints dealt with judicial procedure and were thus eligible for resolution by a *requête civile* at a parlement, the existence of still other grounds for *cassation* in their request entitled them to consolidate all their grievances into a single action at the council.[71] The

---

[67] *Arrêt sur requête* of 3 December 1714, AN, V⁶ 834, no. 15.

[68] For other examples of this type of case, see the *arrêts sur requête* of 23 April 1676 (AN, V⁶ 626, no. 20) and 18 September 1705 (V⁶ 802, no. 4) as well as the *arrêt* between parties of 19 March 1714 (V⁶ 831, no. 23; see with the related *arrêt sur requête* of 29 May 1713, V⁶ 828, no. 26).

[69] *Arrêt* between parties of 17 December 1714 (AN, V⁶ 834, no. 8) and its related *arrêt sur requête* of 19 March 1714 (V⁶ 830, no. 5).

[70] For the other three cases, see the *arrêt sur requête* of 28 September 1695 (AN, V⁶ 755, no. 19), 14 September 1705 (V⁶ 802, no. 28), and 7 December 1705 (V⁶ 802, no. 4). It is interesting that the latter two cases as well as La Gonnière's concerned complaints about criminal sentences. Several jurists of the eighteenth century believed that not all kinds of criminal sentences could be challenged by a *requête civile*: for details on this complicated matter, see Daniel Jousse, *Commentaire sur l'ordonnance civile du mois d'avril 1667* (Paris, 1757), 618–620. If this was true in the seventeenth century, then perhaps one or more of these three cases actually belonged at the council as a matter of law, thus further dispelling any suspicion that the council wished to undermine the use of *requêtes civiles* in the parlements.

[71] An especially clear statement along these lines appears in the *arrêt* pertaining to the case of Bernard de Genevois cited above in this chapter, n. 40.

Conseil Privé certainly knew how to make such a distinction: upon receiving requests for *cassation* that met the criteria for a *requête civile* and did not raise larger questions about the judges' conduct, the council simply converted the petitioner's request into a *requête civile* and remanded the case to the appropriate parlement.[72] For their part, the parlements had no reason to fear that actions in *cassation* for procedural reasons posed an appreciable threat to their right to hear *requêtes civiles*. Between 1701 and 1715, at least three parlements requested and received permission to abbreviate the procedures for judging *requêtes civiles* because substantial backlogs of these cases existed on their dockets![73]

An especially creative way in which the council approached the task of enforcing the new procedural legislation in the parlements was to inform the judges about the procedures it considered to be particularly important and whose violation was likely to result in *cassation*. The chancellors assumed the responsibility for communicating with the parlements on this matter. Sometimes their correspondence took the form of circular letters, as when Boucherat warned eight provincial parlements in 1687 that the council was determined to nullify judgments rendered in violation of royal legislation that both limited the types of litigation the courts could judge in expensive special sessions and prohibited the magistrates from requiring litigants to deposit judicial fees prior to the final judgment of cases.[74] Such letters of general intent could be addressed to a single parlement: in 1707, Pontchartrain reviewed six procedures then in use in the criminal chamber of the Parlement of Rennes that he believed were contrary to the ordinance of August 1670, notably its provisions for judging forgery pleas. He encouraged the judges to reform their conduct rather than risk *cassation* of their sentences.[75]

More so than his predecessors, Pontchartrain also discussed specific cases pending at the council, occasionally explaining in detail to a parlement the reasons why the council had nullified one of its judgments. In 1711, for

---

[72] For example, see the case of Jean La Roque cited above in this chapter, n. 43 as well as the *arrêt sur requête* of 13 March 1685, AN, V⁶ 686, no. 11. Sometimes the council actually remanded petitioners to a parlement to pursue a *requête civile* even when these parties had presented grounds for *cassation* other than violations of the codes of 1667 and 1670: see two *arrêts sur requête* of 27 February 1685 in V⁶ 686, nos. 17 and 23.

[73] For the Parlement of Bordeaux, see several letters of Pontchartrain to La Tresne and Dalon in 1703, 1709, and 1711 in: BN, MSS. Fr. 21122, fols. 208v–209; 21130, fols. 719–720, 812–813; 21133, fol. 184; 21140, fols. 265–266. For the Parlement of Toulouse, see the letter to Riquet, 23 March 1701, ibid., 21140, fols. 98–99. For the Parlement of Paris, see the declarations of 12 January 1710 and 1 May 1715 in *Catalogue général des livres imprimés de la Bibliothèque Nationale: Actes Royaux* (7 vols.; Paris, 1910–1960)—hereafter *Actes Royaux*—nos. 24089 and 25868.

[74] Boucherat to the first presidents of the parlements, 8 November 1687, AN, V¹ 580, pp. 234–235.

[75] Pontchartrain to the Parlement of Rennes, 17 June 1707, BN, MSS. Fr. 21141, fols. 737–743v. For similar letters, see: Le Tellier to Fieubet (Toulouse), 18 December 1679, ibid., 5267, pp. 142–143; Boucherat to Marin (Aix), 21 October 1686, AN, V¹ 578, p. 356.

example, the Parlement of Toulouse ordered the arrest and imprisonment of a solicitor (*procureur*), Antoine Gravière, for having ignored a deliberation of the court and continued procedures in a case after the deadline for such activity had expired. In his request to the council, Gravière raised seven separate objections to the parlement's conduct, claiming (among other things) that he was never properly informed of the court's deliberation and its results, that the deadline the judges wished to enforce lacked legal foundation, and that procedural rules dictated that only persons accused of having committed serious crimes should suffer imprisonment during trial. The council overturned the parlement's rulings in this case. But in a series of letters addressed to the court's first president, Pontchartrain indicated precisely which of Gravière's grounds for nullification had convinced the council to act as it did (the issue of unwarranted imprisonment being the most crucial).[76] In a similar communication to the Parlement of Aix in 1705, the chancellor did not miss an opportunity to review some of the procedural rules for transferring litigation from one chamber of the court to another.[77] Because petitioners normally cited several reasons for seeking the nullification of a parlement's judgment, letters like these eliminated any ambiguity about which of a party's grievances had favorably impressed the council.

A request for *cassation* did not even have to be successful to elicit comments from this chancellor. In 1711, Pontchartrain informed the Parlement of Besançon that although an action against one of its sentences had recently failed, the council was nevertheless disappointed that while judging the case in question the *parlementaires* had violated an edict of June 1706 that determined how divisions of opinion (*partages*) within the court were to be resolved in litigation concerning royal waterways and forests. The message was clear: the council would not turn a blind eye to contravention of this edict in the future.[78] The Parlement of Bordeaux had received a similar warning in 1701. In this year, an action against one of its judgments had failed at the council—the petitioner's grounds, according to the chancellor, were "insufficiently clear and precise." Nevertheless, Pontchartrain notified the judges that while examining the paperwork for this case, the council had learned that this parlement was apparently in the habit of making too many kinds of legal decisions without holding formal hearings, acting instead on simple requests filed by litigants. If the judges did not mend their

---

[76] Pontchartrain to Bertier, 1 June, 9 November, and 6 December 1711, BN, MSS. Fr. 21134, fols. 468–470v, 904–905v, 976–977v. *Arrêt sur requête* of 8 May 1711, AN, V⁶ 822, no. 22. The chancellor was particularly distressed that the parlement had delegated a councillor in the court to arrest and search Gravière. To Pontchartrain, having a judge act in this fashion was dishonorable.

[77] Pontchartrain to Gassandy, 25 September 1705, BN, MSS. Fr. 21124, fols. 566v–568v. *Arrêt sur requête* of 14 September 1705, AN, V⁶ 802, no. 1. For another letter along these lines, see Le Tellier to Brûlart (Dijon), 17 September 1668, BM, Dijon, MS. 541, fols. 327v–328.

[78] Pontchartrain to Doroz, 18 July 1711, BN, MSS. Fr. 21134, fols. 609–611v.

ways and adhere to procedural rules, the chancellor cautioned, they could expect the nullification of their judgments.[79]

One should not exaggerate the extent to which this correspondence gave the parlements even unofficial access to the council's deliberations. The chancellors exercised great discretion in deciding when to contact the parlements, and even Pontchartrain, who excelled in preparing clear and informative letters, wrote in detail about only a few cases of *cassation* each year. The council had no intention of divulging the judicial reasoning behind more than a handful of its decisions, and it never restricted its own freedom of action by leading the magistrates to believe that procedural violations that were not the subject of special comment would be exempt from *cassation*. Nor should one lose sight of the disciplinary purpose of the chancellors' remarks. With this said, however, the fact remains that the chancellors' letters opened an important line of communication between the Conseil Privé and the parlements, lifting in at least a few cases the veil of secrecy that surrounded decision-making in the council and thereby enabling the judges to avert some challenges to their judgments before they occurred. To be sure, the chancellors did not write to the parlements exclusively about matters of judicial procedure: cases of *cassation* involving other grounds also prompted an occasional letter.[80] But given the large number of procedural rules and the confusion that could have resulted had the *parlementaires* lacked any information about the council's sense of priority in enforcing them, even limited contacts between the parlements and the Conseil Privé had beneficial consequences for their mutual relations. Local as well as central archives provide examples of parlements, having once received a letter from the chancellor, revising their traditional practices to conform to his advice. Such occurred at Rennes, for instance, after the judges had received Pontchartrain's letter of 1707 mentioned above, and in 1711 the Parlement of Bordeaux responded to the nullification of one of its sentences by voting to adhere in the future to provisions in the ordinance of August 1669 that restricted the kinds of cases the *parlementaires* could remove from the lower courts.[81] The parlements were presumably

---

[79] Pontchartrain to La Tresne and Dalon, 26 and 31 January 1701, ibid., 21120, pp. 111–113, 136–137. It is interesting that the chancellor was highly critical of the court's conduct in this case, accusing the judges of "affectation" and a "denial of justice." And yet the request for *cassation* failed, thus underscoring the point made earlier about the council's reluctance to nullify parlementary judgments on grounds of inequity.

[80] For example, see Pontchartrain's letters of 7 February 1710 to Le Mazuyer and to the Parlement of Toulouse regarding the enforcement of an edict of December 1691 dealing with the registration of ecclesiastical acts: ibid., 21131, fols. 215v–218v. With this letter, see the *arrêt* between parties of 3 February 1710 (AN, V⁶ 818, no. 12) and the related *arrêt sur requête* of 21 October 1707 (V⁶ 810, no. 5).

[81] Archives Départementales (hereafter AD), Ille-et-Vilaine, 1 Bf 1222 ("'grand' chambre: arrêts"—16 August 1707); Pontchartrain to the Parlement of Bordeaux and to Dalon, 22 July and 15 August 1710, BN, MSS. Fr. 21132, fols. 763–767v, 840 (see with the *arrêt* between parties of 21 July 1710—AN, V⁶ 819, no. 24—and the related *arrêt sur requête* of 27 March 1708—V⁶ 811, no. 18).

willing to accede to the council's wishes so long as the judges also received satisfaction on issues that they considered to be important, such as the abbreviation of procedures for judging *requêtes civiles* alluded to previously (and this is only one of many examples of the judges obtaining official changes in procedural rules).[82] Such signs of cooperation stand in marked contrast to the animosity that had soured the parlements' contacts with the Conseil Privé in the years before 1661.

Without question, the best method for the Conseil Privé to enforce royal legislation on judicial procedure without provoking serious conflict with the parlements was to consider nullifying their judgments for only the most "important" (to use a favored word of the era) procedural infractions. Exactly what in the council's view constituted an important as opposed to a minor violation of judicial procedure obviously varied from one case to another according to the particular circumstances involved. This situation, when coupled with the absence of the council's judicial reasoning in its *arrêts*, prevents us from ever defining with absolute precision criteria that were themselves constantly changing. If the letters of the chancellors shed at least some light on the problem, it seems that when the council reviewed allegations of procedural error, it took into account not only the gravity of a violation in principle—whether a court had flagrantly transgressed widely accepted norms of judicial conduct, for example, or whether the judges had ignored previous warnings by the council—but also the extent to which a specific infraction had determined the final outcome of litigation before a parlement.[83]

What is certain, however, is that the council exercised its discretionary power within limits that were sufficiently narrow to prevent charges of procedural irregularity from becoming an easy route to *cassation*. The conversion of some requests for *cassation* into *requêtes civiles* is one indication of this, as is the evidence in the chancellors' letters that even well proven violations of procedural rules did not always ensure that the council would nullify a parlement's sentence. Indeed, there is reason to believe that the majority of requests for *cassation* that raised questions of procedural error were unsuccessful. Of the 50 cases in which this issue appeared either alone or with other grounds for *cassation*, we have 15 final decisions (11 *sur requête* and four between parties), and only five of these pronounced nullification (seven parties lost their bid for *cassation* while three others

---

[82] As just one of scores of possible examples of the *parlementaires* securing the modification of procedural rules, it was the *procureur général* of the Parlement of Paris, Achille de Harlay, who both suggested and helped to draft the declaration of December 1680 concerning writs of personal citation (*ajournement personnel*) in criminal affairs: Jousse, ed., *Recueil chronologique des ordonnances*, 1: 466–468; Le Tellier to Harlay, 14 February, 21 and 25 November, and 3 December 1680, BN, MSS. Fr. 17415, fols. 130, 211, 215, 217.

[83] To observe the council operating within these criteria, see the letters of the chancellors cited in the previous notes as well as the letters of Pontchartrain to Morant (Toulouse; 31 March 1700), La Bedoyère (Rennes; 12 November 1702), and Le Bret (Aix; 24 April 1714) in: BN, MSS. Fr. 21119, pp. 247–248; 21121, fols. 531v–533v; 21139, fols. 375v–376v.

were advised to pursue a *requête civile* before a parlement). If one bears in
mind that documentary evidence for procedural violations was relatively
easy to assemble, at least when compared to that needed to sustain the
other grounds for *cassation*, it would stretch the imagination to assume
that the unsuccessful petitioners in these actions had absolutely no foundation for their grievances. Moreover, even in the 30 cases in which allegations of procedural error supplemented still other grounds for *cassation*,
there is no indication that petitioners padded their complaints with lengthy
lists of minor infractions. Quite the contrary, requests to the council consistently focused on those aspects of judicial procedure that were either
inherently complex or especially crucial to the final outcome of cases: in
criminal affairs, for example, the formalities associated with receiving appeals and with converting civil cases into criminal ones; in civil matters,
such issues as the assessment of court costs and the way in which a parlement handled a litigant's challenge of a particular magistrate sitting on a
case.[84] It is possible, of course, that the *parlementaires* simply made few
mistakes in implementing most judicial procedures, thus giving litigants
little cause to complain. This could account for the almost total absence of
complaints about the judges' observation of rules on such routine matters
as the preparation of trial documents and the granting of delays during
litigation. In view of the council's record in interpreting the other grounds
for *cassation*, however, one suspects that in the realm of judicial procedure
as well petitioners clearly understood that only especially compelling reasons could convince the Conseil Privé to nullify a parlement's judgment.

Turning to the final ground for *cassation*—the violation of royal legislation
(excluding that pertaining to judicial procedure discussed above)—familiar
patterns emerge in the council's conduct. Certainly, the Conseil Privé did
not dissuade litigants from making complaints of this type. Twenty-one of
the 74 *arrêts sur requête* under consideration mention this issue, nine of
them citing it as the sole reason for a petitioner's recourse to the council.
As with the other grounds for *cassation*, these complaints also appear
throughout the nine years represented in the primary sample. In addition,
the spectrum of royal acts the parlements were alleged to have violated in
their legal decisions was quite broad, ranging from such legislative mon-
uments of Louis XIV's reign as the ordinances for commerce (March 1673)
and marine (April 1681), to more specific laws like the edict of February
1683 mentioned earlier that regulated the distribution of sums resulting

---

[84] The titles of the ordinance of April 1667 that petitioners cited most frequently in their
complaints were 1 (*De L'Observation des ordonnances*), 6 (*Des Fins de non-procéder*), 24 (*Des
Récusations des juges*), 31 (*Des Dépens*), and 35 (*Des Requêtes Civiles*). In the ordinance of
August 1670, the most frequently cited titles were 9 (*Du Crime de faux*), 20 (*De La Conversion
des procès civils en procès criminels*), and 26 (*Des Appellations*). Addressing this problem with
statistical precision is difficult because some petitioners referred to the two codes without
citing specific titles and articles. Most petitioners did provide this information, however, so
the list above is accurate.

from the sale of crown offices.[85] Even official acts of very limited scope, such as letters patent of 1655 confirming the statutes of the saddlers' guild of Rennes, attracted the attention of petitioners.[86]

But if the council gave litigants wide latitude to submit requests for *cassation*, at the same time it not only made the actual nullification of sentences difficult to achieve, but it also attempted to limit the instances when *cassation* would apply. On the one hand, the rate of success in these cases was hardly more impressive than that associated with the other grounds for *cassation*. The 21 cases include ten final decisions (six *sur requête* and four between parties), half of which pronounced nullification. This is a modest number if we bear in mind that two of the five victories involved royal legislation concerning jurisdiction, which we have already noted the council was anxious to enforce.[87] On the other hand, an examination of the dates of the legislation that petitioners cited in their complaints reveals that the Conseil Privé was most interested in defending royal acts of recent vintage, those that were presumably well known to the *parlementaires*. Seventeen of the 21 *arrêts sur requête* referred to legislation issued after 1654, and only five parties claimed that the parlements had violated royal decrees that had appeared before that date.[88] The Conseil Privé apparently gave litigants little incentive to comb the legal heritage of France for ancient or esoteric statutes upon which to build a case against the parlements' judicial decisions.

In defining and interpreting the grounds for *cassation*, therefore, the Conseil Privé viewed this legal remedy as an extraordinary expression of the king's sovereign justice to be applied sparingly and within narrow limits. Whether all the patterns we have observed in the council's conduct were new to Louis XIV's personal rule or had their origins in previous decades is something that only a thorough study of *arrêts* from the first half of the century will determine with precision. There can be no doubt, however, that the king's forceful assertion of conciliar supremacy over the sovereign courts in 1661 did not usher in an age characterized by the unbridled and arbitrary nullification of parlementary sentences. This was true not only when the council dealt with the more traditional grounds for *cassation*—the violation of private law, for example, or errors in establishing

---

[85] For examples, see the cases cited above in this chapter, nn. 36 and 41 as well as the *arrêts sur requête* of 18 September 1705 (AN, V⁶ 802, no. 5), 7 December 1705 (V⁶ 802, no. 7), 31 December 1714 (V⁶ 834, no. 11), and 14 January 1715 (V⁶ 834, no. 3).

[86] For examples, see the *arrêts sur requête* of 21 October 1705 (AN, V⁶ 802, no. 2) and 19 March 1714 (V⁶ 831, no. 8).

[87] See the cases cited above in this chapter, nn. 36 and 58, as well as the *arrêt sur requête* of 7 January 1715 (AN, V⁶ 834, no. 10) and two *arrêts* between parties of 7 September 1705 (V⁶ 802, no. 13) and 22 December 1705 (V⁶ 802, no. 14; see with the related *arrêt sur requête* of 29 September 1704, V⁶ 798, no. 10).

[88] Nor was the pre-1654 legislation cited obscure. Adrun Moret, for example, alleged that the Parlement of Paris had violated an ordinance of 1551 on the attachment of real property (*saisie réelle*), a well known piece of legislation. *Arrêt sur requête* of 3 December 1714, AN, V⁶ 834, no. 2.

proper jurisdiction—but also when it ruled on matters for which it had little previous experience, such as the enforcement of the monarchy's substantial legislation on judicial procedure.

Still other aspects of the council's jurisprudence on *cassation* revealed a concern for the parlements' interests. When the council received a complaint that was politically sensitive or that threatened to undermine the legitimate authority the parlements exercised on the local level, the chancellor and his colleagues took steps to spare the judges any public embarrassment. In 1709, for example, the Parlement of Aix prosecuted one of its members— the councillor Sauveur de Michaelis—for extortion and prevarication in his post, sentencing him *in absentia* to banishment and various monetary penalties. Michaelis complained in a request to the council that serious procedural irregularities had marked his trial. Pontchartrain believed that Michaelis was guilty as charged but correct in his allegations—the procedure against him, the chancellor informed First President Pierre Cardin Le Bret, "has appeared to be entirely ridiculous, without rules, without principle, full of passion and partiality, and without any spirit of justice."[89] Nevertheless, Pontchartrain postponed a decision on the request for four years, working all the while with local notables to arrange a settlement that would enable the court to punish this councillor for his crimes without subjecting the judges to the humiliation of having their original sentence officially nullified. "All things being equal," the chancellor remarked to the public minister (*procureur général*) of the court, André de La Garde, "[the council] will always willingly act more favorably toward an entire parlement than toward an individual."[90] Only when an arrangement was made in 1713— involving a new trial for Michaelis and a reduction in the original penalties against him in return for his resigning office—did the council officially consider, and then reject, his request.[91]

Less dramatic but equally demonstrative of the council's approach was a case involving the *sénéchaussée* of Figeac, two of whose magistrates complained in 1709 that the Parlement of Toulouse had violated royal legislation and exceeded its jurisdiction by ordering them to return judicial fees that they had properly assessed in a case regarding the possession of a benefice. Pontchartrain informed the parlement that the council found the complaint fully justified, but that it would not nullify the court's sentence on the condition that the *parlementaires* themselves receive the two officials as

---

[89] Pontchartrain to Le Bret, 24 August 1709, BN, MSS. Fr. 21130, fols. 707v–711.

[90] Pontchartrain to La Garde, 22 July 1712, ibid., 21136, fols. 644v–646.

[91] This complex and intriguing case can be followed in nearly two dozen letters that Pontchartrain wrote to Le Bret, La Garde, the Archbishop of Aix, and Michaelis himself between 1709 and 1714 throughout ibid., 21129–21130, 21135–21136, and 21138–21139. See also the *arrêt sur requête* of 13 November 1713 in AN, V⁶ 830 as well as Bibliothèque Méjanes (Aix), MS. 989 (one of the "Tables des Délibérations du Parlement"), entry for "mercuriales, corrections et admonitions."

complainants and eventually rule in their favor. In this way, justice would be served without the council giving the appearance of publicly infringing upon the parlement's right to supervise the conduct of lesser judges.[92]

There is perhaps no better illustration of the council's desire to accommodate the parlements on the matter of *cassation* than its jurisprudence regarding two subjects that had generated heated parlementary criticism before 1661: the council's practice of retaining some cases for final judgment after having nullified the judicial sentences of the parlements; and its policy of pronouncing *cassation* solely on the basis of a petitioner's request without always calling for additional procedures. On the first issue, the judges understandably protested a threat to their material interests, the removal of litigation translating into lost fees. But the *parlementaires* also believed that the council's conduct undermined their power and prestige in a more fundamental way, claiming that whenever the council exceeded its regulatory functions and acted as an ordinary court of law—in effect inserting itself as another layer in the traditional judicial hierarchy—it not only usurped the legitimate authority vested in other institutions, but it encouraged litigants to assume that they could circumvent the parlements' right to judge cases in last resort. That the council occasionally retained jurisdiction over litigation involved in cases of *évocation de justice* and *règlement de juges* only aggravated parlementary resentment.[93]

The *parlementaires* of the 1640s and 1650s never alleged that the retention of cases at the Conseil Privé was the normal practice, and the council's own *arrêts* from that era show that most legal actions were resolved then as they were later in the century. Upon ordering *cassation*, the council either sent the parties to another parlement in order to have their cases retried or, less frequently, it simply pronounced nullification and left the parties to their own devices. In cases of *évocation de justice* and *règlement de juges*, the council confined itself to determining proper jurisdiction within the system of ordinary courts.[94] Nevertheless, the removal of litigation

---

[92] See Pontchartrain's letters to officials in both courts on 29 December 1709 and 28 January and 1 February 1710 in BN, MSS. Fr. 21130, fols. 1107–1109v, 1112–1115v; 21131, fols. 170–173, 183–184v. See also the *arrêt sur requête* of 9 September 1709 in AN, V⁶ 816, no. 9.

[93] Of course, there were instances when the Conseil Privé quite legitimately judged the merits of litigation. This was so, for example, when another council awarded it jurisdiction in a particular case or when litigation concerned such matters as the possession of royal offices, appeals from the rulings of the provincial intendants in civil matters, and certain conflicts between lesser judicial officials concerning their general functions. See, for example, the *arrêts sur requête* of 3 July 1669 (AN, V⁶ 554, no. 25), 25 October 1695 (V⁶ 755, no. 10), 7 September 1705 (V⁶ 802, no. 5), and 18 March 1715 (V⁶ 834, no. 9). Problems with the parlements arose when the council assumed jurisdiction over litigation that was already pending in the parlements (as was the case with *évocations de justice* and *règlements de juges*) or had already been judged there (as in cases of *cassation*).

[94] For these principles in operation before 1661, see the *arrêts* from 1647 and 1656 throughout AN, V⁶ 215, 319, and 326.

from the parlements for final judgment at the council was a problem serious enough to have figured prominently in the judges' memoranda of mid-century, and even a modest sample of *arrêts* issued before 1661 discloses examples of the practice.[95] For this reason, the virtual cessation of this activity during Louis XIV's personal rule was highly significant, sufficient in itself to have improved the council's relations with the parlements. Not a single action in *cassation* against a parlement's judgment in the primary sample resulted in the council retaining final jurisdiction over a case, and this generalization applies to *évocations de justice* as well. Only in two cases of *règlement de juges* in which parlementary jurisdiction was at stake did the council keep a case for final judgment. But in each instance, the litigation in question concerned administrative matters for which ample precedents existed to justify the council's decision.[96] Furthermore, even when it did retain final jurisdiction over an occasional case, the council could reverse itself at a later date and return litigation to a parlement.[97] We shall see that other councils were more willing to retain cases, although in limited number and only in special circumstances. As regards the Conseil Privé in particular, it definitively laid to rest any suspicions the judges might have had about its intention to compete with the parlements as an ordinary court of law.[98]

The council was less inclined to discontinue pronouncing *cassation* solely on the basis of a petitioner's request. After all, if the issues in a complaint were clear and could be resolved immediately by an *arrêt sur requête*, it made little sense to burden a petitioner's adversaries with the expense and inconvenience of further proceedings. Moreover, the nullification of parlementary judgments "on the simple request of parties" (as contemporaries put it) was the exception rather than the rule even before 1661.[99] One suspects that the parlements' opposition to the practice stemmed less from

---

[95] For example, see the *arrêts* between parties of 22 February 1656 (AN, V^6 319, no. 22) and 27 June 1656 (V^6 326, no. 146) as well as several "arrêts de rétention" scattered throughout V^6 319.

[96] One case, involving a *règlement de juges* between the Cour des Aides of Montauban and the Parlement of Toulouse, concerned an appeal from a ruling by one of the intendant's subdelegates; the precedent for the council keeping this case was its well established right to hear appeals from the rulings of the intendants themselves. In the other example of retention, the council itself was (along with the Parlement of Toulouse) one of the bodies eligible to resolve a dispute regarding a royal official's functions. See the *arrêts* between parties of 20 February 1685 (AN, V^6 686, no. 45) and 23 September 1695 (V^6 755, no. 14).

[97] As it did on 2 August 1664 after the Parlement of Paris objected to the retention at the Conseil Privé of litigation involving one Jeannet d'Absac: AN, X^{1A} 8664, fols. 133–134.

[98] René Guillard, an *avocat* at the council whose *Histoire du conseil du roy* ends with the reign of Louis XIV, noted the "circumspection" with which the council retained cases (pp. 79–80). For the general principle that the council would not judge the *fond* of litigation, see the *règlement* of January 1673, arts. 76–78. On a related issue, the primary sample contains no examples of the council removing cases from the parlements and sending them to the provincial intendants, the Requêtes de l'Hôtel, or commissions of the council (unless the parties were involved in ordinary cases of *règlements de juges*).

[99] See above, this chapter, n. 94.

principled objections than from the strong sentiments of mistrust the judges harbored against the council in those years. Certainly, the Conseil Privé gave the parlements little cause for alarm during Louis's personal rule. As noted previously, even in cases of *cassation* that concerned routine jurisdictional issues, the council did not normally use *arrêts sur requête* to provide definitive decisions. Instead, these *arrêts* usually summoned all the litigants involved in a disputed parlementary judgment to contest a petitioner's complaint fully before the council. This policy of allowing both sides in a dispute to present evidence prior to a conciliar decision was especially prevalent in the more serious cases of *cassation*. Of the 67 *arrêts sur requête* in the primary sample that concern these more serious cases, only 20 (or 30 percent) resolved an action at this stage of the proceedings; and in only eight of these 20 cases did the council rule in favor of the complaining party (nine *arrêts* rejected outright the request for *cassation* while three others converted actions into *requêtes civiles* for the parlements to adjudicate). Ever mindful of the important role that the *parlementaires* played in maintaining public order, the council only very rarely nullified a parlement's criminal sentence by an *arrêt sur requête*.[100] In addition, for those few individuals who did see a parlementary judgment in their favor overturned without their having had the opportunity to contest the matter at the council, a judicial procedure known as *opposition* enabled them to request the council to reconsider its decision. Examples of parties having successfully pursued this remedy appear throughout the council's *arrêts*.[101] The *parlementaires* also enjoyed the right to initiate such proceedings in order to defend one of their judgments that they believed the council had

---

[100] Only six of the 67 *arrêts sur requête* concerning serious cases of *cassation* dealt with criminal affairs (a number that rises to ten of 74 if we include the seven *arrêts sur requête* traced from the ten *arrêts* between parties drawn from the primary sample). Only one of the six *arrêts sur requête* nullified a parlement's sentence, and this was in response to a request filed by a plaintiff rather than by a defendant in a forgery case at the Parlement of Bordeaux: AN, V⁶ 802, no. 28 (14 September 1705). As regards the general paucity of criminal matters among the cases of *cassation* at the Conseil Privé, this could have resulted from a number of circumstances: the fact that the parlements judged more civil cases than criminal ones; the lack of financial resources on the part of most convicted criminals to initiate proceedings at the council; the care with which the parlements judged criminal cases; and the simplicity of criminal as opposed to civil procedures, thus reducing the chances for error.

[101] For example, see the *arrêts sur requête* of 3 July 1669 (AN, V⁶ 554, no. 32) and 16 May 1676 (V⁶ 626, no. 35) as well as the *arrêt* between parties of 3 December 1714 (V⁶ 834, no. 18). Just how often parties pursued *opposition* against *arrêts sur requête* pronouncing *cassation* is impossible to determine. By definition, an action in *opposition* referred to an *arrêt sur requête* issued on an earlier date, and these earlier dates will never all fall within the chronological limits of even the most reasonable sample of conciliar *arrêts*. But the very existence of *opposition* means that any statistics concerning how often actions in *cassation* either succeeded or failed at the council will necessarily be weighted in favor of petitioners who succeeded. After all, if a petitioner won *cassation* by an *arrêt sur requête*, his opposite party might have secured a revision of the council's decision at a later date through *opposition*. This situation actually underscores a point made earlier in this study: most requests for *cassation* at the Conseil Privé were unsuccessful.

nullified too precipitously.[102] In this as in the other aspects of its jurisprudence on *cassation*, the Conseil Privé tempered its broad discretionary authority with a fundamental respect for the integrity of the parlements' judicial decisions.

---

[102] The primary sample contains no examples of the parlements undertaking *opposition* against the council's *arrêts sur requête* that pronounced *cassation*. But other sources attest to the practice: (1) decisions by individual parlements to pursue this legal remedy (see the *procureur général*'s report to the Parlement of Grenoble on 7 September 1715 in AD, Isère, B 2313 ["Jurisprudence et Délibérations du Parlement," 1545–1786], fols. 81–82); (2) the *arrêts* of other councils (see the *arrêt en commandement* of 11 January 1672 in AN, E 1766, in which the Parlement of Paris successfully opposes an *arrêt* that the Conseil Privé had issued in *cassation*); (3) Pontchartrain's letters to Bertier (Toulouse; 9 November 1711) and to Le Bret (Aix; 24 April 1714), in which the chancellor notes explicitly that the parlements can pursue *opposition* (BN, MSS. Fr. 21134, fols. 904–905v and 21139, fols. 375v–376v; see the related *arrêts sur requête* of 18 May 1711 and 26 March 1714 in AN, V⁶ 822, no. 22 and 831, no. 5).

V. THE JURISPRUDENCE OF THE CONSEIL PRIVÉ: *ÉVOCATIONS DE JUSTICE* AND *RÈGLEMENTS DE JUGES*

T he same spirit of conciliation that guided the conduct of the Conseil Privé in resolving cases of *cassation* also characterized its jurisprudence on the two other matters that brought it into frequent contact with the parlements—*évocations de justice* and *règlements de juges.* In terms of their quantity alone, these legal actions occupied an important place in the council's activities: several hundred cases of each variety exist in the primary sample, and together they outnumber actions in *cassation* by a ratio of at least five to one.[1] In addition, because *évocations de justice* and *règlements de juges* could result in a parlement losing litigation to another tribunal, the judges understandably showed a keen interest in the council's policies for adjudicating them.

This is not to suggest, however, that *évocations de justice* and *règlements de juges* were as inherently controversial as the nullification of parlementary judgments in last resort. As noted previously, both legal actions were ordinary and indispensable features of orderly judicial administration, settling as they did jurisdictional disputes that the parlements lacked the authority to resolve on their own. Even the most obstinate *parlementaire* determined to defend his court's prerogatives would not deny that litigants were entitled to seek a change in venue if their adversaries had significant family ties to judges in the court of pending litigation. Nor would he contest the right of parties who had identical litigation pending simultaneously in several sovereign courts to proceed before a single tribunal. Indeed, the parlements themselves routinely resolved disputes about such matters as they pertained to the lesser courts located within their areas of jurisdiction. Moreover, as regards *évocations* in particular, councils other than the Conseil Privé normally granted those kinds of changes in venue that were most likely to provoke parlementary opposition—the notorious *évocations de grâce* and *évocations de propre mouvement* that removed cases from the parlements not for reasons of family connections between judges and litigants, but for political considerations and as favors to influential individuals. We shall

---

[1] Owing to their routine nature, it made little sense to count the number of *évocations de justice* and *règlements de juges* in the primary sample; the approximate ratio of five to one is based on selective sampling. However, I did examine every *arrêt* dealing with these legal actions in order to tease out illustrative examples, to determine the broad contours of judicial procedure, and to trace the council's jurisprudence on specific issues, such as the frequency with which it retained litigation for final judgment.

return to these more controversial *évocations* in due course. The point that
bears underscoring here is that the parlements never challenged the legitimacy of *évocations de justice* and *règlements de juges,* nor did they see
anything in the very nature of these legal actions that undermined their
authority. Problems arose only when the judges believed that the rules for
initiating these actions were either unclear or inadequately enforced. They
especially protested when the Conseil Privé, in adjudicating a *règlement de
juges* or in ordering an *évocation,* retained final jurisdiction over a case
instead of designating a tribunal within the ordinary judiciary.

We have already seen that the Conseil Privé resolved the most serious
of these problems—the retention of litigation for final judgment—in favor
of the parlements. There was progress in the area of formal legislation as
well. The first three titles of the ordinance of August 1669 considered in
detail *évocations de justice* and *règlements de juges* in both civil and criminal
affairs, addressing in 66 articles such basic issues as the circumstances in
which litigants were eligible to initiate an action, the documentary evidence
necessary to support a case, and the methods for soliciting conciliar proceedings.[2] This ordinance held no unpleasant surprises for the *parlementaires.* On many subjects—the number of relatives a party's adversary had
to have in a parlement to warrant a change in venue, for example, or the
proof required to establish that identical litigation between the same parties
was pending simultaneously in several sovereign courts—the ordinance
simply restated rules set forth in such previous legislation as the edict of
Chantelou (1545), the ordinance of Blois (1579), and the "Code Michaud"
(1629).[3] Procedural rules too were drawn largely from existing regulations.[4]

When provisions in the ordinance did lack legislative precedents, they
were uniformly restrictive in the sense of limiting a litigant's ability to
pursue these actions. The ordinance clearly aimed to prevent unscrupulous
parties from using proceedings at council as a way to delay the final judgment of their cases in the sovereign courts, especially when the interests
of the crown or the maintenance of public order were at stake. Thus litigants
could not seek *évocations de justice* within two weeks of the conclusion of
a parlement's judicial term, and certain kinds of litigation (notably that
pertaining to the royal demesne) were excluded altogether from changes
in venue arising from a litigant's family ties.[5] Parties also lost their right to
file for *évocations de justice* once the court of pending litigation had begun

---

[2] For the ordinance, see above chap. III, n. 10. The best commentary on this legislation is
Bornier, *Conférences des ordonnances de Louis XIV,* 1: 379–517. It contains useful information
on the articles in the ordinance cited in the notes below.

[3] Ordinance of August 1669, tit. 1, art. 5 and tit. 2, art. 4. For examples of other articles
based on previous legislation, see tit. 1, arts. 6, 9, 10, 18, 35, 37, 38, 40, 43, 45; tit. 2, art. 12;
tit. 3, arts. 6, 7.

[4] For example: tit. 1, arts. 22–24, 30–33; tit. 2, arts. 9, 10.

[5] See tit. 1, arts. 16, 17, 47. It would be interesting to discover the extent to which these
and other articles cited in this paragraph were woven into the council's usages before being
codified in 1669.

to hear evidence in their cases.[6] Over a dozen articles in the ordinance established restrictions such as these, and they were particularly strict when criminal affairs were involved.[7] For example, whereas actions in *évocation de justice* and *règlement de juges* pending at the council in civil cases carried an automatic suspension of procedures in the courts until the council designated proper jurisdiction, the judges were ordered to continue their instruction of criminal cases up to the point of final judgment despite conciliar proceedings.[8]

Legislation issued in subsequent years exhibited the same intent to protect the parlements from both the unnecessary interruption of their judicial business and the chicanery of obdurate litigants. An edict of September 1683 empowered the parlements and other sovereign courts to fine litigants who initiated procedures for *évocations de justice* and then desisted from them without good cause.[9] In a similar vein, a declaration of 13 March 1710 limited the range of family connections in a parlement that an accused criminal could cite in order to justify a change in venue; in this way, relatives of the *procureur général* and of the accused person's own accomplices were excluded from the genealogical accounting that accompanied *évocations de justice*.[10] It is noteworthy that both these measures were drafted in response to requests made by the *parlementaires* themselves.[11] Even the ordinance of August 1669 had come under the scrutiny of the Parlement of Paris before its issuance, and this court was responsible for suggesting several of its restrictive clauses, notably the one prohibiting litigants from filing for *évocations de justice* near the end of a parlement's judicial term.[12]

Still other royal acts, more routine in character, clarified issues that the ordinance of August 1669 had failed to consider. Declarations of 14 August 1687, 23 July 1701, and 15 November 1703 designated which parlements were to receive litigation removed from other parlements as a consequence of *évocations de justice*. The Parlement of Rouen, for example, would receive

---

[6] See tit. 1, art. 19 (this principle is mentioned in the ordinance of 1629, art. 63, but only in 1669 was it stated without ambiguity).

[7] In addition to the articles cited in the two previous notes, see also tit. 1, arts. 11–15, 20; tit. 2, arts. 5, 6, 8; tit. 3, arts. 3, 4.

[8] In cases of *règlement de juges*, the council designated one of the courts whose jurisdiction was in question to continue criminal procedures. For the appropriate articles in the ordinance of 1669, see above chap. IV, n. 19. As another example of restriction in criminal matters, individuals against whom arrest warrants were in effect could not pursue *évocations de justice* or *règlements de juges* unless they surrendered to the authorities: tit. 1, art. 38; tit. 3, art. 4.

[9] Isambert et al., eds., *Recueil général des anciennes lois*, 19: 434–435.

[10] BN, *Actes Royaux*, no. 24168.

[11] Le Tellier to Harlay (Paris), 27 September 1683, BN, MSS. Fr. 17418, fol. 82. Pontchartrain to Du Vigier (Bordeaux) and to D'Aguesseau *fils* (Paris), 9 September and 9 October 1710, ibid., 21130, fols. 762v–763v, 843v.

[12] See an early draft of the ordinance of 1669 with, I believe, the marginal comments of *Procureur Général* Harlay in BN, MSS. Fr. 16485, fols. 159–180 (and see as well the reference to this document in ibid., 17012, fol. 4). Note in particular the concluding remarks on tit. 1 and the comments on draft arts. 20 and 44 (which became arts. 21, 45, and 47 in the final ordinance). These indications illustrate the parlement's influence on the ordinance.

cases evoked from the Parlement of Rennes; litigation removed from the Parlement of Bordeaux would go before the *parlementaires* of Toulouse, and so on.[13] The council's own *règlements* of January 1673, July 1676, and June 1687 refined rules on such technical matters as the submission of documents to the council and the responsibilities of reporting magistrates there.[14]

Finally, and with a touch of irony, the very royal financial policies that the parlements so bemoaned late in the reign had salutary results for at least one aspect of the judges' interests. In return for swallowing the bitter pill of office creations, forced loans, and other similar expressions of the crown's desperate search for funds during the War of the Spanish Succession, at least four parlements between 1705 and 1708 secured an increase in the number of relatives a litigant's adversary had to have among the judges in order to warrant an *évocation de justice* from these courts. As partial compensation for the creation of new offices in the Parlement of Toulouse in 1705, for example, the number of relatives needed to sustain a change in venue was raised from six (the number stipulated in the ordinance of August 1669) to eight.[15] At Aix, where the establishment of a new chamber in Parlement in 1705 was accomplished without the creation of additional judgeships—an operation that cost the *parlementaires* 400,000 *livres*—the number of relatives necessary to justify an *évocation de justice* rose from four to six.[16] The Parlements of Grenoble and Rennes received similar concessions in return for making financial sacrifices.[17] Even the rights of litigants thus did not escape the auction block late in Louis XIV's reign!

Did the Conseil Privé comply with this imposing mass of legislation? Unfortunately, the best source for answering this question—the council's own *arrêts*—does not provide information about every aspect of the council's jurisprudence. Because the *arrêts* do not mention the council's reasoning

---

[13] In chronological order: Isambert et al., eds., *Recueil général des anciennes lois*, 20: 51–52; BN, *Actes Royaux*, no. 20061; Bornier, *Conférences des ordonnances de Louis XIV*, 1: 385–387.

[14] See the *règlements* of 1673 (art. 59), 2 July 1676 (entire), and 1687 (tit. 3) in Bornier, *Conférences des ordonnances de Louis XIV*, 1: 827, 833–834, 843–844.

[15] Edict of January 1705 in Marc-Antoine Rodier, ed., *Recueil des édits, déclarations, arrêts du conseil et du Parlement de Toulouse* (2 vols.; Toulouse, 1756), 2: 307–315.

[16] Bibliothèque Méjanes, MS. 985, entry under "chambres" for 1704–1706.

[17] For Grenoble, where the issue was forced loans, see the edict of April 1706 in BN, *Actes Royaux*, no. 22281. At Rennes the issue was the parlement's payment of 24,000 *livres* to secure the repeal of a tax: AD, Ille-et-Vilaine, 1 Bb 806 (part of the "Table raisonnée des registres secrets"), entry under "parlement" for 3 August 1708. The controller general of finances was in charge of working out the details for these operations: see, for example, documents related to the operations at Grenoble and Aix in AN, G⁷ 246–247, 469 passim. As early as 1661, the Parlement of Dijon received an increase in the parental ties needed to justify an *évocation*, but the reasons for this are obscure: Boislisle, ed., *Mémoriaux du conseil de 1661*, 1: 317, 320–323. As a sign of the times late in Louis XIV's reign, an *arrêt en commandement* of 10 September 1689 (AN, E 1852) declared that if a litigant in a case had lent the judges money to purchase salary raises (*augmentations de gages*), the opposite parties of this litigant could not use these financial ties to the judges as grounds for *évocation*.

for its decisions, the circumstances in a given case that prompted a particular ruling remain obscure. The value of the *arrêts* for tracing the council's policies regarding *évocations de justice* and *règlements de juges* is further diminished because the legal arguments that litigants made in these cases lack the richness and variety of the arguments that parties advanced in cases of *cassation*. When a petitioner attacked a judgment that a parlement had already rendered in last resort, it was obviously in his best interest both to review in detail the conduct of the judges and to search a broad spectrum of potential evidence for compelling reasons that would convince the council to take the extraordinary and delicate step of nullifying a parlementary sentence. We have seen how the diverse and often elaborate arguments of petitioners, when viewed in the light of the various grounds for nullification, breathe life into the council's decisions and reveal important elements of its jurisprudence on *cassation*.

In cases of *évocation de justice* and *règlement de juges*, however, the aims of parties were more modest and the range of legal discourse was much narrower. Litigants in these legal actions came to the Conseil Privé for the resolution of strictly jurisdictional problems, and this restricted the kinds of evidence they presented to the council. In *évocations de justice*, a litigant cited the family connections of his adversary, and this person either denied the existence or the extent of these connections, or he claimed that the substantive issues involved in litigation precluded a change in venue. In *règlements de juges*, parties explained how identical litigation had come before several courts. In either case, such limited information considerably reduces the number of patterns that one can discern in conciliar decisions that lack all reference to the council's reasoning.

Despite these shortcomings, the *arrêts* do offer valuable insights into the council's conduct and policies. The council's reluctance to retain litigation for final judgment is one example of this, and we shall see shortly that the *arrêts* reveal significant features of conciliar procedure. Equally important, the arguments that litigants made in their cases—arguments that are recapitulated either in the *arrêts sur requête* that introduced affairs at council or in the *arrêts* between parties that resolved actions after both sides had contested—are sufficiently detailed to suggest that royal legislation, notably the ordinance of August 1669, provided the touchstone for the council's adjudication of *évocations de justice* and *règlements de juges*.[18]

---

[18] A technical comment about the council's *arrêts* is warranted here. Like actions in *cassation*, cases of *évocation de justice* and *règlement de juges* could be introduced at the council by *arrêts sur requête* and resolved subsequently by *arrêts* between parties. When litigants took this route for introducing cases (which was common in cases of *règlement de juges* but much less so in cases of *évocation de justice*), the historian can use the *arrêts* between parties to locate earlier *arrêts sur requête* that were issued in a given case. One thus has a way to reconstruct the legal reasoning of the parties who initiated an action. Unlike actions in *cassation*, however, cases of *évocation de justice* and *règlement de juges* could be introduced at the council by means *other* than *arrêts sur requête: évocations de justice* by the official notices (*cédules évocatoires*) that litigants desiring a change of venue served their opposite parties; and *règlements de juges*

As if to recognize the council's adherence to the ordinance of 1669, parties consistently related the evidence in their cases to specific clauses in this act. As one example drawn from *évocations de justice*, when Dame Marie Daurat requested in 1670 that the council remove from the Parlement of Paris litigation regarding her deceased husband's estate, she asserted that her opposite parties, Jean and Seraphin du Tillet, had a "great number" of relatives in that court. But she actually listed only those persons whose family ties with the Du Tillets met the criteria for a change in venue as set forth in the ordinance of 1669. Not to be outdone, the Du Tillets relied upon the same legislation to argue, first, that their relationship with some individuals cited in Daurat's request was too remote to justify the transfer of litigation to another parlement, and second, that still other persons listed in the request were relatives common to all parties in the dispute and therefore should be discounted as evidence of excessive consanguinity.[19] Litigants in cases of *règlement de juges* also drew upon the ordinance of August 1669 to substantiate their claims. Robert Quenouille did so in 1715 when he argued that one of his opposite parties in a criminal case, Louise Poirel, had improperly appealed an arrest warrant against her to the Parlement of Paris even though the case was currently pending at the Parlement of Rouen. Citing the ordinance, Quenouille maintained that because the action had originated in a lesser court within the resort of the Parlement of Rouen, this parlement alone was entitled to appellate jurisdiction.[20]

Of course, the fact that parties referred to royal legislation does not in itself prove that the Conseil Privé abided by established rules when it decided individual cases. Fortunately, the *arrêts* offer more direct evidence about the council's intentions. Time and again during Louis's reign, parties successfully sought relief at the Conseil Privé when their adversaries violated the ordinance of August 1669 and its supplementary measures. Did a litigant initiate procedures for an *évocation de justice* and then either desist from them without good cause or fail to bring the action to conclusion

---

by special letters patent acquired at the *Grande Chancellerie* of France. Regrettably, these *cédules évocatoires* and letters patent have not survived in the council's archives. This limits the information one can gather about the reasoning of the parties. Fortunately for the historian, however, the council seems never to have adjudicated cases of *évocation de justice* and *règlement de juges* without allowing both sides in a dispute to present evidence. As a result, the council's archives contain *arrêts* between parties (as well as default judgments) for all the cases it judged on these matters. While the *arrêts* between parties do not repeat in detail the content of the *cédules évocatoires* and letters patent, the review they do provide of the documents each side submitted in evidence is often sufficiently detailed to reveal the general lines of the parties' reasoning. The *arrêts* certainly abound with references to the ordinance of 1669.

[19] *Arrêt* between parties of 18 March 1670, AN, V⁶ 563, no. 1. This *arrêt*, drawn from outside the primary sample, is informative because it shows that the reasoning of intervening parties in an action is summarized in *arrêts*. For examples in the primary sample of parties citing the ordinance of 1669, see below, this chapter, nn. 21–22, as well as three *arrêts* from V⁶ 626: 23 April 1676, nos. 33 and 52; 16 May 1676, no. 14.

[20] *Arrêt sur requête* of 25 February 1715, AN, V⁶ 834, no. 6. For other examples, see the *arrêt* on *requêtes respectives* of 23 April 1676 (V⁶ 626, no. 32) and the *arrêt sur requête* of 7 September 1705 (V⁶ 802, no. 2).

within the specified time limits? If so, the council could be relied upon not only to nullify these procedures and to lift any suspension of proceedings that they had occasioned in the courts, but also to award court costs to the party who had complained and sometimes to fine his adversary.[21] The same response could be expected if a litigant proved that his opposite party had moved for a change in venue after the court of pending litigation had already begun to hear evidence in a case.[22] The council was also willing to revise its own decisions if a party could establish that the facts in an action were different from those upon which the council had originally based a ruling. In 1685, for example, Alexis Davues reminded the Conseil Privé that his opposite parties in litigation concerning the payment of a debt had requested the council to provide a *règlement de juges* between several courts, including the Parlement of Paris. Following standard procedure, the council had suspended further proceedings in the various courts and summoned both sides in this jurisdictional dispute to present evidence. Davues explained that unbeknownst to the council, the Parlement of Paris had already judged part of the litigation in question with the participation of all the concerned parties, thus obviating the need for a conciliar decision about proper jurisdiction. The council evidently agreed, dissolving the action for a *règlement de juges* and instructing the litigants to continue their case before the Parisian *parlementaires*.[23]

The Conseil Privé also demonstrated its compliance with royal legislation on more routine matters. For example, it repeatedly upheld the principle that the instruction of criminal cases should continue in the courts even when cases of *évocation de justice* and *règlement de juges* concerning these affairs were pending at the council.[24] The council also implemented legislation stipulating which parlement was to receive litigation removed from another parlement.[25] In addition, whenever parties raised jurisdictional questions that the *parlementaires* were entitled to resolve on their own, the council simply remanded cases to the appropriate parlement without taking additional action. In 1685, for example, Catherine Robicson requested a *règlement de juges* between two chambers in the Parlement of Paris. Because

---

[21] For example, see the *arrêts sur requête* of 30 September 1695 (AN, V⁶ 755, no. 51) and 14 January 1715 (V⁶ 834, no. 1).

[22] For example, see the *arrêt sur requête* of 21 May 1676, AN, V⁶ 626, no. 5. An *arrêt en commandement* could also uphold this principle, as one dated 8 September 1674 (AN, E 1773) did on the request of the Aix *parlementaires* regarding a criminal prosecution against a merchant accused of peculation who filed a *cédule évocatoire* after the court had already heard evidence against him.

[23] *Arrêt sur requête* of 20 February 1685, AN, V⁶ 686, no. 3.

[24] For example, see the *arrêt sur requête* of 1715 cited above this chapter, in n. 20 as well as the one of 9 July 1669, AN, V⁶ 554, no. 28. See also Pontchartrain to Du Vigier (Bordeaux), 25 February and 1 March 1703 and 9 September 1709, BN, MSS. Fr. 21122, fols. 129v–131v, 136–137; 21130, fols. 762v–763v.

[25] For example, see the *arrêts sur requête* of 14 September 1705 (AN, V⁶ 802, no. 28) and 3 December 1714 (V⁶ 834, no. 17). These are cases of *cassation* sending parties to another parlement for retrial.

her case concerned a jurisdictional dispute within a tribunal rather than between two independent courts, the council followed the ordinance of 1669 and allowed the *parlementaires* to settle the matter.[26] Earlier, in 1668, the council took the same position when it considered a request by Léonard Sandrais, who was involved in a criminal case at the Parlement of Rennes. Sandrais claimed that his opposite party, the *procureur du roi* in a local Breton tribunal, had a prohibitive number of relatives sitting in the parlement's criminal chamber. Rather than invest the time and money necessary to establish this fact through ordinary procedures, Sandrais hoped that the council on its own initiative would transfer the case to the court's *grand' chambre*. The council, refusing to involve itself prematurely in the parlement's internal affairs, denied the request and returned Sandrais to the judges for a ruling.[27]

The chancellors' correspondence with the parlements further corroborates the council's commitment to the orderly adjudication of *évocations de justice* and *règlements de juges*. Sometimes the chancellors answered queries by the judges, offering advice about how best to implement specific regulations. Such letters, often written after consultation with the council or with the king himself, not only helped to introduce royal legislation into the mainstream of judicial administration, but they also enabled the judges to avoid potential challenges to their sentences. In 1682, for example, Le Tellier explained to *Procureur Général* Harlay how the Parlement of Paris should apply two articles in the ordinance of August 1669 to the transfer of cases between chambers in that court, and in 1708 Pontchartrain provided similar information to the Parlement of Grenoble.[28] Boucherat reminded the *parlementaires* of Aix in 1690 that although they had a right to continue the instruction of criminal cases despite actions in *évocation de justice* pending at the council, they were not to proceed to definitive judgment until the council made a final decision about jurisdiction. In 1703, Pontchartrain reiterated the same principle in a letter to the *procureur général* of the Parlement of Bordeaux.[29]

On other occasions, the chancellors discussed specific cases that were currently before the council, often expressing regret for any inconvenience that conciliar proceedings might have caused the judges, but refusing nevertheless to depart from established rules. In 1703, for example, the Parlement of Toulouse notified Pontchartrain that three accused murderers had recently requested the council to grant an *évocation de justice*. Maintaining

---

[26] *Arrêt sur requête* of 13 March 1685, AN, V⁶ 686, no. 16. On this issue, see also Le Tellier to Harlay, 23 July 1679, BN, MSS. Fr. 21118, pp. 73–75.

[27] *Arrêt sur requête* of 18 September 1668, AN, V⁶ 544, no. 11.

[28] Le Tellier to Harlay, 4 April 1682 and 20 February 1683, BN, MSS. Fr. 17417, fol. 33; 17418, fol. 28. Pontchartrain to Bérulle, 18 April 1708, AD, Isère, B 2322 ("Lettres. . . ."), fols. 329–330v.

[29] Boucherat to *gens du roi*, 9 June 1690, AN, V¹ 584, p. 74. Pontchartrain to Du Vigier, 25 February 1703, BN, MSS. Fr. 21122, fols. 129v–131v.

that the claims of these individuals lacked all legal foundation, the court expressed an interest in moving to final judgment of their case. While Pontchartrain readily acknowledged that actions at council could conceivably interfere with the swift punishment of crime, he was unwilling to deny the accused a legitimate recourse at law. How, he asked rhetorically, could the court possibly repair an error if it condemned these persons and later discovered that their request for a change in venue was justified?[30] Pontchartrain took the same position in 1705, when the Parlement of Aix complained that a *procureur* in that court named Castel had avoided penalties against him for three years through various procedural artifices, most recently by having another individual who had entered his case as an intervening party initiate procedures for an *évocation de justice.* However odious Castel's conduct had been in recent years, the chancellor asserted, legal rules alone would determine whether the council decided in favor of a change in venue.[31]

If it appears from these examples that the council did not cater to what the judges perceived to be their immediate interests, it must also be emphasized that in the long run a conciliar policy promoting the consistent enforcement of royal legislation was preferable to the arbitrary treatment of cases about which the parlements themselves had complained earlier in the century. Moreover, the failure of the judges to have their way in some cases should not leave the impression that the council was unwilling to consider seriously parlementary complaints, and even to revise its own decisions, when the judges argued from sound legal principles. If the issues at stake were relatively simple and unambiguous, informal communication with the chancellor could produce fruitful results. In 1678, for example, the council had erroneously empowered the *Grand Conseil* (a Parisian sovereign court not to be confused with the king's councils) to adjudicate a *règlement de juges* between the *Châtelet* of Paris and the *Connétablie de France,* a ruling that deprived the Parlement of Paris of its rightful jurisdiction. Informed of the mistake, Chancellor Le Tellier swiftly arranged for the transfer of the case to the *parlementaires,* assuring Procureur Général Harlay that, "I will let nothing pass before [the council] that could be prejudicial to the authority of Parlement."[32]

In more complicated cases, a parlement could defend its jurisdiction by having its *procureur général* intervene officially. The judges took this step when they believed that a party had so misrepresented the facts in a case

---

[30] Pontchartrain to Caulet, 11 April 1703, BN, MSS. Fr. 21122, fols. 200v–201v. For a similar case whose outcome is unknown, see Languet (Dijon) to Séguier, March 1666, ibid., 17412, fols. 104–105.

[31] Pontchartrain to La Garde, 12 December 1705, BN, MSS. Fr. 21124, fols. 732v–733. Even when denying the judges' requests, however, the chancellor could nevertheless pledge to keep their objections in mind when a case eventually came before the full council: Pontchartrain to Bertier (Toulouse), 12 August 1711, ibid., 21134, fols. 722v–723v.

[32] Le Tellier to Harlay, 6 May 1678, BN, MSS. Fr. 17414, fol. 159.

that only a detailed and formal rebuttal could sufficiently enlighten the council. In 1669, the Parlement of Toulouse had sentenced to death *in absentia* several individuals accused of counterfeiting. Shortly thereafter, these persons had gone before the *grand prévôt* of Languedoc to have their case prosecuted, an act that then enabled them to solicit the Conseil Privé for a *règlement de juges* between the two competing jurisdictions. In a request to the council, the *procureur général* of the parlement argued that when the council had agreed to resolve the jurisdictional dispute, it did not know that these individuals had already been convicted of the charges against them. Although the council ruled that it wished to examine more evidence in this confusing case, it also ordered that pending a final decision the convicted felons would enter the parlement's prisons and remain there while the court implemented procedures to purge them of their contumacy.[33] A similar case appeared at the council in 1695 involving one François Meyer, whom the Parlement of Grenoble had recently sentenced to banishment for the crime of rebellion. After his conviction, Meyer had remained in prison for trial on charges of forgery. As this second case approached conclusion, Meyer attempted to delay final judgment by initiating procedures for an *évocation de justice*. Angered by such chicanery, the parlement's *procureur général* described in a request to council the "frivolous" nature of Meyer's maneuvering, pointing especially to the inappropriate timing of this attempt to secure a change in venue. Within two weeks, the council dissolved all procedures for the *évocation de justice* and informed the court that it could finish this case.[34]

In order to expedite the parlements' efforts to accomplish their aims through ordinary channels, Chancellor Pontchartrain stood ready to consult with the judges before they formally intervened in a case, offering a preliminary opinion about their chances for success or failure.[35] The parlements were neither required to solicit such advice nor bound to follow it. But the very existence of this line of communication, and the fact that the judges availed themselves of it, further testifies to the council's willingness to cooperate with the parlements.[36]

---

[33] *Arrêt sur requête* of 9 July 1669, AN, V[6] 554, no. 28.

[34] AD, Isère, 2B 502 ("arrêts patrimoniaux et criminels. . . ."), fols. 129–130. One can occasionally find among the *arrêts en commandement* successful efforts by the parlements to have cases of *évocation de justice* at the council dissolved: see, for example, two *arrêts* in favor of the Parlement of Toulouse of 27 February and 5 April 1683 in AN, E 1820.

[35] For example, Pontchartrain did this in his letter to La Garde cited above in this chapter, n. 31, advising the *procureur général* that a formal opposition to the council judging the request for *évocation* in Castel's case would probably fail. Sometimes this chancellor also gave a parlement advance notice of a conciliar decision so that the judges could continue a case without having to wait until the council dispatched a formal *arrêt*. For an example concerning the Parlement of Aix and a party's failure to secure a change of venue in a criminal case, see AD, Bouches-du-Rhône (annexe: Aix), B 6065 ("Délibérations de la chambre tournelle"), entry for 28 June 1706.

[36] Of course, a parlement's intervention in a case did not guarantee success: see Pontchartrain to the Conseil Provincial of Artois, 9 April 1712, BN, MSS. Fr. 21135, fols. 334v–336. Moreover,

In adjudicating *évocations de justice* and *règlements de juges*, therefore, the Conseil Privé exhibited a basic respect for the *parlementaires'* authority and dignity as superior magistrates. On the one hand, a substantial body of royal legislation defined clearly and in detail the legal principles for deciding individual cases, legal principles that limited the ability of litigants to challenge a parlement's jurisdiction. On the other hand, there is every reason to believe that the council implemented this legislation, abandoning the controversial practice of retaining for final judgment the cases that came before it and giving the judges ample opportunity to defend their interests. These developments, coupled with the council's jurisprudence on *cassation*, provide a striking example of how the celebrated quest for administrative order associated with Louis XIV's personal rule had advantageous consequences for the kingdom's highest courts of law.

---

the council retained the right to assess court costs against a tribunal whose intervention in a case was deemed to have been particularly unwarranted, a principle that Pontchartrain discussed at length in letters to Boisot and Doroz at the Parlement of Besançon (February and March 1714) and to *procureurs généraux* Pauyot and Dauphin of the Cours des Aides of Rouen and Clermont respectively (22 October and 22 November 1709): ibid., 21130, fols. 872v–874v, 1004–1005v; 21139, fols. 184–188, 235v–240v. All the more reason, then, for the judges to consult the chancellor before entering a case or to intervene only when their legal arguments were sound.

VI. THE CONSEIL PRIVÉ AND JUDICIAL PROCEDURE

The relaxation of tensions between the Conseil Privé and the parlements also stemmed from important developments in the council's own judicial procedures. One cannot review here all the procedural steps that contesting parties and the council itself followed to bring cases to conclusion.[1] There is, to be sure, no lack of legislative texts to consult. As noted previously, Louis XIV's reign was characterized by substantial and persistent efforts to clarify this council's procedures. The ordinance of August 1669, its supplementary measures, and such internal *règlements* as those of February 1660, January 1673, and June 1687 all testify to this reforming activity. But this legislation set forth literally hundreds of rules that could pertain to cases of interest to the *parlementaires,* and still other practices formed a part of the conciliar routine without ever having been officially codified. Not only did many of these rules and practices change over time, but they also varied according to the nature of the legal action and to the circumstances in individual cases. The chancellors wrote only infrequently about procedural matters, and not all procedures have left traces in the council's archives. It is true that the council's *arrêts,* notably those between parties, do list the major procedures followed in a given case. But there is no way to assess on the basis of such information whether all the procedures mentioned were properly implemented or even necessary to resolve a dispute.

For these reasons, the historian of the parlements must be selective when investigating the evolution of the council's procedures, focusing only on issues that occupied an important place in the council's relations with the parlements and for which sufficient evidence exists to draw reliable conclusions. Five aspects of the council's judicial procedure meet these criteria. Their study reveals that the Conseil Privé attempted not only to examine cases carefully before rendering decisions, but also to dissuade impulsive litigants from challenging the jurisdiction or the judgments of the parlements without good cause.

---

[1] There exists no comprehensive study of this council's procedures; the historian of Louis XIV's reign must rely primarily on unpublished documents. While all the authors cited above in chap. II, n. 1 provide some information on procedural matters, only Antoine addresses the subject in a systematic way: his comments on the Conseil Privé appear throughout *Le Conseil du roi sous le règne de Louis XV,* bk. 2, chaps. 1–2. But even his discussion touches on only the major features of judicial procedure, and this only for the eighteenth century.

The first of these procedural issues concerns the attention the Conseil Privé gave to the cases that came before it. During Louis XIV's personal rule, all the royal councils relied upon various subordinate bodies to prepare their work and, in some instances, to render final decisions on certain categories of affairs. Some of these bodies, known as *bureaux*, were permanent committees of council members charged only with examining dossiers and familiarizing themselves with cases in advance of formal council meetings. Other groups, called *commissions*, were empowered to judge specific kinds of cases. *Commissions* deemed to be *ordinaires* were, like the *bureaux*, composed of council members who met on a permanent basis. Commissions that were *extraordinaires* were only temporary, disbanding once the duties assigned them were completed; they occasionally drew their membership from outside the councils. To these *bureaux* and *commissions* one can add still other groups, constituted both formally and informally, that served the councils in various ways: the meetings the king held with his ministers and other principal advisers to formulate policy and to establish the agenda for the *conseils de gouvernement;* assemblies of masters of requests and of *intendants des finances* at which these officials coordinated their work for the councils; and a wide range of *ad hoc* councils and committees that advised the king on special matters, drafted legislation, and accomplished certain administrative tasks.

The number, composition, precise duties, and even official names of all these satellite bodies surrounding the councils evolved throughout the *ancien régime,* a complex subject whose details need not concern us here.[2] We shall concentrate only on the groups affiliated with the Conseil Privé. But it is important to recognize that underlying this aspect of conciliar organization was a logic born of bureaucratic necessity: given the great quantity of business that regularly came before the various councils, some form of committee structure was needed both to increase the efficiency of formal council meetings and to assume some of the responsibility for the daily administration of the realm. For this reason, small groups of council members meeting in various settings for specific purposes had long been a feature of council life.

As regards Louis XIV's Conseil Privé in particular, it worked closely with two kinds of bodies drawn from its own membership: assemblies of masters of requests and *bureaux* composed of councillors of state. When a case came before the Conseil Privé, the chancellor appointed one of the masters of requests to serve as reporting magistrate (*rapporteur*). This official was

---

[2] For an overview of the various subordinate bodies that served the king's councils over time, see: Mousnier, "Le Conseil du roi," 51–53; Boislisle, *Les Conseils du roi sous Louis XIV,* 43–63, 146–172; Antoine, *Le Conseil du roi sous le règne de Louis XV,* 145–175; idem, *Le Fonds du conseil d'état du roi aux Archives Nationales,* 14–23. Two recent studies focusing on specific aspects of the system are Phytilis, *Justice administrative et justice déléguée au XVIIIe siècle,* and Schaeper, *The French Council of Commerce.* Also informative is Coudy, *Les Moyens d'action de l'ordre du clergé,* 145–157.

responsible for gathering together the pertinent documents in the case, communicating with the contesting parties, supervising the flow of procedure, and ultimately for presenting before the entire council an oral report (*rapport*) that summarized the principal issues in the case and offered a recommendation for its resolution. Having heard this report, the assembled members of the council expressed their own opinions about the case and then voted according to the principle of majority rule, with the chancellor breaking any tie votes. Before appearing at the council, however, the reporting magistrate met with other masters of requests serving during one of the council's three-month sessions, or *quartiers*. This group, known as the "assemblée des maîtres des requêtes," examined the case with the reporting magistrate and, through discussion, helped him to refine his views. These assemblies, which were well established in the sixteenth century and continued to meet regularly until the end of the *ancien régime*, ensured that no case came before the entire council without first having received preliminary and collective scrutiny.[3]

During the seventeenth century, the practice gradually appeared of having senior members of the Conseil Privé also examine cases in advance of formal council meetings. After a reporting magistrate had conferred with his colleagues in their assembly of the *quartier*, he then met with one of several *bureaux* staffed by councillors of state. Like the assemblies of the masters of requests, the *bureaux* played a purely advisory role; neither the reporting magistrate nor the council itself was bound by the results of a *bureau*'s deliberations (assuming that a consensus had been reached, which was not required). The principal aims of the *bureaux* were, first, to widen the circle of council members who were familiar with a case before its presentation to the entire council, and second, to provide reporting magistrates with an additional opportunity to clarify their views through group discussion.

These *bureaux* did not originate during Louis XIV's reign. Conciliar *règlements* from the first half of the seventeenth century refer to their existence, although in this era most *bureaux* do not seem to have been attached to a particular council.[4] An important *règlement* of June 1627, for example, created ten *bureaux* serving all the councils. Each of these *bureaux* was charged with examining affairs pertaining to a specific subject, such as

---

[3] For references to these assemblies both before and after Louis XIV's personal rule, see: Valois, ed., *Inventaire des arrêts*, 1: lxi; Mousnier, "Le Conseil du roi," 31; Ormesson, *Journal*, 2: 819, 824; and Antoine, *Le Conseil du roi sous le règne de Louis XV*, 306–307. During Louis XIV's personal rule, the assemblies are mentioned in a *règlement* of 27 October 1674 (in Bornier, *Conférences des ordonnances de Louis XIV*, 2: 832–833) and in the *règlement* of January 1673, art. 79.

[4] For example, the *règlement* of 21 May 1615 (arts. 15–16) speaks of *bureaux* serving both the Conseil Privé and the Conseil d'Etat et des Finances. An exception would be the four *bureaux* created by the *règlement* of 5 August 1619 to serve only the *Conseil de la direction des finances* (which later evolved into the *commission ordinaire* of Grande Direction): Mousnier, ed., "Les Règlements du conseil du roi sous Louis XIII," 149, 156–158.

police, war, Protestants, marine and commerce, and so on. One of these *bureaux,* composed of six councillors of state, reviewed with reporting magistrates cases regarding "justice, contentions et règlements des cours," including cases of *évocation de justice* and *règlement de juges.*[5] By the late 1690s, when documents again describe in detail the formal organization of the *bureaux,* this system had evolved to the point where, depending upon the year, between five and seven *bureaux* were affiliated exclusively with the Conseil Privé. In each of these *bureaux* sat from five to seven councillors of state chosen by the chancellor at the beginning of the year. Two of these *bureaux* had specialized functions, one examining cases dealing with *cassation,* another reviewing cases involving the clergy and ecclesiastical affairs. The other *bureaux,* known simply as "bureaux des parties," examined cases pertaining to the other aspects of the council's jurisdiction.[6]

Precisely when this more elaborate organization emerged remains unknown, but it certainly occurred sometime during the period of Louis XIV's personal rule.[7] In his memorandum of 1665, Councillor of State Verthamon mentioned the existence of a system similar but not identical to the one in place later. After urging the king to create *bureaux* composed of councillors of state and masters of requests "to examine together all the documents related to the requests and other affairs reported by the masters of requests," he noted in passing that, "Chancellor [Séguier] has already begun to implement this system by establishing three or four *bureaux* for each *quartier,* some [being composed] of just one master of requests and one councillor of state, with advantageous results for the welfare of justice."[8] Abbé Dangeau reports that the *bureau* specializing in ecclesiastical affairs was created in 1684, and the first reference to a *bureau* of *cassations* in the *arrêts* examined for this study appears in 1685.[9]

---

[5] Ibid., 169–173.

[6] The *bureaux* serving the Conseil Privé are listed in the *Almanach Royal,* which was first published in 1699, under the rubric, "bureaux des messieurs les conseillers d'état pour la communication des instances des parties." I examined the volumes for 1699, 1705, and 1712. In theory, another *bureau,* the "Conseil de Chancellerie" (see above, chap. II, n. 7), was attached to the Conseil Privé. In practice, however, this body served the chancellor as much as it did this council, and its decisions took the form of *arrêts en commandement* as well as *arrêts simples* of the Conseil Privé. I have thus not included it in this discussion of the *bureaux* affiliated exclusively with the Conseil Privé. For details on this *bureau,* see Antoine, *Le Conseil du roi sous le règne de Louis XV,* 157–160; idem, *Le Fonds du conseil d'état du roi aux Archives Nationales,* 16–17, 63.

[7] The systematic listing of *bureaux* seems to have been rare in the *Etats de la France* that preceded the publication of the *Almanach Royal* mentioned in the previous note. Dent ("The Council of State and the Clergy," 263, n. 1) indicates that the *Etat* for 1694 mentions the *bureaux,* and Boislisle (*Les Conseils du roi sous Louis XIV,* 47, n. 6) reports the same for 1698. But a sampling of *Etats* from earlier years reveals no mention of the *bureaux,* although the council's *arrêts* shows them operating in this era (I thank Professor John Hurt for consulting the *Etats* for 1656 and 1658, and Professor Richard Golden for consulting five volumes for later years).

[8] BN, Clairambault MS. 613, p. 565.

[9] Philippe de Courcillon, marquis de Dangeau, *Journal,* ed. E. Soulié and L. Dussieux (19 vols.; Paris, 1854–1860), 1: 6. For a reference to the *bureau* of *cassations,* see the *arrêt sur requête* of 27 February 1685, AN, V[6] 686, no. 6.

The *bureaux* of councillors of state and the assemblies of masters of requests have left few traces in the council's records. If either group ever maintained archives, which is doubtful given their purely consultative role, these have not survived.[10] Moreover, reporting magistrates presented only oral opinions to the council, and what they said remains unknown owing to the absence of minutes for the council's meetings during the seventeenth century. Fortunately, the council's *arrêts* compensate to some extent for these gaps in documentary evidence. Every *arrêt* the Conseil Privé issued bore the signatures of the chancellor and the reporting magistrate. In addition, the *arrêts* normally mention whether a *bureau* had examined a case before its presentation to the full council; often the councillors of state comprising a *bureau* also signed the *arrêts* pertaining to the cases they had reviewed.[11] Such references do not, of course, inform us about what occurred during a *bureau*'s deliberations. Furthermore, not every *arrêt* mentions a *bureau*'s intervention, thus leaving open the possibility either that some cases did not receive this type of preliminary examination or that those who drafted the *arrêt* failed to record it. Nevertheless, in the absence of other sources the *arrêts* at least indicate the kinds of legal actions that were likely to attract a *bureau*'s attention, important information for determining how the Conseil Privé handled cases involving the parlements. Insofar as the masters of requests in their assemblies are concerned, as a general rule the *arrêts* do not refer to their participation; their traditional involvement in all cases coming before the council no doubt obviated the need for such a formality. As will be noted briefly below, however, there were some legal matters that the masters of requests resolved in their assemblies without consulting either a *bureau* or the entire council. *Arrêts*

---

[10] Antoine, *Le Fonds du conseil d'état du roi aux Archives Nationales*, 63.

[11] The signatures of the chancellor and the reporting magistrate appear at the very end of an *arrêt*, after the council's decision (*dispositif*), the chancellor signing on the left, the reporter on the right. The participation of the reporter is noted at the end of the introductory section (*exposé*) of the *arrêt*, normally with this phrase or a close variation: "Oui le rapport de Sieur X . . . , maître des requêtes ordinaire de son hôtel, commissaire à ce député, et tout considéré." If the *arrêt* refers to the participation of a *bureau* of councillors of state, this notation also comes at this point in the *arrêt*. Sometimes this reference is vague, stating simply that the reporter consulted with councillors of state (sometimes these are mentioned by name) "[aussi] commissaires à ce député." At other times, precise information is furnished about a *bureau*, that the reporter met with "commissaires pour le fait des cassations," or "au bureau de X . . . , conseiller d'état ordinaire," or "au bureau de cassation du Sieur Y . . . , conseiller d'état ordinaire," or "au bureau du Sieur Z . . . , et autres conseillers d'état aussi commissaires à ce député." When one or more members of a *bureau* signed an *arrêt*, they did so below the reporter's signature. Bear in mind that the information given here about signatures applies only to the original *minutes* of the *arrêts* of the Conseil Privé. The *expéditions* of *arrêts*, that is, the copies that were dispatched for parties or published for public consumption (as opposed to the *minutes* conserved in the council's archives and consulted for this study), differed slightly from the *minutes* in their official wording and had their own rules for signatures. Thus, *expéditions* are referred to as "extraits" of the council's registers, and they bear only one signature, that of the secretary of the council charged with dispatching *arrêts*. For details, see Antoine, *Le Fonds du conseil d'état du roi aux Archives Nationales*, 41–42.

pertaining to these matters often bear the signatures of several masters of requests.[12]

The *arrêts* indicate that during Louis XIV's personal rule cases involving the parlements generally followed one of two tracks upon their arrival at the Conseil Privé. The first of these awaited legal actions, like those in *cassation*, that the council had the option of deciding by *arrêts sur requête* without calling all the concerned parties to present evidence. The normal practice in these affairs was to have both the assembly of masters of requests and a *bureau* of councillors of state examine cases early in the proceedings and prior to the issuance of *arrêts sur requête*. This explains why these *arrêts* frequently refer to a *bureau*'s participation in a case (the activity of the assembly being presumed without requiring official mention).[13] Of course, in a formal meeting the council could decide to use an *arrêt sur requête* not to resolve an action but simply to summon the parties. When this occurred, both the assembly and a *bureau* could be expected to review the case once again before the council rendered a final decision by an *arrêt* between parties (thus these *arrêts* too often recall a *bureau*'s participation).[14] In practice, this system ensured that cases of *cassation*—certainly the most sensitive aspect of the council's jurisdiction in the eyes of the *parlementaires*—received preliminary and "double" examination (by the assembly and a *bureau*) prior to any final decision; if a case moved beyond the stage of an *arrêt sur requête*, this examination occurred twice. For this reason, the *bureau* of *cassations* was very busy: "in effect," according to Chancellor Pontchartrain, "the most tiring and disagreeable of all." But he also noted that this *bureau* "more than all the others [contributes to] the welfare of justice and [protects] the honor of the courts whose judgments are attacked."[15]

A second track existed for legal actions the council rarely decided by *arrêts sur requête*. In cases of *évocation de justice* and *règlement de juges*, for example, the council almost always called both sides to present evidence before resolving a dispute with an *arrêt* between parties. *Arrêts* issued in the early stages of these cases, such as those providing interlocutory judgments or those *sur requête* summoning the litigants, were routine in nature. It made little sense to burden the *bureaux*, much less the entire council, with them. Instead, the assembly of masters of requests, meeting in special session with the chancellor, could decide these matters without seeking further consultation. The fact that several masters of requests routinely

---

[12] When several masters of requests signed the *minutes of arrêts*, they, like the councillors of state in a *bureau*, did so below the reporter's signature at the end of the *arrêt*.

[13] For example, see the *arrêts sur requête* in *cassation* of 27 February 1685 (AN, V^6 686, no. 23), 19 March 1714 (V^6 831, no. 13), and 25 February 1715 (V^6 834, no. 3).

[14] For example, see two *arrêts* between parties in *cassation* in AN, V^6 834: 17 December 1714 (no. 8) and 28 January 1715 (no. 8).

[15] Pontchartrain to La Reynie (who presided over the *bureau* of *cassations* in the late 1690s and early 1700s), 12 December 1708, BN, MSS. Fr. 21128, fols. 1098–1099v.

signed certain kinds of these *arrêts* illustrates the procedure.[16] Once a case neared completion, however, a *bureau* would then normally participate as well before the full council rendered a final decision, as the *arrêts* between parties in these legal actions clearly demonstrate.[17]

In assessing the merits of these procedures, it is important to bear in mind the magnitude of the council's workload. During Louis XIV's reign, the Conseil Privé assembled once or twice a week, and each meeting resulted in an average of 26 *arrêts*.[18] Had the council been obliged to discuss the legal issues involved in each of these cases, its efficiency surely would have suffered. Instead, the division of labor between its satellite bodies enabled the full council to devote most of its attention to cases ready for a final decision, cases that were already familiar to a number of masters of requests and councillors of state in attendance owing to their previous work in the assembly and the *bureaux*. More routine matters were left to the masters of requests and the chancellor, with the entire council simply ratifying their decisions. We shall never know, of course, whether the assemblies and the *bureaux* gave serious and thoughtful attention to all the cases that passed before them; one must always allow for differences in the work habits and abilities of individual council members. But the system itself was sound. Given the various constraints that limited bureaucratic efficiency in the seventeenth century, one would be hard pressed to imagine better ways to have utilized the time and talents of the council's membership.

Furthermore, if the system described here was inherently flexible in that it provided two tracks for the preliminary examination of cases, it could be further modified to take into account any special circumstances that a given case might present. The chancellor could decide, for example, that an affair was sufficiently complex to warrant the attention of more than one *bureau* before the council issued an *arrêt*. Thus, we learn from an *arrêt* between parties resolving a case of *évocation de justice* in 1705 that the reporting magistrate—a Sieur Le Camus—had consulted two *bureaux*— those presided over by Councillors of State Marillac and Le Peletier— before he reported to the entire council.[19] In similar fashion, the chancellor

---

[16] The process whereby the masters of requests and the chancellor alone decided certain issues without seeking further consultation is described in several reform articles the masters of requests presented to Séguier in March 1665: BN, MSS. Fr. 17565, fols. 196–205. The signatures of several masters of requests appear frequently on the *minutes* of *arrêts d'instruction* (such as *référés* and *procès-verbaux*), as well as on default judgments (*congés, forclusions*). Their signatures appear less often on *arrêts sur requête* summoning parties to contest *évocations de justice* and *règlements de juges;* usually just the chancellor and the reporter signed the *minutes* of these *arrêts*. See, passim, the *arrêts* in AN, V⁶ 326, 577, and 790 (from the years 1656, 1671, and 1702 respectively), which I consulted on these subjects.

[17] For illustrative examples, see the *arrêts* between parties of 7 May 1676 (AN, V⁶ 626, no. 45) and 20 March 1685 (V⁶ 686, no. 38).

[18] This figure is based on the primary sample described above in chap. IV, n. 2. A formal council meeting could produce a single *arrêt* (1 December 1714) or as many as 63 (18 September 1668).

[19] AN, V⁶ 802, no. 1 (16 October 1705).

might instruct several *bureaux* to examine the same case, but at different stages of the proceedings. This occurred in the case mentioned previously in which the *grand vicaire* of the Bishop of Langres requested the council to nullify a judgment rendered by the Parlement of Besançon. The *arrêt sur requête* in this case, which ordered additional procedures, refers to the participation of the *bureau* presided by Councillor of State Ribeyère; the *arrêt* between parties that later definitively resolved this affair mentions the intervention of another *bureau*, the one specializing in ecclesiastical affairs chaired by Abbé Bignon.[20] The chancellor also had the authority to involve a *bureau* in a case at a stage where the masters of requests normally acted alone, thereby providing senior members of the council with additional opportunities to monitor the activities of their junior colleagues. This explains why one sometimes finds the participation of *bureaux* mentioned in *arrêts sur requête* that simply summoned parties to contest an *évocation de justice* or a *règlement de juges*.[21]

As a final example of the council's willingness to modify its standard procedures, and this in a way that directly benefited the parlements, Gilbert de Voisins informs us that in the mid-eighteenth century an exception existed to the general rule that *bureaux* only examined cases but did not render final decisions. If, upon initially receiving a request for *cassation*, the reporting magistrate and the members of the *bureau* of *cassations* agreed unanimously that the request lacked merit and should be rejected outright, they could prepare an *arrêt sur requête* to this effect and have the chancellor sign it without consulting the entire council.[22] This expeditious method of denying requests for *cassation* early in the proceedings already existed during Louis XIV's reign, although exactly when it appeared remains an open question.[23] But variations in the official wording of *arrêts sur requête* refusing *cassation* suggest that the practice might have originated in the early eighteenth century.[24]

In addition to promoting the intelligent and flexible use of assemblies and *bureaux*, the council also devoted considerable attention to the activities of the reporting magistrates themselves. No member of the council was more familiar with the legal issues and facts in a given case than its reporter, and for this reason it was in the council's own interest to encourage a

---

[20] See above, chap. IV, n. 56.

[21] My impression from examining the *arrêts* in AN, V⁶ 326 and 577 is that this practice was more widespread after Louis XIV assumed personal rule.

[22] Antoine, "Le Mémoire de Gilbert de Voisins," 29; idem, *Le Conseil du roi sous le règne de Louis XV*, 307, 530–531.

[23] Guillard, *Histoire du conseil du roy*, 95.

[24] In the primary sample of *arrêts*, the *arrêts sur requête* denying *cassation* in the years 1676 and 1685 employ the verb "débouter." By the years 1695 and 1705, this word had been replaced by another phrase, "qu'il sera mis néant sur la requête." In 1714, however, the *arrêts* use either this phrase or the words "non recevable." Did the existence of two phrases in 1714 indicate that some requests for *cassation* were denied by the full council while others were rejected by the *bureau* of *cassations*? If so, the practice probably emerged sometime between 1705 and 1714.

master of requests so designated to fulfill his responsibilities conscientiously and impartially. While no amount of formal legislation could compel diligence on the part of reporting magistrates, at least the council could take steps to define their duties with precision and to rectify the most glaring abuses. Louis XIV's Conseil Privé took action along both these lines. On the one hand, the lengthy *règlements* of February 1660, January 1673, and June 1687 explained in detail even the most routine procedures a reporting magistrate followed to prepare a case for final resolution. Together, these acts exhibited an unprecedented interest in such matters as the time limits for initiating and completing various procedures, the rules for exchanging documents between the contesting parties, the methods for drafting and signing *arrêts*, and even the fees that a reporter's secretary could charge for his services.[25]

On the other hand, Louis's chancellors after Séguier attempted to eliminate the confusion that had previously characterized the distribution of cases and the appointment of reporting magistrates.[26] Traditionally, litigants at the council suggested reporters for their cases, with each side enjoying the right to challenge the other's selections. Until the 1670s, however, the rules governing these formalities were so imprecise as to invite contesting parties, each seeking to gain an advantage over the other, to engage in lengthy and costly disputes aimed at securing the appointment of a master of requests whom they hoped would be favorable to their interests. Reporting magistrates were assigned in rapid succession, and it was not uncommon to find several masters of requests working simultaneously on the same case. The council's clerks (*greffiers*) rather than the chancellor became the masters of this situation, willing to manipulate the relevant paperwork for a party who was prepared to pay handsomely for their assistance.

Information exists on how three of Louis's chancellors addressed these problems. Etienne Aligre, who succeeded Séguier in 1672, began the practice of setting aside one day each week for the distribution of cases. While he continued to allow litigants to challenge the reporting magistrates suggested by their adversaries, he ensured that this process occurred early in the proceedings according to rules guaranteeing prompt and proper notification. He then had his son, the abbé de Saint-Jacques, examine these challenges and weed out those that were frivolous. One of the council's clerks actually

---

[25] For details, see the *règlements* of 1660 (arts. 13, 16, 17, 20, 22, 26, 28, 47, 53, 54, 60, 61, 70, 75, 79), 1673 (arts. 34, 35, 37, 43, 47, 53, 55, 58, 60, 79, 80), and 1687 (arts. 20, 21, 32, 51–79, 91, 97, 107, 119–121, 130, 136). See also the *règlement* of 2 June 1680 in Bornier, *Conférences des ordonnances de Louis XIV,* 2: 834–835.

[26] The following two paragraphs are based on the "Mémoire de ce qui s'est pratiqué au conseil du roy dans la distribution des instances depuis environ quarante ans" (ca. 1700) in AAE, *France* 1081 ("mémoires des expéditions" of the secretaries of state, 1700), fols. 207–210v, which Antoine also discusses in *Le Conseil du roi sous le règne de Louis XV,* 63–67. See also the *règlements* of February 1660 (art. 75), January 1673 (arts. 34–39, 48–50, 58), and June 1687 (arts. 45–50, 143). See also the *règlement* of 2 July 1676 in Bornier, *Conférences des ordonnances de Louis XIV,* 2: 833–834.

lost his post for violating these rules. Chancellors Le Tellier and Boucherat had their own distinctive approaches. Angered by the frequency with which parties challenged the reporters designated by their adversaries, and suspecting that the council's clerks often authorized such challenges in order to direct cases to masters of requests whom they favored, Le Tellier limited litigants to submitting lists of three possible reporters, from which he made the final choice. Boucherat went further still, denying parties any role in the selection of reporting magistrates, permitting them only to indicate those masters of requests whom they considered to be suspect. None of these reforms proved to be entirely successful, not only because each chancellor insisted upon introducing his own usages, but also because the council's clerks still found ways to circumvent the rules. Only in the next reign would permanent regulations emerge for designating and challenging reporting magistrates.[27] But at least these chancellors had begun the process of reducing the disorder that had long attended such important formalities.

A study of all these procedures for examining cases clearly reveals that Louis XIV's Conseil Privé made few structural changes in the system inherited from previous generations. The principal elements of this system—reporting magistrates, assemblies of masters of requests, and *bureaux* of councillors of state—were all in place in 1661, as was the general policy of directing cases along one of two tracks for preliminary review. But a spirit of innovation is evident in the council's efforts to consolidate, refine, and improve upon traditional practices. Whether the *bureaux* were more active during Louis's reign than before is difficult to determine with precision because we cannot assume that the failure of an *arrêt* to mention a *bureau* necessarily means that one did not participate in a case. Nevertheless, it is worth reporting that references to the *bureaux* were far more common in the second than in the first half of the seventeenth century. By the end of Louis's reign, few *arrêts* between parties in cases of *évocation de justice* and *règlement de juges,* or any kind of *arrêt* issued in *cassation,* neglected to mention a *bureau's* participation, a generalization that does not apply to the troubled decades of mid-century. The *arrêts* also indicate that such practices as having several *bureaux* examine the same case, or involving the *bureaux* in matters traditionally referred to the masters of requests alone, had few precedents before Louis's personal rule. Furthermore, it was only in this era that *bureaux* became attached specifically to the Conseil Privé and that some of these *bureaux* acquired specialized functions.[28] Efforts to regulate carefully both the distribution of cases and the activities of reporting magistrates unquestionably represented a new direction.

What is perhaps most remarkable about these developments is that they occurred at all. Surviving records of the council's clerks indicate that the

---

[27] Antoine, *Le Conseil du roi sous le règne de Louis XV,* 304–306.
[28] The comparisons over time made in this paragraph are based on an examination of the *arrêts* discussed above in chap. IV, nn. 2 and 4.

caseload of the Conseil Privé declined dramatically during Louis XIV's personal rule. Lists of *arrêts* issued during the council's January *quartier*, which Kaiser has examined for the years 1623–1673 and Antoine for the period 1700–1775, illustrate this reduction.[29] The council's activity peaked during the years 1654–1660, when the January *quartier* alone issued a yearly average of 1,674 *arrêts*. During the first seven years of Louis's personal rule, 1661–1667, this figure dropped to 1,269, and between 1668 and 1673 it fell to 767. The latter figure corresponds to the annual average of *arrêts* issued during the January *quartier* in the years 1623–1653—772. The decline seems to have been gradual but steady for the remainder of Louis's reign.[30] By the period 1700–1708, the average number of *arrêts* the January *quartier* issued each year was only 236. During the last seven years of the reign, 1709–1715, this figure fell to 174, which represented an 86 percent decline from the years 1661–1667. The reign of Louis XV witnessed a further decrease of about 75 percent from the level achieved at the end of Louis XIV's reign.

Such a long-term trend is not easily explained. Certainly, it did not result from a reduction in this council's authority. Even Antoine, when commenting on the significant decline in the eighteenth century, argues forcefully against an interpretation hinging on this council's "decadence," and we shall see in the following chapter of this study that the Conseil Privé did not lose its traditional jurisdiction regarding the parlements to other council bodies during Louis XIV's personal rule.[31] Two other explanations are more plausible, and they apply equally to the reigns of Louis XIV and his successor. First, a reduction in the council's caseload might have reflected a general decline in the volume of litigation coming before the parlements and other sovereign courts, a decline whose origins historians have begun

---

[29] Antoine, *Le Conseil du roi sous le règne de Louis XV*, 375–376; Kaiser, "The Masters of Requests," appendix, chart 3. Their sources are AN, V⁶ 1224–1229, 1240–1242. Antoine also provides figures from the *quartier* of July, 1700–1768, and these correspond closely to those for the January *quartier*. Lists of the *arrêts* for the October *quartier* have not survived, and those for the April *quartier* end in 1653. The lists for the January *quartier* run from 1579 to 1775; those for the July *quartier*, 1579–1768.

[30] While I have not done so, a historian could use the sources cited in the previous note to develop statistics for the period 1674–1699. That the decline was gradual and steady in those years is clear, however, from the number of cartons used to store the council's *arrêts* each year. With each carton holding roughly 260 *arrêts* (based on this study's primary sample), these figures emerge for five-year periods: 1670–1674 (11.2 cartons); 1675–1679 (7.0); 1680–1684 (6.6); 1685–1689 (6.8); 1690–1694 (6.4); 1695–1699 (5.6). These averages stand in sharp contrast to those for 1665–1669 (14.0) and to those for 1700–1704 (4.0), 1705–1709 (3.8), and 1710–1714 (3.2).

[31] Antoine, *Le Conseil du roi sous le règne de Louis XV*, 364–365. Whether the quantitatively less important aspects of the council's jurisdiction—judging appeals from the rulings by provincial intendants, for example, or resolving precedence quarrels in lesser courts—suffered erosion by other council bodies is something only a full-scale study of all the councils can determine. On the basis of the various kinds of *arrêts* examined for this study, I found no indication that other council bodies attempted or made such inroads.

to trace to the period of Louis XIV's personal rule.[32] Second, the council's own considerable efforts to ameliorate the conditions of its work, to relinquish any pretensions of acting as an ordinary appellate court, and to dissuade litigants from initiating frivolous cases also might have taken their toll on the number of cases the council adjudicated.[33] For our purposes, what merits emphasis is that Louis XIV's Conseil Privé, when confronted with a decrease in the amount of its work, did not relax its efforts to perfect the procedures for examining cases. An increasingly elaborate system mobilized to review fewer cases tended to ensure that affairs regarding the parlements received more careful attention at the end of the reign than at the beginning. In this respect, it is worth noting that the peak of the council's activity came at the very time, the mid- and late 1650s, when its conflicts with the parlements had reached their highest pitch and when doubts about its administrative effectiveness were most pronounced.

Two of the remaining four procedural issues we shall consider also relate to the council's examination of cases, but they pertain exclusively to actions in *cassation*. The first concerns the formalities associated with submitting requests for *cassation*. In order to pursue any legal action at the Conseil Privé, a party required the services of an *avocat* chosen among the *avocats aux conseils*, a corps of 170 officials who, acting as both barristers and solicitors, served as intermediaries between parties and the council, shep-

---

[32] No general consensus exists about the reasons for this decline, and additional research will be necessary before one can speak with assurance on this subject. Existing scholarship suggests that a variety of long and short term forces, both national and regional, combined to trim parlementary caseloads. Examining the situation at the Parlement of Rennes during Louis XIV's reign, Hurt points not only to the general deterioration of economic conditions in the province (aggravated by the crown's wartime fiscal policies), but also to other developments, institutional in nature, that tended to divert litigants from this court: the famous investigative commissions active during the reign and, as regards this parlement's jurisdiction as a cour des aides, the growing authority of the intendants in fiscal affairs after 1689. Hurt, "Les Offices au Parlement de Bretagne," 19–22. Viewing the caseload of the Parlement of Paris over a longer time period (1670–1789), Kaiser too notes the conjuncture of economic and fiscal problems as having been important, at least in Louis XIV's reign. But he raises other possible explanations as well, one being that the proliferation of urban courts of commerce in the early eighteenth century might have reduced the number of appeals coming before this parlement. He also urges historians to seek out possible changes in attitudes toward litigation. Kaiser, "The Deflation in the Volume of Litigation at Paris," 312–318. Whatever its various causes were, the decline in litigation at the parlements seems to have been widespread—the issue figures prominently in Pontchartrain's correspondence—and it seems to have affected all kinds of litigation (except, according to Kaiser, serious criminal prosecutions—*grand criminel*). The onset of difficulties at Paris and Rennes dates to the 1670s and 1680s. By the end of Louis's reign, their caseloads had dropped between 50 and 75 percent depending upon the nature of the legal action.

[33] It serves little purpose to speculate whether the council's reforming activity was more important in reducing its caseload than the decline in litigation at the parlements; the two developments were no doubt complementary. But the importance of the council's own activities is perhaps illustrated by the fact that its caseload began to decline in the 1660s, at least a decade before the Parlements of Rennes and Paris experienced difficulties. Moreover, the overall decline in the council's caseload during Louis XIV's reign exceeded that in the two parlements.

herding the cases of their clients through all the necessary procedures.[34] In principle, a single *avocat* sufficed to handle a party's case. There was, however, an important exception first set forth in the *règlement* of February 1660: henceforth, all requests for *cassation* had to be signed not only by the petitioner's principal *avocat*, but also by two additional consultants selected from the 50 senior *avocats aux conseils*.[35] This requirement, which was repeated in the *règlements* of June 1687 and 3 February 1714, clearly aimed to reduce the number of requests for *cassation* submitted to the council by having the *avocats* refuse to sign, and thereby to weed out, those with little merit.[36]

How many potential actions in *cassation* were cut short in this fashion is, of course, impossible to determine. Enforcement of the requirement was not a problem: *arrêts sur requête* issued in *cassation* after 1660 not only mention a petitioner's previous consultation with three *avocats*, but they sometimes bear their signatures as well.[37] Indeed, an *arrêt sur requête* issued pursuant to a request that had omitted the formality of consultation was itself subject to nullification.[38] There are good reasons to suspect, however, that the rule fell short of meeting the council's expectations. After all, the *avocats aux conseils* had purchased their offices, and it was thus in their own financial interest to encourage rather than to discourage litigation. Surely a petitioner intent upon challenging a parlement's civil or criminal sentence could find two among 50 potential consultants to sign a request. Echoing age-old complaints about the avarice of lawyers, Chancellor Pontchartrain denounced in 1710 the "spirit of chicanery of all kinds" and the "shameful greediness" he detected in the conduct of some of the council's *avocats*, "either in multiplying costs and augmenting dockets for the most insignificant affairs or in taking on the worst cases and then using the falsest colors to sustain them."[39] Four years later he even considered

---

[34] The functions of *avocats aux conseils* were transformed into royal offices in 1643, and in 1644 their number was fixed at 200, reduced to 170 by the *règlement* of January 1673. Mousnier, "Le Conseil du roi," 52; Boislisle, *Les Conseils du roi sous Louis XIV*, 39. For a review of the privileges and duties of the *avocats*, see Antoine, *Le Conseil du roi sous le règne de Louis XV*, 244–247. The older study by Emile Bos, *Les Avocats aux conseils du roi: Etude sur l'ancien régime judiciaire de la France* (Paris, 1881), should be used with caution. To the best of my knowledge, procedures at the Conseil Privé during the personal rule of Louis XIV were written, so the *avocats* functioned mostly as solicitors. Guillard, *Histoire du conseil du roy*, 143, suggests that the *avocats* could plead before the *bureaux*, but I have found no evidence of this.

[35] *Règlement* of 1660, art. 14. An examination of the council's *arrêts* before 1660—for example, AN, V⁶ 319 and 326—provides no examples of this rule being in force before this date.

[36] *Règlement* of 1687, art. 43. *Arrêt en commandement* of 3 February 1714, AN, E 1974.

[37] For example, see the *arrêt* on *requêtes respectives* of 20 May 1676 (AN, V⁶ 626, no. 25) and the *arrêt sur requête* of 25 February 1715 (V⁶ 834, no. 3). The reference to the *avocats* (and their signatures, if present, on the *minutes*) appear near the end of the introductory portion (*exposé*) of the *arrêt*.

[38] For this issue as grounds for *opposition* against one of the council's own *arrêts*, see the *arrêt sur requête* of 7 May 1676, AN, V⁶ 626, no. 37.

[39] Pontchartrain to the syndic of the community of *avocats aux conseils*, 7 December 1710, BN, MSS. Fr. 21142, fols. 1198–1199v. For an example of an *avocat*, one Rupin, losing his

reducing the number of senior *avocats* eligible to consult from 50 to 20 because too many *avocats* were willing to sign requests for *cassation* "without having seen anything."[40] The fact that the council sometimes denied requests for *cassation* at the stage of an *arrêt sur requête* without even summoning all the parties to contest a complaint suggests that at least a few requests lacked plausible legal reasoning.

On the other hand, we should not exclude the possibility that conferring with several *avocats* might have deterred some parties from pressing hopeless cases; perhaps just the prospect of paying additional legal fees prompted a sense of caution.[41] Moreover, to assume that the *avocats* lacked any sentiments of honor or of obligation toward their clients would be as presumptuous as claiming that they were all paragons of virtue. A request for *cassation*, duly signed by three *avocats*, was not necessarily groundless or the result of poor legal advice simply because it ultimately failed. We have seen that the council was not generous in pronouncing *cassation* and that occasionally it even ruled against petitioners who had substantiated their contentions. Insofar as the parlements were concerned, however, the requirement of prior consultation worked only to their advantage: any hurdle placed in the paths of petitioners tended to make the nullification of judgments more difficult to achieve.

The other procedural issue concerning the council's examination of cases of *cassation* more directly engaged the attention of the parlements. Like the *arrêts* of the Conseil Privé, the civil and criminal sentences of the parlements (and, indeed, of all the other tribunals in the realm) did not mention the judicial reasoning, or *motifs*, behind the magistrates' judgments.[42] As a result, when members of the council examined requests for *cassation*, they lacked any precise indication why a court had decided a given case in a particular way. For most actions in *cassation*, the council did not consider this absence of information to be crucial. The documents that parties submitted in evidence, which included copies of sentences and other pertinent

---

office for violating conciliar *règlements*, see the *arrêt en commandement* of 2 March 1677, AN, E 1788.

[40] Pontchartrain to Le Pelletier (presiding magistrate in the *bureau* of *cassations*), 19 December 1713, BN, MSS. Fr. 21138, fols. 1107–1110. This letter, which the chancellor wrote in preparation for the *arrêt* of February 1714 cited above in this chapter, n. 36, should be read in conjunction with this *arrêt*. Only in 1738 was the number of senior *avocats* eligible to sign requests for cassation reduced to 30: Antoine, *Le Conseil du roi sous le règne de Louis XV*, 289–290. But the *arrêt* of 1714 did attempt to stimulate assiduous conduct among the *avocats* by requiring that those who signed such requests be prepared to justify their conduct before the council.

[41] Certainly, parties who felt confident about their complaints did not object to this rule. Thus Mathurin Goeslin, whose case is cited above in chap. IV, n. 31, spoke of the requirement for consultation as a way to prevent chicanery and "to defend the integrity [*établir la sévérité*] of *arrêts contradictoires*."

[42] For an informative overview of this aspect of judicial life in *ancien régime* France, see Tony Sauvel, "Histoire du jugement motivé," *Revue du Droit Public et de la Science Politique en France et à l'Etranger* 71 (1955): 5–53.

trial papers, usually contained enough information for the council to determine whether the judges had violated one of the principles that constituted grounds for *cassation*.

In some cases, however, the council believed that the evidence was sufficiently ambiguous or that the complaints about a court's conduct were
so serious as to warrant contacting the judges directly about their rationale
for a particular judgment.[43] In these cases, the council instructed the *procureur général* of the court whose sentence was under attack to submit a
written report that explained the judges' judicial reasoning and addressed
the charges made by the complaining party.[44] The logical place for this
order, known as a "demande de motifs," was in the *arrêt sur requête* the
council issued after a request for *cassation* had already passed before the
three *avocats*, the reporting magistrate, the assembly of the masters of requests, and one of the *bureaux*. The call for *motifs* was not obligatory. Thus,
an *arrêt sur requête* might terminate an action for or against a petitioner
without ordering any additional procedures, in which case a formal request
for *motifs* was unnecessary. Or the council could use an *arrêt sur requête*
to summon all the litigants involved in a disputed judgment to contest a
complaint fully, and this without making any reference to a need for *motifs*.
In this instance, a case then progressed to a final *arrêt* between parties
without the judges themselves participating in conciliar proceedings. If the
arrêt sur requête did call for the submission of *motifs*, however, this order
appeared either alone in the *arrêt* or in conjunction with the summoning
of parties.[45] After the *procureur général* sent in his report, the council was
then in a position to render a final decision on the case (although it had
the option even at this stage of summoning the complainant's opposite
parties if this had not been done earlier).

The council acted with great circumspection when querying the *parlementaires* about their judicial reasoning. Owing to both its prestige and its
proximity to the council, the Parlement of Paris, whose jurisdiction included
nearly half of the realm, was actually exempt from submitting written
reports. If the council sought enlightenment from these judges, the master
of requests who served as the reporting magistrate for a case could visit
the court and collect information orally.[46] Insofar as the other parlements

---

[43] The principle that the council did not consider it necessary to request *motifs* when the
issues in a petitioner's complaint were clear is mentioned in a letter of Pontchartrain to Le
Bret (Aix), 24 April 1714, BN, MSS. Fr. 21139, fols. 375v–376v.

[44] For a general discussion of this procedure, especially in the eighteenth century, see Sauvel,
"Les Demandes de motifs," and Antoine, *Le Conseil du roi sous le règne de Louis XV*, 324–327,
351–353.

[45] For examples of an order for *motifs* without summoning the parties, see the *arrêts sur
requête* of 3 July 1669 (AN, V⁶ 554, no. 13) and 19 March 1714 (V⁶ 831, no. 13); for *motifs*
requested simultaneously with the summoning of parties, see the *arrêts sur requête* of 9 March
1685 (V⁶ 686, no. 22) and 21 October 1705 (V⁶ 802, no. 13). The call for *motifs* appears in
the decision portion (*dispositif*) of the *arrêt*.

[46] This principle is stated clearly in a letter of First President Lamoignon to *Procureur Général*
Harlay, 30 September 1666, BN, MSS. Fr. 17413, fol. 33.

were concerned, the council did not request *motifs* in most cases. Of the 74 *arrêts sur requête* examined previously in connection with "serious" cases of *cassation*, 20 provided final decisions while 13 others involved the Parlement of Paris. Of the remaining 41, 17 (or 41 percent) called for *motifs*. As one might expect, the procedure was utilized even less in more routine cases. Of the 27 *arrêts sur requête* examined earlier in this category, seven gave final decisions and two others involved the Parisian *parlementaires*. Only four of the remaining 18 *arrêts* (or 22 percent) ordered the submission of *motifs*. In addition, the entire procedure unfolded in an atmosphere of secrecy. Contesting parties did not have access to the reports that *procureurs généraux* submitted, and the *arrêts* between parties that terminated cases never revealed the contents of these reports. Because in theory *motifs* were drafted by the *procureur général* and not by the court as a whole, the parlements did not retain copies in their archives.[47] The Conseil Privé itself did not preserve these reports systematically: some survive from the eighteenth century, but none from the reign of Louis XIV.[48]

Such secrecy, while certainly an intelligent concession to parlementary sensibilities, proves frustrating to the historian interested in determining how the parlements and the Conseil Privé itself viewed this procedure. On one level, the *parlementaires* could hardly have been expected to show enthusiasm for a tangible reminder of the council's disciplinary authority, especially when this authority might benefit a litigant so impertinent as to challenge a judgment rendered in last resort by superior magistrates who thought highly of their own dignity. A university professor called upon by a dean to justify in detail a student's grade given months previously might appreciate the judges' uneasiness. Indeed, Pontchartrain's correspondence contains several examples of the chancellor reprimanding *procureurs généraux* for procrastinating in submitting their reports.[49]

One should not too hastily conclude, however, that the parlements were hostile toward the call for *motifs*. Delays in submitting reports did not

---

[47] Antoine, *Le Conseil du roi sous le règne de Louis XV,* 326. My research in the judicial archives of the Parlements of Aix, Dijon, Grenoble, Paris, Rennes, and Rouen uncovered no copies of *motifs* sent by the *procureurs généraux* to the council.

[48] AN, V⁶ 1163–1164 contain a few *motifs* for years after 1728. Antoine, *Le Fonds du conseil d'état du roi aux Archives Nationales,* 60, n. 1, notes that in the council's archives, *motifs* are usually attached to the relevant *arrêts* between parties, but such is unfortunately not the case for Louis XIV's reign. According to Sauvel, "Les Demandes de motifs," 544–547, *motifs* took the form that one might expect: sometimes a *procureur général*'s report was lengthy and reviewed a case in detail; at other times, the *motifs* simply addressed a petitioner's grounds for *cassation*.

[49] The council normally gave a *procureur général* two months to submit *motifs,* yet at times some had not done so after as long as eight months or even two years! Pontchartrain to Des Mesples (Pau), 13 December 1707, and to Du Vigier (Bordeaux), 14 July 1711, BN, MSS. Fr. 21126, fols. 1014–1015; 21134, fol. 607. In a letter to Doroz (Besançon), 17 June 1711, the chancellor complained about "the lack of punctuality shown by the *procureurs généraux* of most parlements in satisfying conciliar *arrêts* enjoining them to submit *motifs* for the judgments of their courts against which parties are proceeding in *cassation*." Ibid., 21133, fols. 517v–518.

necessarily reveal a spirit of obstinacy. *Procureurs généraux* prepared their
reports after consulting the judges and the reporting magistrate who had
rendered the judgment under attack.[50] Bringing together magistrates who
were unaccustomed to explaining their reasoning, and this for the purpose
of recalling facts and circumstances in a case judged months before, must
have been a time-consuming and tedious affair. Even judges who had
agreed on the final disposition of a case might have done so for different
reasons.[51] Furthermore, if the parlements opposed the procedure, they never
made this known. The council's practice of soliciting *motifs* was well established by the end of the sixteenth century, and it was certainly in use
in the decades preceding Louis XIV's assumption of personal rule.[52] Yet
the parlements' memoranda of mid-century, which were so detailed in
outlining the judges' many grievances against the councils, made not a
single reference to the "demande de motifs." This silence no doubt stemmed
from the fact that while a call for *motifs* might have inconvenienced the
judges, it nevertheless afforded them the opportunity to defend their conduct and to rebut the allegations made by the complaining party.

The Conseil Privé certainly viewed the procedure in this positive light.
There are, of course, many aspects of the council's collective thinking on
this matter that will forever remain obscure. Because the council's own
arrêts do not explain the judicial reasoning behind decisions, the circumstances that prompted a request for *motifs* in one case but not in another
are unknown. The *arrêts* reveal no patterns in this respect: the council's
archives contain many cases raising identical grounds for *cassation* but
differing in whether they entailed a call for *motifs*.[53] Nor do the *arrêts*
indicate how important a *procureur général*'s comments were in determining
the final outcome of a case. Nevertheless, the traces of the procedure in
the chancellors' correspondence, notably in that of Pontchartrain, leave no
doubt about the council's good intentions. In 1700, for example, Pont-

---

[50] Each parlement no doubt had its own particular usages for drafting *motifs*. Those in use
at Bordeaux are discussed at length in Pontchartrain to Du Vigier, 29 April 1706 and 9 March
and 26 April 1712, ibid., 21125, fol. 311; 21135, fols. 317v–318, 355v–356v. In practice,
probably the most important person in the preparation of *motifs* was the judge who had been
the reporting magistrate for the judgment under attack.

[51] Petitioners had six months from the date that a judgment in last resort was delivered to
them to submit requests for *cassation*: see the *règlements* of January 1673 (art. 66) and June
1687 (art. 38). Given the various delays a request might encounter once at the council, the
parlementaires were in effect being asked to recall their reasoning for judgments they might
have rendered as long ago as a year in the past. Sauvel, "Les Demandes de motifs," 542–
543, reviews the practical difficulties that judges experienced in preparing *motifs*.

[52] Antoine, *Le Conseil du roi sous le règne de Louis XV*, 324; Sauvel, "Les Demandes de
motifs," 534. For an example, see the *arrêt sur requête* of 11 February 1656, AN, V⁶ 319, no.
153.

[53] For example, *arrêts sur requête* of 3 and 10 July 1669 (AN, V⁶ 554, nos. 13, 58) mention
procedural and jurisdictional grounds for *cassation* and include a call for *motifs*, whereas *arrêts
sur requête* of 13 September 1668 (V⁶ 544, no. 16) and 27 February 1685 (V⁶ 686, no. 6) refer
to the same grounds but do not order *motifs*. Similarly, *arrêts sur requête* of 20 May 1676 (V⁶
626, no. 17) and 19 March 1714 (V⁶ 831, no. 1) both raise a violation of law as grounds for
cassation, but only the former includes a call for *motifs*.

chartrain notified the *procureur général* of the Parlement of Rennes that a case was pending at council in which the complaining party had accused the *parlementaires* of illegally judging litigation of limited scope and monetary value in costly special sessions. The council had just ordered the submission of *motifs* in this case, and the chancellor was anxious to read them, "so that I can see if anything can justify such extraordinary conduct, conduct that would dishonor the parlement if the fact is such as has been averred."[54] Eight years later, the chancellor notified the first president of this court that a petitioner had recently complained that one of the ten *parlementaires* who had judged his case was his creditor; if proven, this violation of law would provide a "decisive and convincing" reason to nullify the parlement's judgment. Owing to his "friendship and consideration" for the judges, however, Pontchartrain wished to allow them to explain their side of the story.[55]

Complementing this absence of confrontational language was the fact that a court's *motifs* could indeed rescue a sentence from potential nullification. Pontchartrain could be quite explicit about this. To draw another example from his correspondence with the Breton *parlementaires*, in 1700 the council rejected a request for *cassation* even though the complaining parties had clearly established one of their grounds (a serious irregularity in judicial procedure involving a reporting magistrate's failure to communicate a pertinent document to the other judges). Pontchartrain noted that the council had decided to uphold the parlement's sentence in part because the *motifs* submitted by the *procureur général* were "so reasonable."[56] The efficacy of *motifs* is also suggested by an examination of the ten *arrêts* between parties considered earlier in connection with the "serious" cases of *cassation*. Two of these cases entailed a prior request for *motifs*, and in both instances the council eventually ruled against the complaining parties.[57] None of this should imply, of course, that the submission of *motifs* always worked to the advantage of the parlements, as Pontchartrain's correspondence also makes clear.[58] Nevertheless, that the procedure could

---

[54] Pontchartrain to La Bedoyère, 18 August 1700, BN, MSS. Fr. 21119, pp. 827–828.

[55] Pontchartrain to Brilhac, 18 July 1708, ibid., 21128, fols. 754–756. The chancellor perhaps had good reason to treat the Parlement of Rennes with respect, having served as this court's first president earlier in his career. Note that in this case, Pontchartrain informally solicited *motifs* before the council even issued an *arrêt sur requête*. For another example of such early requests for *motifs*, see his letter to Le Bret (Aix), 3 March 1714, ibid., 21139, fols. 201v–202v. Most often, however, *motifs* were solicited formally in the *arrêts sur requête*.

[56] Pontchartrain to De Lasse and to La Bedoyère, 5 May 1700, ibid., 21119, pp. 361–363. For other examples of *motifs* having been solicited in cases that were eventually resolved in the parlements' favor, see Pontchartrain to Le Mazuyer and to the Parlement of Toulouse, 7 February 1710, and to Doroz (Besançon), 18 July 1711, ibid., 21131, fols. 215v–218v; 21134, fols. 609–611v.

[57] *Arrêts* between parties of 26 September 1695 (AN, V⁶ 755, no. 22) and 28 January 1715 (V⁶ 834, no. 8).

[58] See Pontchartrain to La Bedoyère (Rennes), 12 November 1702, and to Le Mazuyer (Toulouse), 29 December 1709, BN, MSS. Fr. 21121, fols. 531v–533v; 21130, fols. 1107–1108.

tip the scales in a parlement's favor, and this even when petitioners had substantiated their contentions, indicates the weight the council was disposed to accord the judges' opinions.

Two final procedural matters warrant attention because they reveal the council's willingness to respond favorably to the judges' grievances of mid-century. One concerns the *parlementaires'* belief that parties who initiated and then lost legal actions at the council should pay heavy fines, and the other pertains to the council's practice of frequently suspending the enforcement of parlementary judgments while actions in *cassation* were pending. On the first issue, the principle that unsuccessful appellants to the parlements and other sovereign courts should pay a fine was well established in French law. Royal legislation to this effect dated to the early sixteenth century, and the statutory amount was 75 *livres*. The rationale for this rule was that the prospect of paying fines would deter litigants from pursuing frivolous appeals. Over the years, however, the judges had become lax in imposing fines. Not only did they fear a reduction in their caseloads—an important concern for magistrates who collected personal fees, or *épices*, for the litigation they judged—but they also believed that considerations of equity should weigh heavily in the decision to fine an appellant—the fact that an appeal was unsuccessful did not necessarily mean that it lacked all legal merit. The subject of fining appellants attracted renewed interest during Colbert's tenure as controller general of finances. An edict of August 1669 established a system of appeal fines that applied uniformly to all the sovereign courts of the realm. Henceforth, litigants who wished to initiate appellate proceedings in the sovereign courts first had to deposit 12 *livres* with the tax farm for the royal demesne. If the appeal subsequently failed, this sum passed automatically to the crown as a fine. The only discretionary power the magistrates retained in this matter was the right to fine appellants 75 *livres* if the circumstances of a case so warranted.[59]

One may be justifiably cynical about the intent of this legislation and argue that Colbert was more interested in augmenting royal revenue than in curtailing litigation. In view of the numerous and potentially high costs associated with litigating in the sovereign courts, the sum of 12 *livres* was relatively insignificant and probably not sufficient to make prospective appellants reassess their plans. But the monarchy was far more serious about discouraging litigants from challenging judgments that the sovereign courts had already rendered in last resort. Thus the ordinance of April 1667 required parties who initiated actions in *requête civile* to make an advance deposit of 450 *livres*, a substantial sum representing a comfortable annual income for an urban or rural bourgeois family. If the *requête civile* then failed, this deposit automatically became a fine, with 300 *livres* going to

---

[59] The edict, which provides a concise history of appeal fines, is in Isambert et al., eds., *Recueil général des anciennes lois,* 18: 336–339.

the crown and 150 *livres* to the petitioner's adversaries.[60] For the reasons stated above, the judges generally opposed all these obligatory deposits and fines, and Colbert had to overcome stiff resistance in several parlements before he secured the implementation of the new rules.[61]

It was against this background that the Conseil Privé itself adopted a policy of assessing mandatory fines. The parlements had already called upon the council to do this during the era of the Fronde (conveniently ignoring any inconsistency in hoping to avoid such a requirement themselves), and the king's ministers could hardly have touted the advantages of a system imposed with difficulty on the sovereign courts in the late 1660s and early 1670s had not the council that dealt primarily with judicial affairs also fallen into line. In addition, we have seen that the Conseil Privé exhibited a genuine interest in deterring parties from pursuing frivolous actions; introducing fines was certainly consistent with this desire. The ordinance of August 1669 took the first step in this direction by establishing a fine of 300 *livres* against parties who began procedures for *évocations de justice* and then either lost their cases or desisted from them without good cause.[62] The council's *règlement* of January 1673 was more rigorous still, applying to parties who initiated cases of *évocation de justice* and *cassation* the same rules that pertained to litigants who pursued *requêtes civiles* at the sovereign courts: an advance deposit of 450 *livres* and the forfeit of this sum (300 *livres* to the crown, 150 *livres* to the opposite parties) if the action subsequently failed.[63] The reason for attaching fines to these two legal actions was "because there is even greater justification for condemning to fines those who file poor requests for *évocation* and *cassation* [than for penalizing those who lose *requêtes civiles*] because [petitioners in the former

---

[60] Ordinance of 1667, tit. 35, arts. 16, 39. The amounts of the deposit and fine were reduced by half when petitioners challenged default judgments.

[61] For a general idea of this opposition, see a declaration of 21 March 1671 (in Isambert et al., eds., *Recueil général des anciennes lois*, 18: 427–431), which reiterated the provisions of the edict of 1669 and the ordinance of 1667 on the subject of appeal fines. See also the letters addressed to Colbert from several parlements in the early 1670s throughout BN, Clairambault MS. 759 (especially the documents concerning the Parlement of Toulouse, pp. 71–98v), as well as an *arrêt en commandement* of 5 November 1678, which nullified portions of over 70 judgments at the Parlement of Aix that violated the legislation of 1669 and 1671 (AN, E 1795). In a forthcoming book on the Parlement of Rennes, which will contain information on the other parlements as well, Professor John Hurt will place the parlements' hostility toward mandatory appeal fines within the larger context of parlementary opposition to Colbert's financial policies in the late 1660s and early 1670s. My own work in the judicial archives of six parlements (see above, this chapter, n. 47) indicates that the appeal fines were implemented by the parlements during the 1670s.

[62] Ordinance of 1669, tit. 1, art. 35.

[63] *Règlement* of 1673, arts. 62, 68, 70–72. The amounts of the deposit and fine were reduced by half when petitioners sought the nullification of default judgments. An *arrêt en commandement* of 22 April 1673 ordering the *avocats* of the council to abide by these rules is in AN, E 1770. The council's *règlements* issued throughout Louis's reign also established deposits and fines for other kinds of legal actions, such as *récusation*, *inscription en faux*, and *tierce opposition*. These did not figure prominently in cases involving the parlements, however, and thus they are not considered in this study.

actions] abuse . . . the authority of the king's council, because the costs they cause [their adversaries] are higher, and because they interrupt even more the course of justice."[64] The adoption of mandatory fines was a novel policy for the Conseil Privé. While it had always possessed the authority to impose fines, it had rarely done so. A summary examination of *arrêts* from the years 1647, 1656, and 1660 reveals no mention of fines, and the primary sample for 1668 yields only one instance, a fine of 200 *livres* against a party who had lost his bid for an *évocation de justice*.[65]

Tracing the implementation of these rules is a complicated affair. It is clear that the council quickly abandoned one aspect of the system—the requirement that a deposit of 450 *livres* precede the initiation of actions. An *arrêt* of 27 October 1674 officially relieved parties of this formality, and both Boucherat and Pontchartrain testified to its demise.[66] The reason— and it was one the parlements themselves had mentioned regarding the advance sums required to pursue *requêtes civiles*—was that parties should not be denied recourse to legal remedies solely because they lacked the funds to make deposits.[67] Only late in the reign did the council change its position on this matter, and it did so in a way that both benefited the parlements and demonstrated the council's renewed interest in discouraging litigants from attacking judgments rendered in last resort. Responding to Pontchartrain's concern that too many requests for *cassation* were ground- less, an *arrêt* of February 1714 reintroduced the requirement that deposits precede the initiation of procedures for *cassation*. Upon presenting the council with a request for *cassation*, a complaining party now had to deposit 150 *livres*, this sum passing to the crown as a fine if the request failed at the stage of an *arrêt sur requête*. If, however, the *arrêt sur requête* did not pronounce on the merits of the request but instead summoned all the con- cerned parties to contest the complaint, the petitioner was required to de- posit an additional 150 *livres* before further proceedings commenced. The

---

[64] These words are taken from an *arrêt* of September 1698 that will be discussed below: Bornier, *Conférences des ordonnances de Louis XIV*, 2: 862–864.

[65] *Arrêt* between parties of 18 September 1668, AN, V[6] 544, no. 18 (and the fine was in favor of the opposite party, not the crown). The generalization for the years 1647, 1656, and 1660 rests on an examination of V[6] 215, 319, 325–326, and 400 (dossier for 27 February 1660 only).

[66] Bornier, *Conférences des ordonnances de Louis XIV*, 2: 832–833; Boucherat to Le Bret (Aix), 30 June 1691, AN, V[1] 585, p. 235; Pontchartrain to La Porte (Metz), 2 June 1711, BN, MSS. Fr. 21133, fols. 474v–475v.

[67] As the *arrêt* of September 1698 (see above, this chapter, n. 64) explained, deposits fell into disuse "because it has been judged that it was necessary to give all the king's subjects the liberty to approach his throne, that is, to have recourse to the justice and authority of his council." The parlements, however, never received the right to dispense with advance deposits in cases of *requête civile*. But for an idea of their reasoning on the matter, see Le Tellier to Fieubet (Toulouse), 14 January 1680, BN, MSS. Fr. 5267, pp. 156–157. Noted the chancellor: "The issue of the poverty of the king's subjects in your resort who are incapable of depositing [fines] in order to pursue a *requête civile* was carefully considered when the ordinance [of April 1667] was formulated . . . [but] one has preferred to all these considerations the security [*repos*] that a [parlementary] judgment [in last resort] provides families."

total sum of 300 *livres* was then divided equally between the crown and the opposite parties if the council ultimately rejected the request in a final *arrêt* between parties.[68] While the *arrêt* of 1714 thus reduced the potential fine from 450 to either 300 or 150 *livres*—a concession to Pontchartrain's desire not "to appear too harsh [*dur*] and to carry things too far against those who seek *cassation*"—the restoration of deposits unquestionably placed yet another obstacle in the paths of those who wished to challenge the sentences of the sovereign courts. Commenting on this implication, though with considerable hyperbole, one petitioner went so far as to intimate that the judges were now free to violate royal legislation with impunity![69]

If the council relaxed the requirement for advance deposits during most of Louis XIV's reign, it remained committed—at least in its public pronouncements—to imposing fines on those who initiated and then lost cases of *évocation de justice* and *cassation*. The *règlement* of June 1687 reiterated the rules set forth in January 1673 on this subject, and still other *arrêts* worked out the technical details for the bookkeeping associated with recording fines.[70] The council's own judicial decisions, however, tell a more complicated story of enforcement. The *arrêts* in the primary sample for the years 1676, 1685 and 1695 reveal that only about two-thirds of all unsuccessful actions in *évocation de justice* entailed fines; the ratio dropped to approximately one in eight for unsuccessful actions in *cassation*. One hesitates to place too much confidence in these figures because in theory fines were mandatory and imposed automatically as soon as an action was lost. The failure of an *arrêt* to mention a fine thus does not necessarily mean that one was not intended. All that can be said with assurance is that the council did assess fines and that parties who contemplated initiating an action had to bear this in mind.

---

[68] These amounts were reduced by half when a petitioner sought the nullification of default judgments. For the *arrêt* of 1714, which should be read in conjunction with Pontchartrain's letter to Le Pelletier in 1713, see above, this chapter, nn. 36 and 40. The chancellor wished to reintroduce deposits because he hoped "that parties will no longer continue to present poor requests [for *cassation*] as frequently as they have presented them for sometime now to the council."

[69] According to Jean Benet, who maintained in December 1714 that the Parlement of Aix had violated the marine ordinance of 1681 while judging his litigation, part of the reason why the judges had contravened this legislation was because "the council cannot doubt . . . that the parlement has believed it can dispense with enforcing [this] ordinance [of 1681] because it knows that requests for *cassation* are heard with great difficulty at the king's council since the *règlement* of last February established many obstacles [to winning *cassation*]." See above, chap. IV, n. 36.

[70] *Règlement* of 1687, arts. 34, 44. In order to facilitate the collection of fines, an *arrêt en commandement* of 12 March 1683 established registers in which *avocats* were to record information about the identity and addresses of parties involved in legal actions that could entail fines: AN, E 1818. Another *arrêt en commandement* of 7 August 1684 stated that the amounts of fines would be those set forth in the *règlement* of 1673 even if the council's *arrêts* adjudicating cases failed to stipulate these amounts: Bornier, *Conférences des ordonnances de Louis XIV*, 2: 837–838.

Nevertheless, there is good reason to believe that the council exercised discretion in imposing fines. Ironically, the council seems to have adopted the same policy the judges had followed before Colbert introduced his reforms: consider the question of equity and penalize only those parties whose cases clearly lacked solid legal foundation. For example, one occasionally discovers in the council's archives an *arrêt* in which a fine was originally imposed, but then deleted, suggesting that the reporting magistrate or a *bureau* had penned in a preliminary penalty that was later discarded in a formal council meeting.[71] Boucherat himself indicated that equity mattered in the council's attitude toward fines. In a letter to the first president of the Parlement of Aix discussing *évocations de justice*, the chancellor noted that, "one no longer deposits the sum of 450 *livres* when one begins [procedures for *évocation*], but when the council judges the *évocation*, if it is not good and according to the rules, one rejects the petitioner with a fine and court costs *according to the merit and the circumstances of the affair* [italics mine]."[72] That litigants themselves maintained that fines were not intended unless *arrêts* specifically mentioned them further suggests that the council did not wish to impose fines in all eligible cases.[73] Indeed, it was precisely this ambiguity, arising in part from the council's own practice and in part from the desire of parties to find loopholes, that led the council to issue an *arrêt* of 3 September 1698 which stated unequivocally that fines were mandatory and should be considered officially imposed even if the *arrêts* failed to mention them. Parties were relieved of fines only if the council pronounced this explicitly.[74] The fact that the *arrêts* in the primary sample from the years 1705 and 1714–15 occasionally contain such phrases as "néanmoins sans amende" and "néanmoins l'amende rendue sans tirer à conséquence" demonstrates the council's adherence to this policy.[75] But such relief appears rarely: by the end of Louis's reign the imposition of fines had become the rule at the Conseil Privé.

We shall never know, of course, the extent to which advance deposits and the prospect of paying fines deterred litigants from initiating legal actions at the council. From the vantage point of the parlements, however, the implications of the regulations on these matters were the same as those stemming from the requirement that requests for *cassation* bear the signatures of three *avocats*: any formality that made a litigant's recourse to the council more difficult tended to enhance the independence that the *parlementaires* enjoyed in exercising their judicial functions.

---

[71] For example, the *arrêt* on *requêtes respectives* of 13 March 1685, AN, V⁶ 686, no. 20. Fines are mentioned in the *dispositif* portion of the council's *arrêts*.

[72] See above, this chapter, n. 66.

[73] The *arrêt* of 1698, cited above in this chapter, n. 64, discusses the views of litigants toward fines.

[74] Ibid.

[75] For example, see the *arrêt* between parties of 4 December 1705 (AN, V⁶ 802, no. 7) and the *arrêt sur requête* of 3 December 1714 (V⁶ 834, no. 5).

The *parlementaires* also received satisfaction on the issue of the council's practice of suspending the enforcement of their judgments while actions in *cassation* were pending. The question of ordering a suspension, or *surséance*, arose at the point in conciliar proceedings when the council, having examined a request for *cassation*, was prepared to issue an *arrêt sur requête*. If the council wished to terminate an action at this stage, it did not make a ruling on suspension: the *arrêt* either rejected the petitioner's request outright or nullified the judgment under attack without further deliberation. But when the council decided, as it did in most cases, to use an *arrêt sur requête* not to resolve an action but instead to order additional procedures—summoning the parties to contest, for example, or calling for the submission of *motifs*—it could also suspend the enforcement of the judgment in question until a final *arrêt* between parties eventually settled the case.[76]

The parlements did not oppose orders for suspension in all legal actions that came before the Conseil Privé. We have seen that in pending cases of *évocation de justice* and *règlement de juges* the normal practice was to postpone all procedures in the courts (or at least the final judgment of criminal cases) until the council completed its work. Such postponement was acceptable to the judges because these legal actions were jurisdictional disputes that unfolded *before* a court had issued a judgment in last resort. But to suspend the enforcement of sentences rendered *after* the full instruction of cases had already occurred in the sovereign courts was, in the view of the *parlementaires*, objectionable on two counts. First, a liberal policy of granting suspensions gave unscrupulous litigants an incentive to initiate procedures for *cassation* in the hope of delaying, even if only temporarily, the enforcement of judgments against them. This in turn threatened the interests of litigants who had already won their cases in the sovereign courts, often at great expense. Second, the judges maintained that by ordering a suspension the council seemed to imply that one of their judgments was somehow flawed even though the complaining party had yet to establish this. Should not the judicial wisdom of superior magistrates rather than the allegations of discontent litigants be accorded the benefit of the doubt while cases of *cassation* were pending?[77] For its part, the council found suspensions useful for political as well as for strictly legal reasons. In periods marked by conflict between the sovereign courts and the central administration, the procedure enabled the council to delay the implemen-

---

[76] The order for *surséance* appears in the *dispositif* portion of *arrêts sur requête*.

[77] As the Parlement of Bordeaux noted in its memorandum of 1656, whenever the council suspended the enforcement of judgments (or pronounced *cassation* solely on the basis of a petitioner's request), "the sovereign courts are denied their authority, their *arrêts* [become] useless to parties . . . [and the parlement becomes] contemptible [*méprisable*]." BN, MSS. Fr. 17315, fols. 167–171v. In a speech before the Parlement of Paris in August 1658, *Avocat Général* Talon claimed that *surséances* were "infinitely vexatious" to litigants and that legal actions at the council involving suspensions "degenerate into a vexation in which the repose and security of the king's subjects and the honor of the judges to whom he has communicated a portion of his sovereign authority . . . are equally concerned." AN, X^{1A} 8391, fols. 207v–217v.

tation of controversial judgments while it leisurely considered their merits and implications. But even in calmer times the possibility always existed that the immediate enforcement of a parlementary judgment might do irreparable harm to a petitioner with a potentially strong case. In these circumstances, considerations of equity outweighed the risk of offending the judges.

Because the procedure of *surséance* pitted the discretionary authority of the council against the dignity of the sovereign courts, the controversy surrounding its proper use was both heated and prolonged. Responding to strong pressure exerted by the magistrates, the monarchy had prohibited the practice as early as May 1579 in the ordinance of Blois; the council's own *règlements* of May 1615 and January 1630 as well as the royal declaration of October 1648 had followed suit.[78] In practice, however, the council had frequently ignored this legislation. An examination of *arrêts* issued immediately prior to Louis XIV's assumption of personal rule indicates that the council suspended the enforcement of parlementary judgments in about half of all cases of *cassation* that continued beyond an *arrêt sur requête*.[79] The Parlement of Paris was so concerned about this development that it devoted an entire section of one of its memoranda of midcentury to complaints about the "surséance de l'exécution des arrêts du Parlement et du jugement des procès."[80]

The judges had far less reason to complain after 1661. Not that the Conseil Privé ever intended to relinquish completely an important aspect of its discretionary authority. The *règlements* of January 1673 and June 1687 reiterated past prohibitions, but they also contained an escape clause authorizing the procedure "by the express order of His Majesty," a highsounding phrase that in practice gave the council wide latitude to act as it saw fit.[81] Nevertheless, if the council retained the right to suspend the enforcement of judgments while cases of *cassation* were pending, it exercised this right with a greater sense of discrimination than it had shown in previous years. The *arrêts* reveal that the procedure remained common only in cases referred to earlier in this study as "routine," those in which the complaining parties questioned neither the conduct of the magistrates in judging litigation nor the legitimate right of the parlements to decide certain kinds of legal issues. Of the 27 *arrêts sur requête* examined in this category, seven gave final decisions and thus did not offer a ruling on suspension. Of the remaining 20 *arrêts*, eight (or 40 percent) suspended the enforcement of judgments while the council implemented additional procedures. It is important to recall, however, that these cases usually involved relatively

---

[78] Mousnier, ed., "Les Règlements du conseil du roi sous Louis XIII," 150, 187; Isambert et al., eds., *Recueil général des anciennes lois*, 14: 404; 17: 80, 92.

[79] This generalization, subject to further refinement, is based on a summary examination of two cartons of *arrêts* from 1656: AN, V⁶ 319, 325.

[80] BN, n.a.f. 7982, fol. 334^A-H.

[81] *Règlement* of 1673, art. 65; of 1687, art. 40.

minor complaints of a jurisdictional nature pertaining to the timing rather than to the legal merits of parlementary sentences: petitioners alleged that the parlements had judged litigation while cases of *évocation de justice* were pending at the council, for example, or they claimed that the judges had decided cases after the council had already transferred jurisdiction to another tribunal.[82] Because the very existence of appropriate jurisdiction was at stake in these cases, the council's decision to suspend the enforcement of judgments was neither unreasonable nor contested by the parlements.[83]

But as soon as petitioners departed from routine jurisdictional issues in their requests for *cassation* and instead raised fundamental questions about the conduct and authority of the parlements, the Conseil Privé revised its previous policy and became increasingly reluctant to suspend the enforcement of judgments during conciliar proceedings. Put another way, a party who tapped the full range of grounds for *cassation* and thereby challenged the *parlementaires* on the subjects they presumably knew best—law, royal legislation, judicial procedure, equity, and unusually subtle or complex questions of jurisdiction—did so after 1661 with little prospect of securing a *surséance*. Of the 74 *arrêts sur requête* examined earlier in connection with these "serious" cases of *cassation*, 20 provided final decisions and thus did not raise the subject of suspension. Of the remaining 54 *arrêts*, only eight (or 15 percent) suspended the enforcement of a parlementary sentence.[84] Significantly, only one of these eight *arrêts* appears in the primary sample after 1676, and this involved a case in which suspension was automatic, the *arrêt sur requête* having joined a request for *cassation* to a pending action for an *évocation de justice*.[85] By the second half of Louis XIV's personal rule, therefore, the practice of suspending sentences in all but the most minor and routine cases had for all practical purposes disappeared; any incentive for litigants to pursue *cassation* as a way to delay the enforcement of judgments against them had evaporated.

Furthermore, even in those years when the council still ordered an occasional suspension in a serious action in *cassation*, it did so only for a narrow range of cases. In four of the seven cases mentioned above from the 1660s and 1670s, the complaining parties asserted that a parlement

---

[82] For examples of *surséances* in "routine" cases of *cassation*, see the *arrêts sur requête* of 18 September 1668 (AN, V⁶ 544, no. 53), 10 July 1669 (V⁶ 554, no. 57), and 20 February 1685 (V⁶ 686, no. 33).

[83] In his speech before the Parlement of Paris in 1658, *Avocat Général* Talon recognized the legitimacy of *surséances* in these kinds of cases. See above, this chapter, n. 77.

[84] That the council before 1661 frequently suspended the enforcement of parlementary sentences even during "serious" cases of *cassation* is illustrated by the fact that the dossier for 18 February 1656 alone contains at least three such *surséances*: AN, V⁶ 319, nos. 33, 127, 153.

[85] *Arrêt sur requête* of 22 December 1705, AN, V⁶ 802, no. 2. In a letter of 2 March 1714 to one Mirot, a councillor in the Parlement of Bordeaux, Pontchartrain noted that the council's request for *motifs* did not automatically entail the suspension of a judgment; a *surséance* took effect only when the council's members explicitly ordered it, he continued, "which they almost never do." BN, MSS. Fr. 21139, fols. 197v–198v.

had exceeded its jurisdiction in a major way, having decided legal matters that fell completely outside its legitimate competence. Three of these cases were initiated by clerics.[86] We have already noted, however, that the council was particularly interested in defending the clergy's interests when important jurisdictional issues were at stake. The order for suspension in these cases thus comes as no surprise. The point that bears underscoring is that even this modest exercise of the council's discretionary authority diminished as the reign progressed.

It is possible, of course, that the council continued to suspend the enforcement of judgments when a failure to have done so might have irreparably harmed a party. One can easily imagine the council according this grace to petitioners who challenged criminal sentences pronouncing the death penalty. Unfortunately, the absence of cases like this in the primary sample precludes testing this hypothesis. Nevertheless, even if we grant the possibility that the execution of sentences was suspended in certain criminal cases, the council must have acted with great restraint. The primary sample as well as Pontchartrain's correspondence contains several examples of petitioners attacking sentences that ordered incarceration during trial, judicial torture and, graver still, a term in the king's galleys. In none of these cases did the council suspend the execution of the sentences in question while it considered the merits of the request for *cassation*.[87] Of the eight *arrêts* cited above in which the council did suspend a judgment while a serious case of *cassation* was pending, only one involved a criminal affair: in May 1676, a convent in Dijon claimed that the parlement of that city had violated the constitution and statutes of the spiritual community by ordering that a nun involved in a criminal case be transferred there from another religious house.[88] One suspects, however, that the suspension in this case resulted more from the clerical status of the complaining parties than from the severity of the sentence in question. Whether cases of *cassation* concerned civil or criminal matters, therefore, Louis XIV's Conseil Privé pursued a highly selective policy toward suspending the enforcement of

---

[86] *Arrêts sur requête* of 13 September 1668 (AN, V[6] 544, no. 16), 3 July 1669 (V[6] 554, no. 13), and 20 May 1676 (V[6] 626, no. 17). For the other case involving a jurisdictional issue, see the *arrêt* between parties of 21 May 1676 (V[6] 626, no. 10) and the related *arrêt sur requête* of 16 October 1675 (in V[6] 622). For the other three cases involving *surséance* (which involved complaints about a parlement's interpretation of law, royal legislation, or judicial procedures), see the *arrêts sur requête* of 13 September 1668 (V[6] 544, no. 38), 10 July 1669 (V[6] 554, no. 58), and 23 April 1676 (V[6] 626, no. 20).

[87] For petitioners protesting their detention during trial, see the *arrêts sur requête* of 7 May 1676 (AN, V[6] 626, no. 29) and 31 January 1691 (V[6] 726, no. 3; see the related *arrêt* between parties of 26 September 1695, V[6] 755, no. 22). For a petitioner attacking a sentence condemning him to the galleys, see the *arrêt sur requête* of 7 December 1705 (V[6] 802, no. 4: the council sent this case to the Requêtes de l'Hôtel for a preliminary opinion about whether this case warranted *révision*, that is, re-examination by the court that rendered the judgment). For the principle that filing a request for *cassation* did not suspend the execution of a sentence condemning a petitioner to judicial torture, see Pontchartrain to Arbel, *procureur du roi* at the Présidial of Lons-le-Saulnier, 23 April 1711, BN, MSS. Fr. 21133, fols. 343–345v.

[88] *Arrêt sur requête* of 20 May 1676, AN, V[6] 626, no. 17.

parlementary sentences. In so doing, it removed yet another source of conflict with the kingdom's highest courts of law.

Procedural reform thus directly contributed to improved relations between the Conseil Privé and the parlements. It also complemented important developments in the council's jurisprudence. In deciding individual cases, the council showed restraint in pronouncing *cassation* and adhered to established rules when adjudicating *évocations de justice* and *règlements de juges*. In the realm of judicial procedure, this prudent conduct found its counterpart in serious efforts to improve internal efficiency, to discourage litigants from initiating legal actions of dubious merit, and to ensure that cases involving the parlements received careful examination. Part of the inspiration for reform certainly came from the judges: the introduction of fines and the diminished use of suspensions are examples of the council responding to specific parlementary grievances. But the chancellor and his colleagues were also capable of acting on their own initiative to address problems that had attracted little attention outside the council in the past. Ongoing refinements in the system of *bureaux* and assemblies, a closer supervision over the activities of reporting magistrates, the judicious use of *motifs*, and a greater participation of *avocats* in cases of *cassation* all testified to a firm resolve within the council to eliminate disorder from its proceedings and to shed its image as an arena of chicanery. Both sides profited from this enterprise. By promoting orderly and intelligent change in judicial procedure, the council avoided potentially bitter conflicts with the judges and enhanced the integrity of its own judicial decisions. For the parlements, the prospect of a superior authority intervening in their judicial business seemed far less threatening when the council gave numerous indications of its intention to respect their dignity and traditional judicial functions and to remind litigants that recourse to the council's regulatory and disciplinary powers was not a matter to be taken lightly.

VII. THE BEHAVIOR OF THE OTHER COUNCILS: AN OVERVIEW

The spirit of accommodation toward the parlements that was so evident in Louis XIV's Conseil Privé would have reduced historical significance had the other sections of the king's council, when they performed duties normally associated with the Conseil Privé, treated the judges in a markedly different fashion. It could be argued, of course, that the activities of other council bodies have only a limited bearing on the present study. To a large extent this is true. After all, the Conseil Privé handled the overwhelming majority of *cassations*, *évocations de justice*, and *règlements de juges* that pertained to the parlements, and the patterns described in the foregoing pages would remain important under any circumstances. Nevertheless, for a number of reasons an investigation into the other major record groups of the king's councils—the *arrêts en commandement* issued by the *conseils de gouvernement* and the *arrêts simples* "en finance" rendered by the various council bodies involved in the administration of royal revenues—is warranted even if the large size of these collections dictates that such an investigation be restricted in scope.

The very power and prestige of the *conseils de gouvernement* draw our attention to these bodies. The king sat personally on the Conseil d'En haut, the Conseil des Dépêches, and the Conseil royal des Finances with various combinations of his ministers, secretaries of state, and other leading royal officials and advisers. The members of these councils, meeting either in formal session or on an individual basis with the king, considered all manner of domestic and foreign affairs. No problem pertaining to the general administration of the realm, however seemingly insignificant, was ineligible for their attention. We have already noted that the *arrêts en commandement* issued by these councils dealt with a broad range of issues of interest to the parlements, from judicial finances and the interpretation and enforcement of royal legislation to the internal operation of courts and the resolution of conflicts over competence or precedence.

As regards instances when the activities of these high councils overlapped those of the Conseil Privé—the subject of greatest concern to us here— the *conseils de gouvernement* rarely adjudicated *évocations de justice* and *règlements de juges* pertaining to the parlements: with few exceptions, these legal actions were the exclusive preserve of the Conseil Privé.[1] In deciding

---

[1] Thus, *arrêts en commandement* dealing with these matters, like those of 9 May 1662 and 15 February 1667, are rare: *Répertoire*, 11: 111; 18: 98.

two other matters, however, Louis XIV's highest councils played a far more prominent role. First, when parlementary sentences or administrative orders concerned royal finances or other public affairs, the *conseils de gouvernement* rather than the Conseil Privé usually examined requests for *cassation* and pronounced nullification. Even when the parlements had decided strictly private litigation between contesting parties, a certain fluidity of responsibility within the council system meant that at least some requests for *cassation* that administrative logic would dictate belonged at the Conseil Privé came instead before the high councils. Second, while the *conseils de gouvernement* dealt infrequently with *évocations* based on the family ties between litigants and their judges, these councils did assume primary responsibility for ordering the more controversial *évocations de grâce* and *évocations de propre mouvement*. It will be recalled that these *évocations*, granted either on the request of parties or on the king's own initiative, transferred cases from one tribunal to another either as a favor to influential persons or because the litigation at stake was deemed to be sufficiently important or politically sensitive to warrant a change of judges. Determining how the *conseils de gouvernement* exercised their power to order *cassations* and *évocations* will indicate whether the basic respect for the parlements' judicial authority that characterized the conduct of the Conseil Privé also penetrated into the very highest levels of the central administration.[2]

An examination of *arrêts simples* "en finance" serves the same broader purpose. During Louis XIV's personal rule, these *arrêts* were an important vehicle for both establishing and enforcing royal policies regarding the administration of the king's revenues. Several council bodies were empowered to issue them, the most notable being the Conseil d'Etat et des Finances, the Conseil royal des Finances, and the ordinary *commissions* of Grande and Petite Direction. As the reign progressed, however, a more significant source of *arrêts* became the meetings that the king held with the controller general of finances and that this official held in turn with his principal collaborators (especially the *intendants des finances*, the *intendants de commerce*, and the various *bureaux* involved in the administration of finances). Indeed, one of the most important institutional developments of Louis XIV's reign was the concentration of authority over royal finances in the hands of the controller general and the officials who directly served him.

---

[2] In the following pages, I assess the policies of the *conseils de gouvernement* in terms of the *arrêts en commandement* they issued, as if the two—the high councils and these *arrêts*—were synonymous. I well recognize that this is only partially true because one of the *conseils de gouvernement*—the Conseil royal des Finances—also issued *arrêts simples* "en finance." But equating the high councils with the *arrêts en commandement*, which I have done for clarity of presentation, does not jeopardize the validity of the conclusions that follow, and this for two reasons. First, this study ends with a brief examination of *arrêts simples* "en finance"—these documents have thus not been ignored. Second, we shall see that the judicial activities of the parlements do not figure prominently in the *arrêts simples* "en finance." As a result, the *arrêts en commandement* do provide an accurate profile of the relations between the parlements and the high councils, at least in matters pertaining to *évocations* and *cassations*.

This trend, which was already apparent during Colbert's ministry and became even more pronounced during the tenure of his successors, worked to the detriment of council bodies that had previously shared financial jurisdiction. The decline and ultimate demise of the Conseil d'Etat et des Finances by the end of the century was one indication of this, as was an ever decreasing consultative role played by the Conseil royal des Finances. The virtual exclusion of the chancellor from financial matters and a rising proportion of *arrêts simples* "en finance" being reported by the controller general also signaled that the king's finances, in the words of Antoine, "constituted a world apart in the monarchy."[3] Exercising his celebrated *métier de roi*, the king of course kept abreast with the resolution of major problems and continued to determine the general direction of policy. The Conseil royal des Finances still debated certain important issues, and the two Directions, often employing the complex judicial procedures associated with the Conseil Privé, adjudicated at least some litigation of a financial nature. But increasingly *arrêts simples* "en finance" (and even many of those *arrêts en commandement* issued by the Conseil royal des Finances) expressed decisions reached in an administrative fashion by the controller general and the services at his disposal.

For our purposes, the growing independence of what was in fact a burgeoning ministry of finances is important because it allowed, at least in theory, wide latitude for arbitrary action against the parlements, even in the realm of judicial administration. One must certainly not exaggerate this potential. In an era when war finance often dominated public policy and when the *parlementaires* themselves were under considerable pressure to contribute substantial sums to royal coffers, the controller general and his staff had little reason to antagonize the parlements by carelessly interfering with their ordinary internal operation. Nor did the daily administration of finances at the highest levels normally require such interference. The vast majority of *arrêts simples* "en finance" concerned such subjects as levying taxes, supervising the conduct of local financial officials, resolving disputes about the possession of royal offices, ordering payments from various royal accounts, and interpreting and enforcing the leases of tax farms.[4] While decisions about these and other financial matters might well have affected the judges' interests in the broadest sense, they rarely raised serious questions about the parlements' exercise of their strictly judicial functions. Like

---

[3] Antoine, *Le Conseil du roi sous le règne de Louis XV*, 408. Astute discussions of the changes that swept financial administration at the highest levels can be found in ibid., 58–61, 67–75, and bk. 2, chap. 3, as well as in McCollim, "The Formation of Fiscal Policy," chap. 2.

[4] As noted previously, before Louis XIV assumed personal rule, the *arrêts simples* "en finance" dealt with affairs of domestic concern beyond just financial matters. But the emergence of the Conseil des Dépêches, which specialized in general domestic administration, and the gradual disappearance of the Conseil d'Etat et des Finances after 1661 meant that during Louis XIV's personal rule the *arrêts simples* "en finance" only rarely dealt with matters unrelated to royal finances. This is yet another reason why *évocations* and *cassations* concerning the parlements do not figure prominently among these *arrêts* after 1661.

the *conseils de gouvernement*, the bureaucratic apparatus surrounding the controller general did at times find it necessary to nullify a judicial sentence or to order an *évocation de grâce* or *de propre mouvement*. But such actions were more likely to affect courts with primarily financial jurisdiction, such as the cours des aides, than common law courts like the parlements.[5] Nevertheless, the king's finances constituted a vast domain within the royal administration, and *arrêts simples* "en finance" contain some *évocations* and *cassations* pertaining to the parlements. For this reason, even a study focusing on the activity of the Conseil Privé cannot afford to neglect these documents.

The archival holdings of *arrêts en commandement* and *arrêts simples* "en finance" are enormous. Between 1661 and 1715, the *conseils de gouvernement* together issued some 35,000 *arrêts*, and the *arrêts simples* "en finance" number more than 130,000 for the same period. An extensive examination of these vast collections is certainly beyond the scope of this study. Instead, my intention in the following pages is far more modest—to delineate the broad outlines of how council bodies other than the Conseil Privé handled *évocations* and *cassations* pertaining to the parlements. When considering the *arrêts en commandement*, the discussion relies heavily upon a descriptive index of these documents supplemented by some sampling of the original *arrêts*.[6] The use of an index obviously increases the margin for error and

---

[5] Bear in mind that the Parlements of Grenoble, Metz, and Rennes also exercised the functions of cours des aides, which means that these courts might be more heavily represented in *arrêts simples* "en finance" than the other parlements. My sampling of these *arrêts*, to be discussed below, did not show this to be the case, but I leave open the possibility for the historian who would undertake a detailed study of these documents.

[6] For information on the archival holdings of the *minutes* of *arrêts en commandement* and the manuscript index (*Répertoire*) for these documents, see above, chap. II, n. 6. Details on the format and official wording of these *arrêts* are in Antoine, *Le Conseil du roi sous le règne de Louis XV*, 342–361; idem, *Le Fonds du conseil d'état du roi aux Archives Nationales*, 34–42. Based on my own research in the *minutes* of these *arrêts* for the period of Louis XIV's personal rule, I offer the following observations for future researchers (although historians working in a given period of the reign should expect some variations). First, while *arrêts simples* (whether "en finance" or issued by the Conseil Privé) bear the phrase "Le Roi *en* son conseil . . . ," at the beginning of the decision (*dispositif*) portion of these *arrêts*, the *arrêts en commandement* employ the phrase, "Le Roi *étant* en son conseil. . . ." This difference, plus the fact that the *arrêts en commandement* are catalogued together in the upper-number registers of AN, *série* E, makes it impossible to confuse *arrêts en commandement* with *arrêts simples*. Second, *arrêts en commandement* could be issued either at the request of parties (*arrêts sur requête*) or on the initiative of the *conseils de gouvernement* (*arrêts de propre mouvement*): Antoine, cited above, provides information on how to recognize each type by its official wording. Third, within the *arrêts en commandement*, those issued by the Conseil royal des Finances can be easily recognized by the fact that almost all of them were reported by the controller general of finances—his participation is usually noted explicitly at the end of the introductory (*exposé*) portion of the *arrêt*—and by the fact that the controller general as well as the chancellor signed these *arrêts*. Do note, however, that other members of this council could also sign and occasionally report these *arrêts*. Furthermore, if a group of councillors of state examined an affair before an *arrêt* was issued, the *arrêt* will mention the participation of these "commissaires" and sometimes bear their signatures. Fourth, the historian unfortunately has no reliable way to distinguish between *arrêts* issued by the other two *conseils de gouvernement*—the Conseil d'En haut and the Conseil des Dépêches. The *arrêts* issued by these two councils usually bear only the

makes any conclusions drawn subject to future refinement and revision. But the index does give access to the general content of thousands of *arrêts* for selected years before and after 1661. The broad contours of the policies pursued by the *conseils de gouvernement* toward *évocations* and *cassations* thus become apparent. Unfortunately, the *arrêts simples* "en finance," like the *arrêts* of the Conseil Privé, lack an adequate descriptive index; one must consult the original *arrêts*.[7] Because these *arrêts* only infrequently

---

chancellor's signature, and the reference to the reporter is normally vague, a phrase like "Ouï le rapport. . . ." Because the Conseil d'En haut issued few *arrêts*, however, one may assume as a working proposition that all but a few *arrêts en commandement* (except, of course, those issued by the Conseil royal des Finances just discussed) emanated from the Conseil des Dépêches and were reported by the secretary of state in whose volume the *arrêt* is located (although the secretaries of state did not themselves sign the *minutes* of the *arrêts* they dispatched). But the researcher must allow for the possibility that someone other than this secretary of state—another secretary of state, for example, or perhaps the chancellor—was the reporter. In short, the secretary of state who dispatched an *arrêt* was probably, but not necessarily the reporter. Unfortunately, the *arrêts* themselves rarely provide specific information on this subject. Bear in mind, however, that if someone who was not a member of these two councils reported an occasional *arrêt*—a councillor of state or, less often, a master of requests—his participation will be mentioned in the *arrêt* and his signature will accompany the chancellor's (the *arrêt* will also mention and sometimes bear the signatures of any councillors of state who examined an affair as "commissaires"). Fifth, *arrêts en commandement* of whatever variety and issued by any *conseil de gouvernement* exist for at least half the days in a given year: it is thus impossible to determine whether an *arrêt* resulted from a formal council session or from a private meeting between the king and council members. Sometimes a marginal notation, such as "le roi a ordonné la signature de cet arrêt," indicates that an *arrêt* was decided outside a formal session; but such references are rare. Sixth, the above comments about the signatures on *arrêts en commandement* pertain only to the original *minutes* of these documents, which were consulted for this study. The *expéditions* of *arrêts* that were dispatched for parties or published for public consumption differed slightly in their official wording and had different rules for signatures. Thus, *expéditions* were called "extraits" of conciliar registers, and they bear only one signature, that of the secretary of state who dispatched them. For details, see Antoine, *Le Fonds du conseil d'état du roi aux Archives Nationales*, 41–42. Seventh, while *arrêts en commandement* occasionally provided interlocutory judgments or called for further procedures and reports, most gave final decisions on cases and issues. This makes sense given the executive powers of the *conseils de gouvernement*. Finally, the index (*Répertoire*) of *arrêts en commandement* takes no note of all these distinctions and nuances: it indicates only the date and archival location of *arrêts* and provides brief descriptions of their contents. Historians interested in exploring in depth the activities of the *conseils de gouvernement* should consult the original *arrêts*. For the general discussion contemplated here, the *Répertoire* provides adequate information, although I will cite some of the more than one thousand *arrêts en commandement* I have consulted in connection with other research projects. In the notes below, I will cite the original *arrêts* as well as the *Répertoire* when I have consulted both; otherwise, I will cite only the *Répertoire*.

[7] For information on the archival holdings of the *minutes* of these *arrêts* and their index, see above, chap. II, n. 11. These *arrêts* exhibit a great variety of formats and official wordings because a number of council bodies over time were empowered to issue them. Some *arrêts* are like those of the Conseil Privé, bearing the stamp of an elaborate judicial procedure: *arrêts sur requête* resolving cases or ordering additional procedures (calling parties to contest, for example, or requesting the submission of *motifs*); *arrêts d'instruction*; *arrêts* between parties (*contradictoires*), and so on. Others are like the *arrêts en commandement*, giving executive decisions in the form of *arrêts sur requête* and *arrêts de propre mouvement*. For some details on the structure of *arrêts simples* "en finance," consult the works of Antoine cited in the previous note. As a general rule (one must always allow for exceptions when dealing with conciliar *arrêts*), during Louis XIV's personal rule *arrêts* emanating from the Conseil d'Etat et des Finances (before its disappearance) and from the two Directions were reported by the

mention the judicial activities of the parlements, the sample examined here is small—316 *arrêts* selected from two years, 1674 and 1710.[8] While generalizations based on such a small sample must be considered tentative, the patterns these documents reveal are sufficiently clear to inspire a reasonable degree of confidence.

During Louis XIV's personal rule, the *conseils de gouvernement* never abandoned the practice of ordering *évocations de grâce* and *de propre mouvement*. To have done so would have created practical difficulties for the daily administration of the realm, limiting the ability of the king and his highest officials to resolve certain important or unforeseen problems as they arose. It also would have denied the monarchy one of its essential prerogatives, the right to remove litigation from the law courts being a crucial component of the king's sovereignty. Even during the heated controversies between the high judiciary and the central administration in the era of the Fronde, the parlements never challenged the fundamental legitimacy of *évocations*, although they certainly protested their frequency.

The index of *arrêts en commandement* clearly shows the continuation of *évocations* after 1661. If we select seven years between 1662 and 1709—years that were marked by peace as well as by war, and years that together include the tenure of all the secretaries of state and controllers general who served the Sun King—the index indicates that the *conseils de gouvernement* issued 4,477 *arrêts*, or a yearly average of 639.5 *arrêts*.[9] The entries for 33 of these *arrêts* state explicitly that cases were removed from the parlements, for an annual average of 4.7 *évocations*. If we add to these 33 *arrêts* another 27 *arrêts* for which the index does not mention the court experiencing the removal of litigation—prudence dictates that we assume at least some of these *évocations* affected the parlements—the seven years yield a total of 60 *évocations* that either did involve or might have involved the parlements.[10] The annual average of *évocations* then rises to 8.5. The majority

---

masters of requests who, along with any councillors of state who reviewed a case, signed the *minutes* of these *arrêts* with the chancellor. *Arrêts simples* "en finance" emanating from the Conseil royal des Finances and from the services attached to the controller general of finances were usually reported by this official, who signed the *minutes* of these *arrêts* with the chancellor (along with any councillors of state who reviewed a case or issue). The number of *arrêts* reported by the controller general increased dramatically in the course of Louis's reign, as can be seen in McCollim's table, "Council Versus Minister," 70–71. For details on the official wording and signatures of the *expéditions* of these *arrêts* (as opposed to the original *minutes* consulted for this study and discussed in this note), see Antoine, *Le Fonds du conseil d'état du roi aux Archives Nationales*, 41–42.

[8] AN, E 500 (October 1676) and 859[A] (2–20 January 1714). I chose these volumes at random, supplementing them with a summary examination (without preparing statistics) of a dozen other volumes for certain years between 1660 and 1710 (E 339[C], 349[C], 383[B], 571[B], 604[A], etc.) and with the index for the *quartier* of July 1708 (E 1683[160]).

[9] The years, with the number of *arrêts* issued, are: 1662 (304); 1667 (786); 1678 (704); 1686 (839); 1696 (743); 1703 (532); and 1709 (569). I chose these particular years at random.

[10] In examining the *Répertoire*, I counted as *évocations* only those entries in which this word is used explicitly. It is possible, of course, that other *arrêts* removed litigation from the parlements but that the index failed to note this: one can find, for example, entries in which the king "retient" cognizance of an affair (are these *évocations*?). Any statistics drawn from an index

(34) of these *évocations* presumably retained litigation for final judgment at the councils, while the remainder transferred jurisdiction to other parlements (13), to provincial intendants (6), to the Grand Conseil (5), or to still other tribunals (2).

We shall consider in due course the issues that gave rise to these *évocations* as well as the impact of *évocations* on individual parlements. What bears underscoring at this point is that whether one chooses the lower figure of 4.7 *évocations* per year or the higher figure of 8.5, the fact remains that the king's highest councils did not engage in an orgy of indiscriminate interference in the judicial business of the parlements. The frequency with which these councils ordered *évocations générales*, which are not included in the figures presented above, confirms this impression. It will be recalled that these *évocations* were a type of *évocation de grâce* that transferred from one jurisdiction to another *all* the litigation, both pending and future, that the concerned parties might have during a specified time period (usually three years and subject to renewal). Because their scope was broader than that of other *évocations*, which pertained only to specific litigation already pending in the courts, *évocations générales* were sorely resented by the parlements. During the seven years under consideration, the index of *arrêts en commandement* indicates that the *conseils de gouvernement* granted or renewed 11 *évocations générales* that withdrew litigation from the parlements, for a yearly average of 1.5 *évocations générales*. Even if we include an additional 16 *évocations générales* for which the index does not mention the court suffering the removal of litigation—prudence again dictating that we assume at least some of these *évocations* involved the parlements—the annual average of *évocations générales* increases to only 3.8.[11] While the index does not state the destination of litigation in 11 of these *évocations*, the remaining 16 sent cases either to other parlements (9), to the royal councils (3), to the Grand Conseil (2), to a provincial intendant (1), or to a lesser tribunal (1).

---

should be treated gingerly as a matter of course. But the inclusion in the figures given here of a second category of *évocations*—those in which the court suffering the removal of litigation is not named—should compensate for any *évocations* from the parlements that the index fails to mention. After all, the councils evoked cases from all levels of the judiciary, and it is highly unlikely that *all* the *évocations* in this second category applied to the parlements. The distribution of the 60 *évocations* by year is: 1662 (6); 1667 (12); 1678 (20); 1686 (11); 1696 (5); 1703 (1); and 1709 (5). Examination of the *Répertoire* for two additional years in the 1670s (1674 and 1677) confirms the impression that this decade witnessed the greatest number of *évocations* during Louis XIV's personal rule. Why this was so remains unclear and is a subject worthy of future research; perhaps we observe here the last vestiges of parlementary opposition to Colbert's financial policies.

[11] In order to identify *évocations générales*, I used the following criteria: the use of these words in the *Répertoire*; the mention of an *évocation* for a specific time period, such as three years; and references to *évocations* of cases (*procès*) "mus et à mouvoir," "intentés et à intenter," and that a party "a et peut avoir." The distribution of the 27 *évocations générales* by year is: 1662 (6); 1667 (0), 1678 (10); 1686 (7); 1696 (0); 1703 (2); and 1709 (2). Once again, the most active decade appears to have been the 1670s.

However low all these figures are in absolute terms, the question remains how they compare with those for the years preceding Louis XIV's assumption of personal rule. If we take seven years between 1643 and 1660, for example, the index of *arrêts en commandement* indicates that the *conseils de gouvernement* of that era issued 1,249 *arrêts*, or a yearly average of 178.4 *arrêts*.[12] The entries for 26 of these *arrêts* state explicitly that litigation was removed from the parlements, for an annual average of 3.7 *évocations* (as opposed to a yearly average of 4.7 for the seven years after 1661). If we add another 27 *arrêts* for which the index does not indicate the court from which litigation was evoked, the seven years yield a total of 48 *évocations*, or an average of 6.9 *évocations* per year (as compared to an annual average of 8.5 after 1661).[13] Nearly half (22) of these *évocations* presumably retained cases for final judgment at the councils, while the remainder transferred jurisdiction either to other parlements (25) or to the Grand Conseil (1). As regards the *évocations générales* that the *conseils de gouvernement* granted or renewed during the seven years under consideration, the index notes that 20 pertained to the parlements (for an annual average of 2.8 *évocations* as opposed to 1.5 for the seven years after 1661). If we include another four *évocations générales* for which the index does not specify the court suffering the removal of cases, the annual average rises to 3.4 (as compared to 3.8 after 1661).[14] The destination of litigation, once evoked, is known for all 24 *évocations:* other parlements (20), the royal councils (2), and the Grand Conseil (2).

At first glance, then, it appears that the number of *évocations de grâce, de propre mouvement,* and *générales* affecting the parlements increased slightly during the period of Louis XIV's personal rule. There is evidence to suggest, however, that just the opposite occurred and that the parlements fared far better than a simple counting of *arrêts en commandement* indicates. It must be remembered, for example, that Louis's personal rule witnessed

---

[12] The years, with the number of *arrêts* issued, are: 1643 (147); 1645 (157); 1648 (181); 1651 (247); 1656 (130); 1658 (209); and 1660 (178). I chose (at random) years between 1643 and 1660 first, because *évocations* were a hotly contested subject in the two decades before Louis XIV assumed personal rule, and second, because few *arrêts en commandement* exist for the years before 1640 (a point to which I shall return). Note that a published index of *arrêts en commandement* issued between 1643 and 1661 does exist: Michel Le Pesant, ed., *Arrêts du conseil du roi, règne de Louis XIV, inventaire analytique des arrêts en commandement, tome I (20 mai 1643–8 mars 1661)* (Paris, 1976). Because Le Pesant does not describe the content of *arrêts* in the same wording as the *Répertoire*, and because he included some *arrêts* that are not located in the collections of the secretaries of state in AN, *série E*, I relied upon the *Répertoire* for my sampling both before and after 1661. This ensures the use of a uniform source for both time periods: the handwritings in the *Répertoire* are the same throughout the entire index. But researchers should be aware of Le Pesant's index, and I shall make occasional reference to it in the notes below.

[13] The distributions of the 48 *évocations* by year is: 1643 (4); 1645 (6); 1648 (4); 1651 (15); 1656 (2); 1658 (7); and 1660 (10). The concentration of *évocations* in 1651, at the height of the Fronde, should cause little surprise.

[14] The distribution of the 24 *évocations générales* by year is: 1643 (0), 1645 (2); 1648 (0); 1651 (18); 1656 (1); 1658 (1); and 1660 (2). Once again, *évocations* were most numerous at the height of the Fronde.

the creation not only of an additional *conseil de gouvernement* (the Conseil royal des Finances), but also of two new parlements (at Besançon and Tournai) and two more provincial "sovereign councils" with parlementary jurisdiction (those of Artois and Alsace). A natural consequence of these creations would be an increase in the number of *évocations* found among the *arrêts en commandement* after 1661, and this without signaling the existence of a governmental policy aimed at making further inroads into the caseloads of the parlements.[15]

Even more important, the *arrêts en commandement* issued before Louis XIV assumed personal rule contain only a small portion of the *évocations* the monarchy actually granted. As a result, any assessment of the crown's overall policy toward *évocations* before 1661 that rests solely on these *arrêts* risks seriously underestimating the number of *évocations* the parlements experienced. There were two reasons for this situation. First, the *conseils de gouvernement* were not alone in ordering *évocations de grâce, de propre mouvement,* and *générales.* The Conseil d'Etat et des Finances, which issued *arrêts simples* "en finance," was directly involved in ordering these *évocations,* not only because judicial opposition to royal financial and administrative policies during the ministries of Richelieu and Mazarin prompted the removal of cases from the parlements, but also because the authority this council enjoyed in domestic affairs extended beyond strictly financial matters.[16] As for the Conseil Privé, its *arrêts* indicate that even before 1661 it dealt primarily with *évocations de justice,* leaving decisions about the more controversial *évocations* to other councils. But there were exceptions to this general rule, and in any case we have already noted that this council occasionally evoked to itself for final judgment the litigation involved in the legal actions it adjudicated, thereby provoking protests from the parlements.[17] Second, before the Conseil des Dépêches enjoyed a stable existence from the late 1640s and the Conseil royal des Finances was established in 1661, the monarchy simply issued fewer *arrêts en commandement* than it did in subsequent years (a fact illustrated by the figures presented above on the total number of these *arrêts* issued during two seven-year periods

---

[15] For example, of the 33 *évocations de grâce* and *de propre mouvement* in the sample after 1661 in which the parlement experiencing the removal of litigation is identified, one pertained to the Parlement of Besançon, two others to the Parlement of Tournai. If these *évocations* are set aside, the annual average of *évocations* from the parlements falls from 4.7 to 4.3, which edges us closer to the figure of 3.7 for the seven years sampled before 1661.

[16] Bonney, *Political Change in France,* 20–21, notes how the Conseil d'Etat et des Finances was involved in *évocations* during the ministries of the two cardinals. For such activity during the reign of Henry IV, see Valois, ed., *Inventaire des arrêts,* index under "évocations," "conseil du roi: évocations," and "conseil d'état: évocations." Pagès, "Le Conseil du roi sous Louis XIII," 15, 31–32, notes how the Conseil d'Etat et des Finances enjoyed an administrative competence beyond financial matters.

[17] To cite just a few examples of the Conseil Privé granting *évocations* other than those *de justice* before 1661, see the *évocation générale* pertaining to illegal assemblies of the nobility in AN, V⁶ 391 (dossier for 12 September 1659), and the *évocation de grâce* in favor of the Bishop of Condom in V⁶ 399 (dossier for 23 January 1660).

before and after 1661).[18] In the first half of the century, the kings and their ministers were thus accustomed to using all kinds of *arrêts*, not just those *en commandement*, to express decisions reached even at the highest levels of government, decisions that pertained to *évocations* as well as to other important matters.[19]

In short, when the index of *arrêts en commandement* indicates that during seven years between 1643 and 1660 the parlements experienced an average of 3.7 or 6.9 *évocations* per year (or between 1.5 and 3.4 *évocations générales*), it must be understood that these removals of litigation were only the tip of an iceberg. The proof exists not only in the various collections of conciliar *arrêts*, all of which contain *évocations*, but also in the memoranda that several parlements submitted in the 1650s to defend their jurisdiction from encroachments by the councils. In explaining their grievances, the judges often listed by date of issuance the *arrêts* they opposed. But few of the *évocations* mentioned in these lists will be found among the *arrêts en commandement*: a ratio of one to nine would be a conservative estimate.[20]

For the period after 1661, however, the index of *arrêts en commandement* is a far more reliable source for determining how often the parlements experienced *évocations de grâce, de propre mouvement*, and *générales*. Without ever having made a public pronouncement on the matter, Louis XIV nevertheless seems to have considered these *évocations* to have been so important that, with few exceptions, only the councils he personally attended were empowered to order them. The existence after 1661 of three such councils, whose members met regularly either in formal session or alone with the king, allowed for the implementation of this policy. A growing number of *arrêts en commandement* provided the vehicle for the king and his highest advisers to express their decisions. While this concentration of

---

[18] The *Répertoire* shows clearly the increase in the number of *arrêts en commandement* issued over time. The annual average of *arrêts* issued, broken down by decade (with numbers rounded off), is: 1640–1649 (115); 1650–1659 (169); 1660–1669 (609); 1670–1679 (823); 1680–1689 (854); 1690–1699 (830); and 1700–1710 (581). It is true that some *arrêts en commandement*, especially those issued before 1661, are not mentioned in the *Répertoire* because they are located in collections other than AN, *série* E. But the number of such *arrêts* is not large. In his *Arrêts du conseil du roi*, Le Pesant includes less than 200 *arrêts* (of a total of 3,263) that are not located in the collections of the secretaries of state. If these *arrêts* were included in the figures given here, they would not change significantly the marked difference between the number of *arrêts* issued before and after 1661. Note also that the monarchy issued few *arrêts en commandement* before 1640: the *Répertoire* mentions only 316 *arrêts* issued during the entire period, 1611–1639.

[19] Ormesson mentions this in his *Journal*, 1: 246–247 (January 1645).

[20] For example, using two memoranda submitted by the Parlement of Paris (BN, MSS. Fr. 17315, fols. 104–105v, 139–152v), I took a random sample of nine *évocations* of civil cases during the single year 1656 and looked for them in the *Répertoire* and in Le Pesant, ed., *Arrêts du conseil du roi*: only one of these nine *évocations* (one of 8 January involving the secretary of the Duc de Mercoeur) appears in either of these two sources. A check for three *évocations* in 1655 reveals none issued by an *arrêt en commandement*. Indeed, one memorandum submitted by the Parisian *parlementaires* (BN, MSS. Fr. 17288, fols. 523–537v) actually names the masters of requests who reported *évocations*, thus providing yet another indication that councils other than the *conseils de gouvernement* ordered *évocations*.

authority in the *conseils de gouvernement* has left some traces in the administrative correspondence of the era, it is reflected most clearly in the paucity of *évocations* pertaining to the parlements that one finds among the *arrêts* of other council bodies during the period of Louis's personal rule.[21] We have already noted, for example, that the Conseil Privé virtually abandoned its practice of retaining litigation for final judgment. Moreover, if the sample of its *arrêts* examined earlier in this study is any indication, one will search in vain for *évocations de grâce, de propre mouvement,* and *générales* in the records of this council after 1661. For its part, the Conseil d'Etat et des Finances ceased functioning altogether during the second half of the seventeenth century, its duties having been assumed largely by the controller general and his aides. *Arrêts simples* "en finance" continued to exist, of course, but they dealt almost exclusively with financial affairs and, as we shall see shortly, a random sample of these documents reveals little interference with the caseloads of the parlements. This is not to say that the controller general lacked the authority to remove an occasional case regarding royal finances from a parlement. But he was not compelled to use an *arrêt simple* "en finance" to do so: an *arrêt en commandement* issued by the Conseil royal des Finances served the same purpose and had the additional advantage of conveying the king's personal approval.[22] As for the non-financial jurisdiction of the fading Conseil d'Etat et des Finances, it passed to the *conseils de gouvernement* (particularly the Conseil des Dépêches that specialized in domestic affairs), thus providing yet another reason to search for *évocations* among the *arrêts en commandement.*[23]

To be sure, details on the precise timing of these developments and on the total number of *évocations* the parlements experienced throughout the seventeenth century must await a comprehensive study of all manner of conciliar *arrêts*, a task that only a team of researchers could aspire to accomplish. On the basis of the information presented here, and viewing *évocations* from the vantage point of the parlements, the worst that could be said is that the tempo of *évocations* increased, but only slightly, during the period of Louis XIV's personal rule. A far more plausible interpretation,

---

[21] In two letters discussing *évocations générales*, Chancellor Pontchartrain referred to the activity of the king in a *conseil de gouvernement*. A letter of 30 September 1703 to Suduyrault, first president of the Cour des Aides of Bordeaux, indicates that the king personally considered requests for these *évocations*. BN, MSS. Fr. 21122, fol. 578v. A letter of 17 July 1712 to Compong, a *lieutenant* at the royal court of Orthez, instructed that requests for *évocations générales* be submitted to the appropriate secretary of state (for Orthez, this was Torcy), a route that suggests the intervention of the Conseil des Dépêches. Ibid., 21135, fols. 618–619.

[22] Unfortunately, the *Répertoire* does not indicate which *arrêts en commandement* were issued by the Conseil royal des Finances. But for examples of this body ordering *évocations*, see the original *arrêts* of 23 November 1678 (AN, E 1794; *Répertoire*, 44: 257) and 12 October 1697 (E 1901; ibid., 86: 185). For this council pronouncing *cassation*, see the *arrêts* of 20 July 1687 (E 1842; ibid., 63: 37) and 26 September 1690 (E 1859; ibid., 69: 205).

[23] On the Conseil d'Etat et des Finances and the Conseil des Dépêches, and the impact that the latter had on the former, see Mousnier, "Le Conseil du roi," 31–32, 44–46, 49, and Kleinman, "Changing Interpretations of the Edict of Nantes," 542, n. 4.

however, and one that takes into account not simply the number of *évo-cations* mentioned in the index of *arrêts en commandement* but also important changes in the jurisdiction of the various councils after 1661, is that the removal of litigation from the parlements actually decreased, perhaps dramatically so. And why should it have been otherwise? The king and his highest advisers sought to curtail the political activities and ambitions of the *parlementaires*, not to diminish their legitimate judicial authority. As parliamentary opposition to royal financial and administrative policies waned during Louis's reign, the *conseils de gouvernement* could afford to adopt a more moderate position on ordering *évocations*.

If, as seems likely, the number of *évocations* from the parlements declined during the period of Louis XIV's personal rule, it is equally important to note that the impact of *évocations* on individual parlements varied considerably. Years might pass before most parlements even experienced an *évocation de grâce* or *de propre mouvement*. Of the 33 *évocations* in the sample after 1661 that identify the parlement which lost litigation, 14 pertained to the Parlement of Paris, a number that is hardly surprising given the fact that nearly half the realm fell within this court's jurisdiction.[24] The Parlement of Toulouse, which had the second largest territorial resort in the kingdom, experienced ten *évocations*.[25] None of the other parlements, however, suffered more than two *évocations* during the seven years under consideration, and some parlements (Aix, Metz, and Pau, for example) are not mentioned at all in the index for these years.[26] Even the Parlements of Paris and Toulouse did not experience the removal of cases every year in the sample.[27] Furthermore, when a *conseil de gouvernement* did remove litigation from a parlement, it could later restore original jurisdiction either

---

[24] For examples of *évocations* from this court, see five entries from 1667 in *Répertoire*, 18: 160, 278, 328, 352, 411.

[25] For examples of *évocations* from this parlement, see three entries from 1686 in ibid., 60: 340; 61: 323, 364. The figure of ten *évocations* from this court (including one pertaining to the chambre de l'édit attached to this parlement) is high even if this court's area of jurisdiction was large. Perhaps these *évocations* reflect conflicts between local authorities, a point I will discuss below in connection with *évocations générales*.

[26] Nor are the provincial sovereign councils of Alsace, Artois, and Roussillon mentioned in the sample. The Parlements of Rouen, Bordeaux, Grenoble, Rennes, and Tournai experienced two *évocations* each; those of Dijon and Besançon, one each. Considered in this way, the total number of *évocations* is 36 instead of 33 because some *évocations* pertained to more than one court. Note that in the seven years sampled before 1661, *évocations de grâce* and *de propre mouvement* were somewhat more evenly distributed among the parlements. Of the 26 *évocations* that identify the parlement losing litigation, 14 applied to Toulouse (one of which was from the local chambre de l'édit), four to Rennes and to Grenoble (including one pertaining to its chambre de l'édit), three to Paris, and one each to Pau and Rouen (the total of 27 stems from the fact that one *évocation* concerned two parlements).

[27] In the seven years under consideration here, the Parlement of Paris experienced no *évocations de grâce* or *de propre mouvement* in 1696 and 1703; the Parlement of Toulouse experienced none in 1703. Bear in mind, of course, that the index refers to 27 other *évocations* that do not identify the court that lost cases. If this information were known, it would change the figures offered in this paragraph, but the broad generalizations would no doubt remain the same.

on the request of parties or in response to complaints by the judges. On 11 May 1667, an *arrêt en commandement* evoked from the Parlement of Paris a dispute concerning whether the Order of Cordeliers had the right to supervise the nuns of Mont Sainte Catherine de Provins; but another *arrêt* issued just two days later returned this case to the Parisian *parlementaires*.[28] When in 1671 two other cases were removed from the same parlement, a letter addressed to the king by *Avocat Général* Talon secured their return in short order, complete with assurances from Secretary of State Le Tellier that the king had no intention of authorizing "any *arrêt* that is contrary to the order that should prevail in justice."[29] In 1667, litigation that had been evoked from the Parlement of Toulouse was returned on the request of one of the parties in the case.[30] We shall never know, of course, precisely how often the parlements complained about *évocations de grâce* and *de propre mouvement*, and only a thorough reading of every *arrêt en commandement* issued during Louis XIV's reign would provide statistics on how frequently the high councils reversed their decisions.[31] But these and other examples suggest that lines of communication remained open between the parlements and the highest levels of the royal administration.[32]

Similar patterns characterized *évocations générales*. The uneven distribution of these *évocations* among the parlements was even more pronounced than was the case for *évocations de grâce* and *de propre mouvement*. Eleven of the 27 *évocations générales* in the sample after 1661 identify the parlement losing jurisdiction, and all but one of these 11 removals pertained either to the Parlement of Bordeaux or to the one of Toulouse.[33] Indeed, the identity of the parties who benefited from this royal grace suggests that

---

[28] *Répertoire*, 18: 352, 379.

[29] The king also informed the *parlementaires* that the two cases in question had been evoked by mistake. On this affair, see: AN, X^{1A} 8396, non fol., and U 2424 (part of the index to the Le Nain collection of this parlement's registers), vol. 65, fol. 55 (18 June 1671); *Répertoire*, 29: 353 (13 June 1671); Le Tellier to Talon, 12 June 1671, Archives du Ministère de la Guerre, A^1 258 (part of Le Tellier's correspondence dispatched), fols. 112–113.

[30] *Répertoire*, 18: 159 (6 March 1667). Note also that an *évocation de grâce* or *de propre mouvement* could have limited scope. Thus, an *arrêt* of 11 July 1701 evoked to the council a succession case involving the interpretation of the custom of Artois. But a later *arrêt* of 4 June 1703 made clear that the *évocation* applied only to litigation concerning a single provision (art. 76) in the custom. Ibid., 90: 244; 92: 219.

[31] The *Répertoire* also indicates, for example, that not every challenge to an *évocation* was successful. On 1 June 1709, an *arrêt* evoked from the Parlement of Paris a case concerning the ransom for a ship; an *opposition* to this *arrêt* filed by one of the concerned parties failed on 26 October. Ibid., 98: 207, 467.

[32] Throughout the *Répertoire*, entries refer to the *renvoi* of cases to the parlements (for three examples in 1667 concerning the Parisian *parlementaires*, see 19: 11, 193, 258). Whether this simply means the "referral" of cases to the parlements or the actual "return" of cases previously evoked is unclear. Note only that the *Répertoire* might be a useful source to uncover still other instances of the high councils withdrawing *évocations*.

[33] For examples of *évocations générales* from these two courts, see the following entries in the *Répertoire* for 1662 and 1678: 11: 43, 88, 113, 160; 43: 97; 44: 286, 290. Of the 11 *évocations*, four applied to Toulouse and four to Bordeaux, one applied to both courts, another applied to both Paris and Toulouse, and still another applied to the Parlement of Dijon.

as many as half of the remaining 16 *évocations générales* also involved these two courts.[34] The reason for this concentration is not difficult to establish. The Parlements of Bordeaux and Toulouse are known to have engaged in prolonged and frequently bitter jurisdictional conflicts with other regional institutions and authorities, such as town councils and royal financial officials.[35] That those who dared quarrel with the *parlementaires* wished to have their own litigation heard in other courts was a natural development. Thus, twice in 1662 the *capitouls* of Toulouse secured the transfer of their court cases to other tribunals, and in the same year the *jurats* of Bordeaux did the same.[36] In 1678 and again in 1686 the officials of the Cour des Comptes, Aides et Finances of Montpellier obtained the continuation of an *évocation générale* in their favor to the Parlement of Grenoble.[37] Still other regional authorities in the south and southwest—the *syndic général* of the *pays* of Viverais, the officials of the *bourse* of Languedoc, and the Archbishop of Bordeaux to name a few—also obtained *arrêts* transferring their litigation, both pending and future, from local parlements to other sovereign courts.[38]

What this meant, of course, was that the other parlements rarely experienced an *évocation générale:* only the Parlements of Paris and Dijon are mentioned in the index during the seven years under consideration, and then only once each.[39] This stands in sharp contrast to the situation in the decades before Louis XIV assumed personal rule, when many parlements had experienced *évocations générales* and when some *parlementaires*—those

---

[34] For example, *évocations générales* obtained by the *capitouls* of Toulouse and by the *jurats* of Bordeaux (to be discussed below) certainly applied to the parlements of these towns although the *Répertoire* does not note this explicitly; *évocations générales* of 1678 and 1686 in favor of the *lieutenant général* of the *gouvernement* of Burgundy probably applied to the Parlement of Dijon. Ibid., 11: 128, 146; 43: 174; 61: 379.

[35] Dubédat, *Histoire du Parlement de Toulouse*, 2: 271 ff; Boscheron Des Portes, *Histoire du Parlement de Bordeaux*, 2: 218 ff. I thank Professor William Beik for discussing with me the situation in Languedoc. For an example of the quarrels between the *parlementaires* of Toulouse and the *capitouls* of that city prior to Louis XIV's personal rule, see his *Absolutism and State Power in Seventeenth-Century France*, 193–194. It is likely that local conflicts accounted for *évocations générales* from other provincial parlements as well. On 31 December 1664, for example, the intendant of Burgundy, Claude Bouchu, received an *évocation générale* of all the cases he might have at the Parlement of Dijon because he had frequently clashed with this court in the past over such issues as office creations and the verification of municipal debts. AN, E 1723; *Répertoire*, 13: 524.

[36] See the entries for 23 February, 26 May, and 12 June 1662 in *Répertoire*, 11: 43, 128, 146. Sometimes an official in these parlements obtained an *évocation générale* because of conflicts with his colleagues. On 3 December 1677, for example, *Procureur Général* Le Mazuyer obtained an *évocation* for three years of his litigation from the Parlement of Toulouse to the Parlement of Grenoble because, as his request made clear, he sometimes clashed with his colleagues while enforcing discipline in the court; the bad blood that resulted no doubt led him to doubt that he could receive impartial justice in his own parlement. AN, E 1792; *Répertoire*, 42: 449.

[37] *Répertoire*, 44: 80 (3 October 1678); 61: 214 (30 September 1686).

[38] Ibid., 44: 41, 147 (25 July and 19 September 1678); 92: 136 (8 April 1709). For other examples, see *évocations générales* granted in 1678 for the Bishop of Sarlat (4 February) and for the president of the sénéchaussée of Villefranche and Rouergue (15 August) in ibid., 43: 97; 44: 75.

[39] Ibid., 44: 290 (19 December 1678); 98: 1 (2 January 1709).

of Paris and Aix in addition to those of Bordeaux and Toulouse—had
complained explicitly about this issue in their memoranda of the 1650s.[40]
Furthermore, if the Parlements of Bordeaux and Toulouse unquestionably
bore the brunt of *évocations générales* after 1661, there were nevertheless
compensating features of royal policy that helped to remove some of the
sting from these removals. In the first place, *évocations générales* could be
limited in scope. Thus, while the *jurats* of Bordeaux secured the removal
of their litigation from the parlement of that city in 1662, the *évocation*
applied only to "their private affairs, [those] in their own names only."[41]
The transfer of litigation the *capitouls* of Toulouse obtained in the same
year pertained only to certain financial privileges they enjoyed as municipal
officials.[42] Such restrictions seem to have been rare in the years
before 1661.[43]

Second, and more important, *évocations générales* were by no means
permanent. Not only were many granted for a specified time period, normally three years, but the high councils could withdraw the privilege at
any time. In March 1667, for example, an *arrêt en commandement* revoked
the *évocation générale* the *capitouls* of Toulouse had enjoyed, retaining the
privilege for only a few merchants who had previously participated in
municipal government.[44] In May 1665, the first president of the Parlement
of Toulouse had already thanked Chancellor Séguier for an *arrêt* issued in
April of that year which had suspended "all *évocations générales* that had
heretofore been accorded to many corps, towns, communities, and individuals in [this parlement's] resort."[45] In 1709, the process of withdrawing
évocations générales occurred again. An *arrêt en commandement* of 25 February ordered all individuals and corporations enjoying *évocations générales*
from the Parlement of Toulouse to submit documents justifying the con-

---

[40] For the memoranda of these courts, see above chap. II, nn. 14, 18, and 19. For examples
of *évocations générales* from parlements other than those of Bordeaux and Toulouse in the
seven years sampled before 1661, see *Répertoire*, 3: 62 (Aix; 17 June 1645); 6: 229–231, 233
(Rennes; 6 November 1651); 9: 13 (Dijon; 21 January 1658).

[41] Ibid., 11: 146 (12 June 1662).

[42] Ibid., 11: 43 (23 February 1662). As another example of such restrictions, an *arrêt* of 19
March 1709 stipulated that the Order of Cluny, which enjoyed an *évocation générale* to the
Grand Conseil, could only use this privilege against inhabitants of Bugey and Bresse for
litigation valued over 1,000 *livres*; this, on the request of the *syndics généraux* of these *pays*.
AN, E 1950; *Répertoire*, 98: 103.

[43] The *Répertoire* does not allow a quantitative demonstration of this point. But it is worth
noting that several *évocations générales* from the sample before 1661 had a very broad scope,
encompassing not only a group of people—municipal officials, for example, or members of
a cour des aides—but also at times the immediate relatives and even the servants of these
beneficiaries of *évocations*. For examples from the year 1651 alone, see ibid., 6: 195, 210, 229.
The *Répertoire* after 1661 does not mention such broad *évocations générales*.

[44] Ibid., 18: 149 (3 March 1667).

[45] Fieubet to Séguier, 13 May 1665, BN, MSS. Fr. 17406, fols. 121–122v; *Répertoire*, 14:
185 (27 April 1665). This action was known in Bordeaux: on 25 June the *parlementaires* there
requested the chancellor to issue a similar withdrawal of *évocations générales* from this parlement; the outcome is unknown. Archives Municipales de Bordeaux, MS. 795 ("registre secret,"
1664–1669), pp. 66–71.

tinuation of the privilege; until members of the council reviewed each case on an individual basis, all *évocations générales* from this parlement were suspended.[46] In the following year this investigation had already begun to bear fruit for the *parlementaires:* an *arrêt* of 17 March revoked the *évocation générale* enjoyed by the officials of the Cour des Aides of Montauban.[47]

It remains to define in a general way the issues that generated *évocations.* This is easiest to do for *évocations générales.* The ordinance of August 1669 stated that the king would order these blanket removals of litigation in only "very great and important occasions," a principle Chancellor Pontchartrain reiterated in 1703 when he informed the first president of the Cour des Aides of Bordeaux that, as a rule, Louis XIV opposed granting *évocations générales.*[48] The index of *arrêts en commandement* suggests that royal policy conformed to theory in this matter. That most *évocations générales* issued after 1661 pertained to just two parlements indicates that the *conseils de gouvernement* considered this grace to be highly extraordinary, more a temporary response to particularly bitter conflicts between local elites than a legal device intended to have wide application. The willingness of these same councils periodically to suspend and review *évocations générales,* and this at times on a large scale (as was done for the Parlement of Toulouse in 1665 and 1709), testifies to the desire of the king and his highest advisers to restore original jurisdiction to the parlements once the local tensions that had prompted the removal of cases subsided.

Generalizing about the reasons for *évocations de grâce* and *de propre mouvement* is more difficult. It will be recalled that these *évocations* pertained to specific litigation already pending in the courts. The particular circumstances that resulted in a parlement losing jurisdiction over a given case obviously varied from one *évocation* to another, and the index of *arrêts en commandement* provides few details about these circumstances (although one hastens to add that the *arrêts* themselves are not always clear on this subject).[49] Nevertheless, when read in conjunction with some original *arrêts,* the index does provide sufficient information to support several broad observations about the kinds of cases that were most likely to attract the attention of the king's highest councils.

In general terms, *évocations de grâce* and *de propre mouvement* fell into one of four categories. The largest of these, encompassing at least 19 of the 60 *évocations* drawn from the sample after 1661, includes cases that

---

[46] AN, E 1950; *Répertoire,* 98: 53. The original *arrêt* reviews some of the *évocations générales* this parlement had experienced and refers to the *arrêt* of 27 April 1665.

[47] AN, E 1962; *Répertoire,* 99: 173. The original *arrêt* notes that this revocation was pursuant to the *arrêt* of 25 February 1709.

[48] Ordinance of 1669, tit. 1, art. 1. See also Pontchartrain's letter to Suduyrault cited above in this chapter, n. 21.

[49] For example, on 24 September 1668, a *clerc tonsuré* in the diocese of Paris, a Sieur de Clamart, secured the transfer of a case involving the possession of an abbey from the Parlement of Paris to the Grand Conseil, claiming that he could not get fair justice at the parlement; the reasons for this, however, are not clear. AN, E 1748; *Répertoire,* 22: 175.

involved religious authorities or disputes concerning the possession of church benefices.[50] As the defender of the Gallican Church and its privileges, the monarchy had historically intervened in all manner of affairs regarding the clergy; Louis XIV and his ministers dealt regularly with such matters as clerical discipline, the church's temporal possessions, the limits of ecclesiastical jurisdiction, and the administration of hospitals and other charitable institutions. It comes as no surprise that this activity has left traces among conciliar *évocations*. In 1678 alone, for example, the *conseils de gouvernement* assumed jurisdiction over six cases regarding the possession or administration of various priories in the realm.[51] In 1686, two cases involving the possession of parish cures were transferred from the Parlement of Toulouse to the Conseil Privé for judgment, and in the same year the king decided to settle disputes between the monks of the abbey of Pottier and their treasurer.[52] Still other *évocations* pertained to disputes between bishops and towns: in 1662 such a case involving the Bishop of Agde and the inhabitants of Vézelay was transferred from the Parlement of Paris to the Parlement of Dijon, and in 1709 this latter parlement also received litigation pending at the Parlement of Besançon between the bishop of that city and the inhabitants of Defallans.[53] Still other examples of *évocations* include the transfer in 1709 from the Parlement of Paris to the council of litigation regarding the union of the abbey of Moreuil to the Congregation of Saint Maur; earlier, in 1678, an *arrêt en commandement* had empowered *commissaires* of the council to resolve disputes between the *curé* and the churchwardens of the church of Saint Roch in Paris.[54]

While it would be a mistake to assume that *évocations* such as these posed no threat to the jurisdiction of the parlements, it would be equally erroneous to exaggerate their importance. As already noted, there are good reasons to believe that the total number of *évocations* actually declined after 1661, and the decision of the king and his highest advisers to transfer or to retain jurisdiction in an occasional case in no way signaled a broader attempt to restrict the right of the parlements to hear litigation involving the clergy. We have already remarked that the parlements retained extensive authority in religious affairs during the period of Louis XIV's personal rule, and the fact that clergymen may be found among the petitioners who requested the Conseil Privé to nullify parlementary sentences demonstrates that the judges continued to exercise this authority. Moreover, the example cited above of the Parlement of Paris receiving the return of litigation involving the nuns of Provins illustrates that the high councils were capable

---

[50] In the following paragraphs, nine of the 60 *évocations* in the sample will not be discussed because the *Répertoire* provides insufficient information to place them in a category.

[51] *Répertoire*, 43: 66, 322; 44: 77, 78, 136, 192 (28 January, 27 May, 15 August, 12 September, 17 October). For a similar case, see ibid., 60: 423 (21 June 1686).

[52] Ibid., 60: 340; 61: 142, 323 (13 May, 28 August, 16 November).

[53] Ibid., 11: 199 (30 August 1662); 98: 220 (3 June 1709). For an *évocation* regarding the Bishop of Nîmes, see ibid., 18: 332 (6 May 1667).

[54] Ibid., 43: 67 (28 January 1678); 98: 292 (15 July 1709).

of withdrawing *évocations* in all kinds of cases, including those pertaining to the clergy. Finally, the existence of an *évocation* need not conjure up images of capricious royal conduct; sometimes the removal of litigation from a parlement was intended simply to enforce well established jurisdictional rules. The clergy of Artois, for example, enjoyed the right since 1629 to have certain litigation of a financial nature judged at the Grand Conseil. When in 1672 such a case came before the Parisian *parlementaires*, the clergy requested and received an *évocation* to the proper venue without stirring the least controversy.[55]

Litigation involving the principal aristocratic families of the realm constituted a second category of *évocations*, accounting for 12 of the 60 *évocations de grâce* and *de propre mouvement* drawn from the sample after 1661. Such illustrious names as Foix de Candale, Guise, Epernon, Harcourt, and Lesdiguières appear throughout these *évocations*, and the legal disputes in question usually concerned the succession to property and the satisfaction of creditors.[56] The *conseils de gouvernement* were actually on very solid ground when they intervened in such cases. The monarchy had a long-standing interest in preserving the fortunes of great noble houses, and the parlements themselves never seriously challenged the king's right to exercise this type of stewardship.[57] In addition, the decision to remove cases from the parlements could reflect sound principles of equity as well as the king's natural inclination to grant favors to the *grands*. The high nobility of France often owned property in a number of provinces; the death of a leading family member could easily result in a proliferation of complicated and related suits filed in several courts. The consolidation of this litigation in a single tribunal or at the council itself made perfect legal as well as financial sense. Thus, in 1667 the Marquis de Montsalins requested and secured the transfer of litigation involving the estate of Dame Marguerite de Balayer

---

[55] AN, E 1769; *Répertoire*, 32: 195 (20 October).

[56] For examples, see *Répertoire*, 11: 27 (6 February 1662); 18: 328 (6 May 1667); 44: 22 (11 July 1686); 84: 132 (28 August 1696). *Evocations générales* as well could concern the great nobility: see ibid., 60: 36, 167 (14 January and 13 March 1686).

[57] The memoranda that the parlements submitted in the 1650s rarely mentioned *évocations* in favor of great nobles. When the judges did complain, this was less about the actual removal of cases than about the scope of an *évocation* or the violation of legal technicalities. See, for example, the comments of *Avocat Général* Talon regarding an *évocation* in favor of the Cardinal de Guise in a report to the Parlement of Paris on 6 August 1658; AN, X¹ᴬ 8391, fols. 207v–217v. In January 1707, the Parlement of Aix remonstrated that the intendant of Provence had recently assumed jurisdiction over several affairs, such as municipal elections, that properly fell within the parlement's jurisdiction. The judges conceded without complaint that *évocations* in favor of "great families" had always existed; indeed, they used this traditional practice as leverage against the intendant's less justifiable conduct. AN, B³ 152 (marine: letters received, 1707), fols. 210–221. Even when cases regarding the high nobility remained in the parlements, the king often kept abreast with developments. See, for example, letters written by Colbert and by Jérôme de Pontchartrain (in their capacity as secretaries of state) in 1683, 1701, 1703, and 1706 in AN, O¹ ("maison du roi: dépêches ministérielles") 27, fol. 82v; 362, fols. 218v–219, 347–348; 364, fols. 87v–88; 367, fols. 69v–70. For comments on *évocations* concerning nobles and clerics in the eighteenth century, see Phytilis, *Justice administrative et justice déléguée au XVIIIe siècle*, 34–38, 42–44.

from the Parlements of Bordeaux and Toulouse to the Parlement of Paris.[58]
Similarly, Marie Châtelain, wife of the Marquis de Termes and one of
several creditors of a Sieur Aubert, successfully petitioned the king in 1686
to have litigation concerning the late Aubert's debts that was pending at
both the Parlement and the Châtelet of Paris transferred to the Grand
Conseil.[59] In 1678, the Marquis d'Alluye, governor of Orléans, had several
suits pending simultaneously at the Parlement of Paris, the Châtelet, and
the Requêtes de l'Hôtel; an *arrêt* of 21 December consolidated this litigation
in the parlement's fifth chamber of Enquêtes.[60] It is noteworthy too that a
parlement, having once officially lost cognizance of a case, could still retain
at least partial jurisdiction through the activity of some of its members. In
1696, for example, litigation concerning the estate of the Lur de Salusses
family was pending in both the Parlements of Bordeaux and Paris; on the
request of one of the litigants, an *arrêt en commandement* empowered three
councillors in the *grand' chambre* of the Parlement of Bordeaux to render
a judgment in last resort.[61]

A third category of *évocations de grâce* and *de propre mouvement*, comprising ten of the 60 *évocations* under consideration here, includes a diverse
group of cases that in one way or another concerned the enforcement of
specific royal policies or the supervision of the king's own officials. The
intent to implement policy is illustrated by an *arrêt en commandement* of 8
March 1678, which transferred to the intendant of Burgundy all litigation
pending in any court pertaining to the liquidation of the debts of the city
of Lyon. This *évocation* presaged a general edict of April 1683 by which
Colbert expanded the authority of the provincial intendants in the administration of municipal finances throughout the realm.[62] The crown's efforts
to end factional conflicts in towns and to clarify the lines of local authority
also resulted in *évocations* regarding municipal elections. In 1662 and again
in 1686, for example, disputes stemming from elections in two Langue-
docian towns (Uzès and Cordes) were withdrawn from the Parlement of
Toulouse, one going to the Parlement of Grenoble for judgment and the
other to the council itself.[63] Persons involved in activities of vital concern
to the king and his ministers, such as military procurement and public
finance, could also expect an occasional *évocation* in their favor. In 1667,
one Jean Chirat, who had a contract with the king to manufacture naval

---

[58] AN, E 1749; *Répertoire,* 18: 200 (18 March). In fact, the original *arrêt* notes that previous
conciliar *arrêts* had already empowered the Parlement of Paris to judge appeals in this case.
[59] *Répertoire,* 60: 370 (30 May).
[60] Ibid., 44: 295.
[61] Ibid., 83: 63 (23 January).
[62] Ibid., 43: 156; Nora Temple, "The Control and Exploitation of French Towns During the
Ancien Régime," *History* 51 (1966): 16–34.
[63] *Répertoire,* 11: 40 (20 February 1662); 61: 364 (16 December 1686). The former was
evoked from the Chambre de l'Edit of Castres, which was officially attached to the parlement.
The *Répertoire* does not provide details about these *évocations,* but I thank Professor William
Beik for discussing with me the numerous conflicts that were frequently associated with
municipal elections in Languedoc.

armaments, had litigation pending in three parlements, the Chambre de l'Edit of Dauphiné, and four lesser tribunals, including the Châtelet of Paris. In response to his request, an *arrêt en commandement* of 18 April consolidated all this litigation and sent the parties before the intendant of Burgundy to resolve their differences.[64] In the same year, the king's *fermier général* in the province of Brittany and *payeur des gages* at the Parlement of Rennes, Barthélemy Feret, was embroiled in litigation at this parlement with the seneschal of Rennes and several officials in the parlement itself. The case, which concerned the calculation of debts, had been so bitterly contested that Feret had actually suffered brief imprisonment. Given Feret's status in the king's financial administration, however, and the fact that his adversaries had close ties with the *parlementaires*, the transfer of jurisdiction in this case to a group of councillors of state could have been anticipated.[65]

Evocations pertaining to royal officials could result from an official becoming the subject of a criminal investigation, as occurred in 1696 when an *arrêt en commandement* sent to the intendant of Languedoc all the criminal charges pending at the Parlement of Toulouse against one Sieur La Marque, the king's inspector of manufactures in Haut-Languedoc.[66] Such *évocations* pertaining to criminal affairs exist throughout the conciliar records for Louis XIV's reign, and the original *arrêts* indicate that the *conseils de gouvernement* intervened only in extraordinary circumstances, such as when the parlements were suspected of having committed serious violations of judicial procedure or when passions ran high on the local level and prospects for impartial justice seemed bleak. In 1682, for example, the Parlement of Aix had sentenced to death for duelling the seneschal of Toulon, Maurel de Voullans. In a request to the council, Voullans, who had been condemned *in absentia*, claimed that the *parlementaires* had violated a number of procedural rules while prosecuting his case, including the delegation of one of his creditors to serve as reporting magistrate and the issuance of an arrest warrant before the preliminary investigation of charges was completed. Voullans asked that his case be transferred to another sovereign court for judgment, and an *arrêt en commandement* of 11 September awarded jurisdiction to the Grand Conseil.[67] As another example, the *lieutenant général* of the sénéchaussée of Limoges, a Sieur Vincent, was accused by his colleagues in 1692 of corruption in his post. After the Parlement of Bordeaux had investigated this charge and had begun to prosecute the case, at one point even seizing Vincent's property, Vincent asked the council for a change in venue, asserting that the *procureur général* of the parlement and

---

[64] AN, E 1739; *Répertoire*, 18: 278. The original *arrêt* cites Chirat recalling his service to the king in order to justify this royal grace.

[65] Ibid., 18: 355 (12 May).

[66] Ibid., 84: 157 (11 September).

[67] AN, E 1816 (*Répertoire*, 52: 193); related *arrêt* of 19 September in E 1817 (ibid., 221). For similar cases in which *évocations* occurred only after a parlement failed to resolve a problem or because a jurisdictional dispute between sovereign courts prevented a solution, see the *arrêts* of 18 April 1671 and 12 April 1674 in AN, E 1763, 1778 (ibid., 29: 258; 35: 280).

several *parlementaires* were in active collusion with a "cabal" of Vincent's enemies in Limoges. The following year, after Controller General Pont-chartrain had corresponded extensively with officials on the local level, including the provincial intendant, the Conseil royal des Finances sent the case to the Parlement of Paris, where Vincent was cleared of all charges, reinstated in his post, and awarded damages and court costs. Vindicated, but fearing possible retribution by his adversaries in Bordeaux and Limoges, Vincent then asked the council in 1694 to transfer to other tribunals all his remaining litigation still pending in the two regional courts. An *arrêt en commandement* of 22 September granted this request.[68]

Most *évocations* in favor of royal officials, however, were more routine in nature, involving the removal from the parlements of cases dealing with the definition of the functions of officials or with the transmission of their offices. Examples from the seven years sampled in the index of *arrêts en commandement* include the *évocation* to the council in August 1686 of all disputes between the presidents and the *lieutenant général* of the bailliage of Crépy-en-Valois concerning their respective duties.[69] In January 1709, an *arrêt* transferred from the Parlement of Toulouse to the intendant of Languedoc disputes between the inspector of manufactures in the department of Toulouse and some of his subordinates, the guild wardens of the wool dyers in the town of Daurade.[70] Even minor offices could attract the attention of the high councils: in 1667, an *arrêt en commandement* removed from the Parlement of Paris litigation between two individuals concerning the sale of the office of *précepteur des pages* of the Grande Ecurie de France.[71]

Evocations of this type posed no appreciable threat to the jurisdiction of the parlements. While all the sovereign courts of the realm possessed broad and well established powers within their respective resorts to supervise the conduct of lesser officials, the king's councils legitimately shared this responsibility. Sometimes the resolution of disputes between royal officials required recourse to conciliar authority. Only the councils were empowered, for example, to settle quarrels over precedence or functions within the sovereign courts, and the same rule applied to jurisdictional conflicts either between sovereign courts or between lesser officials subordinate to different sovereign courts.[72] The councils also had the right to establish proper ju-

---

[68] This case can be followed in the *arrêts en commandement* of 9 August 1692, 24 February 1693, and 22 September 1694 in AN, E 1878, 1879, 1888 (*Répertoire*, 73: 203; 75: 174; 80: 139). Pertinent correspondence is in AN, G⁷ 136 (for early 1693). Of course, a case like this could be evoked from one parlement and sent to another: for example, an *arrêt en commandement* of 12 October 1697 in E 1901 (ibid., 86: 185).

[69] *Répertoire*, 61: 133 (12 August).

[70] Ibid., 98: 33 (29 January).

[71] Ibid., 18: 60 (7 March); an *arrêt* decided this case on 9 May (ibid., 339).

[72] For examples among the original *arrêts en commandement*, see those of 15 July 1669 (AN, E 1751; *Répertoire*, 25: 46), 21 December 1671 (E 1764; ibid., 30: 341), 25 November 1687 (E 1842; ibid., 63: 282), and 29 October 1688 (E 1845; ibid., 65: 259). The high councils also decided serious conflicts between the sovereign courts and the lesser tribunals subordinate to them: see, for example, documents on the conflict between the Parlement of Rennes and the

risdiction for the supervision of lesser officials, as occurred in two of the three *évocations* mentioned above. The inspectors of manufactures worked under the authority of the provincial intendants, for example, and thus the intendants rather than the parlements were in the best position to settle disputes between the inspectors and their own subordinates, the guild wardens.[73] All the councils also had extensive experience in judging litigation arising from the sale of royal offices, so the decision to remove from the Parlement of Paris a case dealing even with such a minor office as *précepteur des pages* was not unusual or controversial.[74]

Only when the councils removed cases in which the parlements had a clear and unequivocal claim to jurisdiction, as occurred in the case of the bailliage of Crépy-en-Valois cited above (the Parlement of Paris was the logical place to resolve conflicts regarding the functions of the magistrates in this lesser judicial tribunal), could the king and his highest advisers even be suspected of undermining parlementary authority. But original *arrêts* drawn from throughout the period of Louis XIV's personal rule reveal that the high councils took this step only when the litigation in question threatened to become protracted or overly expensive. In 1688, for example, the king delegated several councillors of state to examine memoranda and to prepare a report concerning a conflict between the presidial courts of Riom and Clermont over the territorial limits of their respective resorts. Not only had this case already been pending at the Parlement of Paris "for many years," but, as Chancellor Boucherat explained to the intendant of Auvergne, the lack of a settlement in this affair had both inconvenienced litigants in civil cases, prompting a number of complaints on the local level, and interfered with the efficient prosecution of crime.[75] In 1676, an *arrêt en commandement* resolved a dispute that had pitted the *jurats* of Bordeaux against the *lieutenant criminal* of the sénéchaussée of that city over the authority each possessed to judge criminal cases. This conflict had come

---

présidial courts in its resort in AD, Ille-et-Vilaine, 1 Ba 65 ("Correspondance"—19 November 1710) and 1 Bb 806 (entry under "parlement"), as well as correspondence between Pontchartrain and the principal parties between October 1710 and January 1711 in BN, MSS. Fr. 21132–21133, passim. Of course, the high councils were always willing to ratify agreements between officials when they cooperated without conciliar intervention. See, for example, two *arrêts en commandement* of 1674: 29 January (E 1773; *Répertoire*, 35: 54) and 15 April (E 1775; ibid., 289). Finally, note that the Conseil Privé too could resolve disputes among judicial officials, especially between lesser royal tribunals and seigneurial courts, and disputes over functions in lesser royal tribunals. See, for example, the *arrêts sur requête* of 21 October 1695 (AN, V[6] 755, no. 17), 7 September 1705 (V[6] 802, no. 5) and 3 December 1714 (V[6] 834, no. 4), as well as the *arrêt* between parties of 23 September 1695 (V[6] 755, no. 14).

[73] On the activity of the inspectors, see Schaeper, *The French Council of Commerce*, 155–162, and Charles W. Cole, *French Mercantilism, 1683–1700* (New York, 1943), 153–161.

[74] For examples of various council bodies deciding matters pertaining to the sale and transmission of royal offices, see the *arrêts* of 3 October 1676 (AN, E 500, fols. 148–153v), 14 June 1684 (E 1827; *Répertoire*, 55: 396), 6 February 1694 (E 1881; ibid., 78: 152), and 16 October 1705 (V[6] 802, nos. 15, 18, 22).

[75] *Arrêt en commandement* of 7 September 1688, AN, E 1847 (*Répertoire*, 65: 143); Boucherat to Vaubourg, 8 November 1687, AN, V[1] 580, pp. 232–233.

before the council only after the parties had already contested at both the Parlement of Bordeaux and the Grand Conseil without having reached a definitive settlement.[76] As a final example, in January 1712 Chancellor Pontchartrain informed the first president of the Parlement of Paris that the king wished to assume direct jurisdiction over litigation that was currently pending at the parlement between the judges of the Châtelet of Paris and those of the bailliage of the Palais de Justice over their respective functions and jurisdiction. Pontchartrain feared that this case, if left to run its course in ordinary justice, would result in lengthy oral pleading, in numerous and costly memoranda submitted by each side, and ultimately in expensive written procedures; the contesting parties, the chancellor noted, should spend their time serving the public rather than litigating against one another. But Pontchartrain made it clear that while the king wanted a speedy resolution to this affair, he did not question the parlement's fundamental right to resolve such disputes. In fact, the chancellor instructed the first president to meet with the *procureur général* and the *avocats généraux* of the court for the purpose of preparing a report on how this litigation should be settled. The king would then simply ratify the results of their deliberations.[77]

That the high councils exercised discrimination in removing cases like these from the parlements is confirmed by the presence among the *arrêts en commandement* of instances when local judicial officials petitioned the king to resolve their differences, only to have the high councils remand the parties to the appropriate parlement for a settlement. This happened in 1683, for example, when the *lieutenant particulier* and the *lieutenant criminel* of the sénéchaussée of Agen, who were quarrelling over their respective functions, were directed to explain their grievances to the Parlement of Bordeaux.[78] In 1687, an *arrêt en commandement* designated the Parlement of Toulouse as the appropriate authority to resolve a jurisdictional dispute between the bishop, the consuls, and the judicial officials of Béziers.[79] The chancellors too in their daily correspondence instructed local judges to settle their differences with one another before their "natural" superiors, the *parlementaires*.[80]

---

[76] AN, E 1785; *Répertoire*, 40: 452 (4 December). As another example, in 1681 the intendant of Languedoc was empowered to settle a dispute between officials in the sénéchaussée of Puy, in part because the chancellor feared that litigation in the courts would only encourage the parties "to maintain their [mutual] animosity." Le Tellier to D'Aguesseau, 4 March 1681, AN, H[1] 1703.

[77] Pontchartrain to Des Mesmes, 19 January 1712, BN, MSS. Fr. 21135, fols. 65–66. For another example of conciliar intervention in a case with the participation of the magistrates, see the *arrêt en commandement* of 12 April 1692 in AN, E 1873 (*Répertoire*, 72: 306). The *arrêt*, which dealt with the territorial jurisdiction of the bailliage of Longwy, was prepared according to advice submitted by the first president of the Parlement of Metz: see the letters of this official, Guillaume de Sève, in AN, G[7] 376.

[78] *Répertoire*, 54: 15 (17 July).

[79] Ibid., 62: 74 (3 February).

[80] See, for example, Boucherat to Contest (intendant of Limoges), 16 July and 15 August 1686, AN, V[1] 578, pp. 139, 212. See also Pontchartrain to the *avocat du roi* at the royal seat

In reviewing this third category of *évocations*, what is most remarkable is not that the king and his highest advisers occasionally removed cases from the parlements in order to enforce specific policies or to exercise direct supervision over royal officials, but rather the restraint they showed in doing so. Ten such *évocations* pertaining to all the parlements of France in a period of seven years was not excessive. Except for the removal of litigation concerning municipal finances, an area in which all regional authorities lost ground to the provincial intendants during Louis XIV's reign, none of the *évocations* mentioned above made permanent inroads into parlementary jurisdiction.[81] Nor did the high councils act without sound justification. Efforts to consolidate dispersed litigation in a single tribunal, to spare royal officials lengthy and costly legal battles regarding their functions and offices, and to encourage the impartial administration of criminal justice represented the legitimate and appropriate exercise of conciliar authority. Even during the Fronde the parlements had never challenged the fundamental legality of *évocations*, just their frequent and arbitrary use. The high councils of Louis XIV took these objections seriously.

A fourth and final category of *évocations de grâce* and *de propre mouvement*, comprising ten of the 60 *évocations* in the sample after 1661, can only be described as miscellaneous because the cases in question shared little in common. In 1667, one Hélie Bonnu, who enjoyed by royal privilege the exclusive right to use a new invention for tanning leather, successfully petitioned the council to assume jurisdiction over cases pending in the courts regarding his privilege.[82] An *arrêt en commandement* of August 1686 sent before a *commission* of the council litigation that two owners of property near the Place des Victoires in Paris, then the site of construction, had at the Parlement of Paris against the municipal government.[83] In 1709, the same parlement lost to the council litigation between two individuals regarding their respective claims to a ransom paid for the English ship, *Helen of Liverpool*.[84] Why the *conseils de gouvernement* took an interest in cases like these is not always clear, and it is best to avoid excessive generalizations. But an examination of some original *arrêts* in this category of *évocations* suggests that, once again, the councils acted with good cause. An excellent case in point was the transfer in 1709 from the Conseil Provincial of Val-

---

of Ax (28 January 1703), to the *lieutenant criminel* at the bailliage of Besançon (19 April 1705), and to the *procureur du roi* at the royal seat of Fougères (22 October 1710) in, respectively, BN, MSS. Fr. 21122, fol. 74; 21124, fol. 349; 21132, fols. 1035–1036.

[81] Nor, according to Maurice Bordes, should we even exaggerate the loss of parlementary jurisdiction over municipal finances: *L'Administration provinciale et municipale en France au XVIIIe siècle* (Paris, 1972), 194. For an example of the continued authority of the parlements in local administration, see Patrice Berger, "French Administration in the Famine of 1693," *European Studies Review* 8 (1978): 101–127.

[82] *Répertoire*, 19: 3 (9 July).

[83] Ibid., 61: 92 (10 August).

[84] Ibid., 98: 207 (1 June). Perhaps this *évocation* resulted from the existence during wartime of a special *commission extraordinaire* of the council (the *Conseil des Prises*) to judge the validity of naval captures: Antoine, *Le Fonds du conseil d'état du roi aux Archives Nationales*, 20.

enciennes to the Parlement of Tournai of a criminal case involving a minor municipal functionary, an usher at the city council of Valenciennes named Nicodème Bourdon. In his request to the council, Bourdon explained that the Conseil Provincial had recently sentenced him *in absentia* to serve three months in prison and to make a public apology to an official of the court whom Bourdon had presumably insulted. Not only did Bourdon question the propriety of the Conseil Provincial judging a case involving one of its own members, he also claimed that his prosecution was marred by procedural errors, including a defective summons and the fact that the public minister at the Conseil Provincial had begun proceedings on his own initiative without the participation of a civil party or a denouncer, conduct that Bourdon asserted was highly irregular in minor criminal cases. Given the gravity of these charges and the obvious passion this case had stirred on the local level, the order for Bourdon to purge his contumacy at Tournai was reasonable.[85]

There is an additional aspect of *évocations* that warrants mention because it further illustrates the restraint with which the king and his highest advisers interfered with the caseloads of the parlements. As indicated earlier, whenever a *conseil de gouvernement* withdrew litigation from a parlement—whether this was by an *évocation de grâce, de propre mouvement,* or *générale*—a number of options existed for establishing new jurisdiction. An *arrêt en commandement* might simply keep the litigation in question within the system of ordinary courts, transferring jurisdiction to another parlement or other sovereign court. The provincial intendants too could receive the authority to judge a case in last resort. If the high councils wished to exercise a more direct supervision over the cases they evoked, still other possibilities were available. The king might decide to judge a case personally in a *conseil de gouvernement* after hearing a report prepared either by one of its members (such as a secretary of state or the controller general) or by a group of councillors of state and masters of requests.[86] Evoked litigation also could go before another permanent section of the king's council that already had the right to judge litigation in last resort, such as the Conseil Privé or one of the Directions of finances.[87] For perhaps as many as a third of the cases

---

[85] AN, E 1946; *Répertoire*, 98: 29 (26 January). Being unsure whether the Conseil Provincial of Valenciennes enjoyed a jurisdiction similar to the provincial conseils souverains (which, as noted above in chap. IV, n. 18, I have counted among the parlements), I have included this case in the sample to be on the safe side. At least two other *évocations* in this miscellaneous category might have resulted from concern in the high councils that a parlement was incapable of rendering impartial judgments: an *évocation* of 16 September 1667 from the Parlement of Toulouse to the one of Grenoble of a case involving the consuls of Montpellier, who had disputed with the *parlementaires* (*Répertoire*, 19: 88); and an *évocation* of 27 June 1662 between the same parlements of litigation involving the Guirand family, some of whose members had quarrelled with the Parlement of Toulouse over the jurisdiction of the *prévôts des maréchaux* in Languedoc (ibid., 11: 155).

[86] For example, see the entries for 13 March 1662, 23 February 1674, and 12 September 1678 in *Répertoire*, 11: 62; 35: 145; 44: 136.

[87] For example, see the entries for 13 May and 16 November 1686 in ibid., 60: 340; 61: 323.

they evoked and retained, however, the high councils appointed special *commissaires* to render final judgment. It is this practice that merits our attention.

Once appointed, these *commissaires*, who rarely exceeded ten in number, formed an official *commission extraordinaire* of the council.[88] The composition and responsibilities of these *commissions* varied. Some were composed exclusively of council members (councillors of state and masters of requests), while others were made up of jurists recruited from outside the councils (such as judges and *avocats* from the parlements and other sovereign courts). Still other *commissions extraordinaires* were "mixed," drawing their membership from both within and outside the councils. The jurisdiction of *commissaires* could extend over a single case or over an entire category of litigation. Although some *commissions extraordinaires* sat for many years, thus giving the impression of permanence, they were all in fact temporary in nature, their authority expiring after they had completed the tasks assigned to them. All kinds of cases—public affairs in which the king's interests were directly engaged as well as litigation between private parties— were eligible for judgment by *commissaires*.[89]

During the reign of Louis XIV, *commissions extraordinaires* empowered to judge litigation were still in a nascent stage of development; only after 1715 did these bodies proliferate and become a commonplace and institutionalized feature of council life.[90] Indeed, the systematic preservation of their archives dates only to the early eighteenth century.[91] Despite these

---

[88] In technical terms, we are dealing here with "commissions extraordinaires de jugement à la suite du conseil." The phrase, "commission extraordinaire de jugement," distinguishes these *commissions extraordinaires* not only from the permanent *bureaux* and *commissions ordinaires* (the two Directions) of the council, but also from the *commissions extraordinaires* "d'avis," which examined affairs and prepared reports but did not judge in last resort. The phrase, "à la suite du conseil," distinguishes the *commissions extraordinaires* considered here from the *commissions extraordinaires* "extérieures au conseil," which were in fact special *tribunaux d'exception* (such as *chambres de justice*) that sat "sur les lieux" in Paris or in the provinces. For details on the "commissions extraordinaires de jugement à la suite du conseil" and their place in conciliar organization, especially in the eighteenth century, see Phytilis, *Justice administrative et justice déléguée au XVIIIe siècle*, 16–21. For a survey of all kinds of *commissions extraordinaires*, see Antoine, *Le Conseil du roi sous le règne de Louis XV*, 162–174. Note that *commissions extraordinaires* could be created either by *arrêts en commandement* or by *arrêts simples* "en finance." I found none in my sample of the latter, so the following paragraphs concern only the *conseils de gouvernement*.

[89] In addition to their diverse composition and jurisdiction, *commissions extraordinaires* exhibited other differences as well. Sometimes an entirely new *commission* was created to judge a case or group of cases, while at other times an existing *commission extraordinaire* was empowered to judge additional affairs. Yet another possibility was to convert one of the permanent advisory *bureaux* or *commissions ordinaires* of the council into a *commission extraordinaire* for specific cases. On all these matters, see Phytilis, *Justice administrative et justice déléguée au XVIIIe siècle*, 53–66, and chap. 2, passim. Phytilis has prepared three graphs tracing various characteristics of the *commissions extraordinaires* established between 1700 and 1789 to judge litigation. One shows that of the 62 *commissions* appointed between 1700 and 1715, 54 dealt with "affaires privées" while eight considered "affaires royales." Ibid., appendix, graph 1.

[90] Ibid., 24, 46, 169–172; Antoine, *Le Conseil du roi sous le règne de Louis XV*, 96–97.

[91] AN, *série V*[7]. For details, see Antoine, *Le Fonds du conseil d'état du roi aux Archives Nationales*, 18–23, 64–76.

gaps in our knowledge, two points are clear about the use of *commissaires* during Louis XIV's reign. First, the *conseils de gouvernement* acted cautiously in appointing *commissaires*, often taking this step only after having solicited and examined preliminary reports on the litigation in question. This explains why *arrêts en commandement* ordering *évocations* to the councils frequently do not mention the ultimate destination of cases; a subsequent *arrêt* established *commissaires*.[92] The existence of these precautions has led one recent historian of *commissions extraordinaires* to conclude that, in the realm of judicial administration at least, Louis XIV employed methods that were far less "authoritarian" than those of his successor, who often appointed *commissaires* without extensive preliminary investigation.[93]

Second, a general rule during Louis XIV's reign—and one that would apply throughout the eighteenth century—was that the appointment of *commissaires* depended upon the consent of all the contesting parties. To be sure, there were numerous exceptions to this rule: *évocations* concerning royal finances and other public affairs did not require this prior agreement, and even private parties occasionally avoided the formality. But there can be no doubt that the high councils intended to implement the rule in most cases, especially in those involving private litigants. Of the 62 *commissions extraordinaires* established between 1700 and 1715 to judge litigation, 46 resulted from the prior consent of the contesting parties.[94] While the situation in previous years is less clear, the index of *arrêts en commandement* does mention *évocations* "du consentement des parties" as early as the 1670s.[95] In his correspondence as secretary of state for the king's household and then as chancellor, Pontchartrain noted Louis XIV's commitment to enforce the consent rule. In 1713, a judge named Guibal at the sénéchaussée of Béziers in Languedoc informed the chancellor that the Parlement of

---

[92] For examples, see: Phytilis, *Justice administrative et justice déléguée au XVIIIe siècle*, 144–145; Antoine, *Le Conseil du roi sous le règne de Louis XV*, 156–157; and in the *Répertoire*, the entries for 12 May and 23 September 1667 (18: 355; 19: 99), and those for 7 May and 25 July 1678 (43: 268; 44: 37). Of the 27 *évocations générales* mentioned in the sample after 1661, three are noted as having been retained at the council, and two of these refer to *commissaires* (see the entries for 14 January and 13 March 1686 in ibid., 60: 36, 167). Of the 60 *évocations de grâce* and *de propre mouvement* in the sample, 34 are noted as having been retained at the council. But only eight of these refer to *commissaires* (for example, see the entries for 28 January and 11 July 1678 as well as 11 September 1696 in ibid., 43: 66, 67; 44: 22; 84: 159). Nevertheless, the *Répertoire* also mentions numerous other *arrêts* that simply appointed *commissaires* without mentioning *évocations;* it is likely that many of these appointments pertained to cases that the high councils had already evoked previously (for examples, see the entries for 25 April, 22 September, and 12 October 1696 in ibid., 83: 252; 84: 185, 223).

[93] Phytilis, *Justice administrative et justice déléguée au XVIIIe siècle*, 144–145. He also notes (p. 60) that in the early eighteenth century the *arrêts* establishing *commissions extraordinaires* were very precise in defining the jurisdiction of these bodies.

[94] Ibid., appendix, graph 2. Phytilis does not indicate how many of these 62 *commissions* dealt with cases evoked from the parlements (as opposed to other tribunals), but the trend in favor of the consent rule is clear.

[95] For examples, see the following entries in the *Répertoire:* 23 February, 18 September, and 12 October 1674 (35: 146; 36: 156, 211); 12 November and 24 December 1677 (42: 386, 496); 25 November 1678 (44: 258); 13 March 1686 (60: 167).

Toulouse had recently joined two of Guibal's cases for resolution by a single judgment. Owing to the complexity of his litigation and to its potentially high cost, Guibal hoped that Pontchartrain would arrange for its transfer to *commissaires* of the council. The chancellor replied that not only did he lack the authority to do this on his own initiative, but that the king would not even consider granting such a request unless all of Guibal's adversaries agreed.[96] A former army officer named Escaich received the same response when he made a similar request in 1712.[97] But even if parties were willing to observe the consent rule, the transfer of their litigation to *commissaires* was not guaranteed. In 1692, for example, the Marquis d'Albyville petitioned the council to assume direct jurisdiction over his litigation with the Duc de Brissac currently pending at the Parlement of Paris. After consulting the king, Pontchartrain denied this request, and he did so without even raising the possibility that Albyville might seek Brissac's consent. Pontchartrain's response summarized well the overall policy of the high councils toward *évocations*: "His Majesty deeply regrets that he is unable to accord you this grace, not being accustomed to depriving [*dé-pouiller*] ordinary jurisdictions of the litigation to which they are entitled in order to have it judged in his council."[98]

Turning to the activity of the *conseils de gouvernement* in the realm of *cassation,* it is important to recall that the Conseil Privé was the principal forum for considering the nullification of parlementary judgments. The conclusions drawn earlier in this study about the policies and practices of this body thus apply to the vast majority of *cassations* the monarchy issued concerning the parlements. Nevertheless, the *arrêts en commandement* reveal that the king's highest councils did occasionally participate in the process of *cassation.* They certainly had the option to do so when the parlementary sentences in question dealt with royal finances and other public affairs. To be sure, the Conseil Privé was not altogether excluded from handling *cassations* relating to these matters, and we shall see shortly that the various council bodies involved in the administration of the king's revenues also at times overturned the judgments of the parlements by *arrêts simples* "en finance." But the fact remains that given their high status and their extensive administrative responsibilities and authority, the members of the *conseils de gouvernement*, meeting either alone with the king or in formal council sessions, were logical candidates to nullify parlementary judgments and administrative acts that jeopardized the enforcement of important royal policies. What is more, even when requests for *cassation* concerned judicial sentences that had decided litigation involving private individuals—the very type of case that usually came before the Conseil Privé—the king and his principal advisers could intervene, although why they chose to do so in some cases but not in others is not always evident.

---

[96] BN, MSS. Fr. 21138, fols. 665–666v (17 July).
[97] Ibid., 21136, fols. 725–726 (9 August).
[98] AN, O¹ 36, fol. 34 (8 February).

One fundamental development is clear from the outset, however: the king's highest councils pronounced far fewer *cassations* after Louis XIV assumed personal rule than before. Consulting the index of *arrêts en commandement*, if we take a sample of eight years between 1643 and 1660, we find that the *conseils de gouvernement* of that era issued 1,385 *arrêts*, or a yearly average of 173.1 *arrêts*.[99] Of these, 111 *arrêts* nullified the judicial sentences and administrative acts of the parlements, for an annual average of 13.9 *cassations* by *arrêts en commandement*.[100] All but a few of these *cassations* had an obvious political purpose. The decades of the 1640s and 1650s witnessed intense conflicts between the parlements and the central administration, the judges employing a variety of tactics—including delays in registering legislation, the issuance of formal remonstrances, and administrative orders to lesser magistrates—to undermine the enforcement of controversial royal financial and administrative policies.[101] The highest officials of Mazarin's administration naturally took a keen interest in this opposition and frequently relied upon *arrêts en commandement* to circumvent it. Did a parlement, having been compelled to accept the creation of a new chamber in the court, then attempt to disrupt the activities and the internal transfer of the judges who composed it? This occurred at Aix in the 1640s, when the *parlementaires* sought to frustrate the operation of a chamber of Requêtes established in 1641. Several *arrêts en commandement* censured this obstructionist behavior.[102] Did the judges at times aspire to supervise the conduct of the provincial intendants by ordering these officials to register

---

[99] With the addition of the year 1653 (136 *arrêts*), the years consulted and the number of *arrêts* issued each year are those listed above in this chapter, n. 12.

[100] The number of *cassations* by year is: 1643 (6); 1645 (11); 1648 (12); 1651 (27); 1653 (12); 1656 (5); 1658 (21); and 1660 (17). By parlement, these figures break down as follows: Toulouse, with the Chambre de l'Edit de Castres (47); Paris (27); Rennes (11); Aix (7); Rouen (7); Bordeaux (6); Dijon (3); Metz (2); Grenoble (1); unclear (1). One *cassation* concerned two parlements, so the total is 112. In this and in another sample of *arrêts* from later years examined below, I have included not only the entries in the *Répertoire* that use the words "casser" and "cassation," but also entries that describe the nullification of parlementary judgments with such terms as "sans s'arrêter à," "sans avoir égard à," "nonobstant," and "lève modifications." I do this because experience with the original *arrêts* leads me to believe that phrases like these in the *Répertoire* usually indicate *cassation* in the original *arrêts*; too, these phrases in themselves indicate nullification even when they appear in the original *arrêts*. In compiling statistics, I have not included the nullification of parlementary *ordonnances*, deliberations, or procedures: I am concerned with the *cassation* of judgments (*arrêts*). Nor have I included references in the *Répertoire* to the nullification of judgments rendered by the chambers of Requêtes du Palais attached to the parlements because these chambers did not judge in last resort. Neither of these exclusions, however, involves many entries. If they were included, the number of *cassations* would rise from 111 to 124, or 15.5 (instead of 13.8) *cassations* per year.

[101] The *parlementaires* could also rely upon their urban police powers, judicial strikes, the reception of appeals from church courts, and the purposeful judgment of litigation against crown interests to oppose royal policies. For a concise review of these obstructionist tactics and the various methods by which the crown could attempt to circumvent them, see Hamscher, *The Parlement of Paris After the Fronde*, 82–86.

[102] For example, see: *Répertoire*, 3: 66 (1 July 1645); several entries under the name of "Charles de Tressemanes-Chasteuil" in Le Pesant, ed., *Arrêts du conseil du roi*, 363; Kettering, *Judicial Politics and Urban Revolt*, 190–197.

their commissions at the parlements? If so, *arrêts en commandement* might be used to deflate such pretensions, as happened at Bordeaux in 1643.[103] Certainly, *arrêts en commandement* frequently blocked efforts by the parlements to interfere with the collection of taxes and other royal levies. The eight years sampled here provide instances of this occurring at the Parlements of Bordeaux, Grenoble, Rennes, Rouen, Paris, and Toulouse.[104] Examples such as these could be multiplied: the historical literature on judicial politics in the era of the Fronde as well as the *arrêts en commandement* recount numerous episodes in the "war of *arrêts*" that raged between the parlements and the king's councils in the decades preceding Louis XIV's assumption of personal rule.[105]

In later years, however, as the *parlementaires* trimmed their political ambitions and gradually abandoned their public opposition to royal policies, the role of the high councils in issuing *cassations* likewise declined. By the mid-1670s, when the process of bringing the magistrates under a greater degree of royal control was virtually complete, few *cassations* regarding the parlements figured among the *arrêts en commandement*—and this at a time, it will be recalled, when the number of these *arrêts* had increased dramatically, when the establishment of a new high council and several additional parlements and provincial sovereign councils had actually increased the opportunity for *cassations* to occur, and when the disappearance of the Conseil d'Etat et des Finances had expanded the non-financial competence of the Conseil des Dépêches in domestic affairs. If we turn to the index of *arrêts en commandement* and take a sample of eight years between 1675 and 1710, we find that Louis XIV's *conseils de gouvernement* together issued a substantial 5,832 *arrêts en commandement*, or an average of 729 *arrêts* per year.[106] But only 23 of these *arrêts*, or an annual average of 2.8 *arrêts*, nullified the judicial sentences and administrative acts of the parlements.[107] There was thus a direct relationship between the political activities

---

[103] *Répertoire*, 2: 124 (21 July 1643). On this issue, see also Bonney, *Political Change in France*, 244–245. For other examples of *cassation* against parlements attempting to interfere with the activities of provincial intendants, see *Répertoire*, 3: 142 (22 November 1645); 6: 220 (24 October 1651). As a related example, when in 1656 the Parlement of Paris ordered two masters of requests to appear before the court to explain their conduct in reporting conciliar *arrêts*, an *arrêt en commandement* voided this order: ibid., 8: 99 (19 October); Hamscher, *The Parlement of Paris After the Fronde*, 101–103.

[104] For several examples, see *Répertoire*, 3: 100, 110; 4: 141, 215, 260, 280; 6: 22, 51, 53, 62, 67, 98, 134, 214, 216, 220; 7: 133; 8: 103, 105; 9: 41, 196, 357, 362, 371, 393, 427, 429, 435, 459, 493. Hamscher, *The Parlement of Paris After the Fronde*, 88–98, describes in detail this court's opposition to royal financial policies in the 1650s.

[105] All the scholarship cited above in chap. I, nn. 2, 4, and chap. II, n. 13 can be consulted in this respect. The particular examples given in this paragraph were chosen to illustrate how existing historical literature can be read in conjunction with *arrêts en commandement*.

[106] The eight years sampled with the total number of *arrêts en commandement* issued each year are: 1675 (899); 1683 (783); 1687 (681); 1690 (864); 1695 (875); 1708 (472); 1709 (569); and 1710 (689). All the controllers general, chancellors, and secretaries of state who served Louis XIV after 1675 are represented in this sample; I chose the particular years at random.

[107] The number of *cassations* per year is: 1675 (4); 1683 (6); 1687 (6); 1690 (1); 1695 (2); 1708 (2); 1709 (1); and 1710 (1). As noted above in this chapter, n. 100, a number of entries

of the parlements and the participation of the high councils in the process of *cassation;* the decline of nullifications by *arrêts en commandement* signaled the resurgence of royal authority during Louis's reign and the emergence of more compliant parlements. But the king and his principal advisers, having achieved this objective, did not press their advantage: so long as the parlements expressed their views and grievances through acceptable and conventional channels, such as negotiating with individual ministers, the king's highest councils showed little interest in ruling on complaints about parlementary judgments. They were content to leave the bulk of this task to the Conseil Privé, with all the safeguards that this implied for the judges' interests.

Why did Louis XIV's high councils order *cassations,* even if only infrequently? Answering this question with precision requires consulting the original *arrêts.* In nine of the 23 *cassations* under consideration here, the councils were motivated by the same considerations that had predominated in earlier years: either the parlements failed to enforce important royal policies or they seriously overstepped their legitimate authority. Most of these *cassations* (six of nine) were issued on the councils' "own initiative," or *de propre mouvement,* which meant that the councils acted in an executive fashion without having received a formal request to intervene.[108] In the course of conducting their ordinary administrative business, the members of the high councils learned, usually from local authorities or the provincial intendants, that a parlement had acted improperly. In 1683, for example, the intendant of Guyenne, who exercised broad powers for billeting the royal troops who passed through his area of jurisdiction, ordered the municipal and royal officials of Tartas not to interfere in this matter. When these officials appealed this order to the Parlement of Bordeaux, and when the judges there agreed to hear the appeal, an *arrêt en commandement* nullified the parlement's decision as having been made "par juge incompé-

---

from the *Répertoire* have been excluded from the sample; had they been included, the number of *cassations* would rise from 23 to 33, or 4.1 *cassations* per year. The distribution of the 23 *cassations* among the parlements is: Paris (4); Toulouse, including the Chambre de l'Edit of Castres (3); Besançon (3); Aix (2); Bordeaux (2); Rouen (2), Chambre de l'Edit of Grenoble (1); Dijon (1); Metz (1); Pau (1); provincial sovereign councils of Artois (1), Tournai (1), and Roussillon (1). Note that if the courts created since 1661 are excluded (Besançon, Artois, and Tournai), the number of *cassations* drops from 23 to 18 (2.2 *cassations* per year), which further underscores the paucity of *cassations* when compared to the sample for the years before 1661. I have not specifically counted the *cassations* pronounced in the 1660s and early 1670s (except for the years 1668–1671 discussed below), but my impression from reading several hundred *arrêts* from this era is that the number of *cassations* issued fell somewhere between the two samples considered here.

[108] For information on how to distinguish *arrêts* issued "de propre mouvement" from those issued "sur requête," refer to the works of Antoine cited above in this chapter, n. 6. Both kinds of *arrêts* could be expressed either by *arrêts en commandement* or by *arrêts simples* (whether "en finance" or those issued by the Conseil Privé). In practice, however, the Conseil Privé issued few *arrêts* "de propre mouvement" (as mentioned above in chap. IV, n. 3): none figured in the discussion of this council earlier in this study. But for a few examples of the Conseil Privé issuing these kinds of *arrêts,* see those of 3 July 1669 (AN, V⁶ 554, no. 33) and 27 February 1685 (V⁶ 686, no. 1).

tant."[109] In the same year, another *arrêt en commandement* withdrew permission that the Conseil Souverain of Tournai had given the town of Solre-le-Château to levy a municipal tax, or *octroi*, on beer; the *arrêt* stated that the king wished that no tax be collected without his prior consent.[110] The high councils could also respond to formal requests filed by private parties. In 1675, for example, the Parlement of Toulouse changed the date for municipal elections in the town of Montgiscard, something a conciliar *arrêt* of 1651 had prohibited. Complaints by local notables resulted in the annulment of this administrative order.[111]

In reviewing cases like these, however, one must not forget how rare they were. That the parlements together experienced in eight years only nine *cassations* pertaining to public affairs underscores their growing submission to royal policies as Louis XIV's reign progressed. This paucity of *cassations* with obvious political intent stands in sharp contrast to the situation that had prevailed during the era of the Fronde, when a single year could witness well over a dozen such nullifications.

The remaining 14 *cassations* concerned private rather than public affairs. The councils issued only two of these *cassations* on their own initiative, the rest having resulted from formal complaints filed by individuals whose litigation the parlements had judged in the course of their routine judicial work. The intervention of the high councils in litigation involving private parties had never been extensive, nor was it during the eight years under consideration here: these 14 cases constitute a majority of *cassations* in the sample after 1675 only because the number of nullifications for political reasons had declined. The only noteworthy exception to this general lack of interest in private cases occurred during the years 1668–1671, when over 25 *arrêts en commandement* nullified parlementary judgments for violations of the code of civil procedure of April 1667. The king and his ministers clearly wished to advertise their intention to enforce this new legislation by censuring at least some contraventions with *arrêts en commandement*—*arrêts* that by definition bore the stamp of the king's personal approval.[112] But even during these years the Conseil Privé remained the

---

[109] AN, E 1822; *Répertoire*, 53: 281 (30 April).

[110] AN, E 1822; *Répertoire*, 53: 210 (1 April). For another example of such "political" *cassation* by *arrêts* "de propre mouvement," see the affair regarding the Parlement of Besançon, which on 19 March 1687 suffered the *cassation* of one of its sentences that had failed to apply the criminal penalties for duelling set forth in a royal edict of 1679: E 1843 (ibid., 62: 151). See also the *cassation* of 21 June 1687 against the Parlement of Paris, which had exceeded its jurisdiction and violated royal legislation of 1669 on manufactures by receiving an appeal from an *ordonnance* issued by the municipal government of Tours: E 1843 (ibid., 62: 296).

[111] AN, E 1781; *Répertoire*, 38: 309 (20 November). Another example of *cassation* "sur requête" comes from the same year: when the Parlement of Aix ordered all bishops and archbishops in its resort to establish their personal residences in the principal towns of their dioceses, the General Assembly of the Clergy, then in session, requested and received the rescission of this order on 9 September: *Répertoire*, 38: 153 (I was unable to consult the original *arrêt* in E 1780).

[112] Many of these *arrêts* have been published in Bornier, *Conférences des ordonnances de Louis XIV*, 1: appendix. The originals are scattered throughout AN, E 1742–1765. For three

principal body responsible for ruling on complaints that the parlements had violated the rules of judicial procedure.

The question remains, then, why the *conseils de gouvernement* participated at all in *cassations* pertaining to the litigation of private individuals. The *arrêts en commandement* do not comment explicitly on this subject, and it is best to avoid excessive speculation. For some cases, the reasons why a high council rather than the Conseil Privé resolved a particular dispute simply remain a mystery. In 1683, for example, the Parlement of Toulouse violated royal legislation on criminal procedure by condemning two men to terms in the king's galleys without having had a sufficient number of judges hear the case. This was a serious breach of judicial procedure, to be sure, but there was no logical reason why an *arrêt en commandement* was necessary to rescind the parlement's sentence. Indeed, the *arrêt* remanded the case to the same judges for a retrial, which suggests that the Toulouse *parlementaires* were under no suspicion of having acted with malevolent intent.[113] Surely, the Conseil Privé had ruled on far graver allegations of judicial misconduct. As another case in point, in the same year the municipal magistrates of Dunkirk sentenced a bourgeois of that town to pay a fine and to serve six months in jail for poor conduct (the conciliar *arrêt* is not more specific about the nature of the charges). This person then appealed to the Parlement of Paris, which agreed to hear the case, summoning all the concerned parties to contest the matter fully and letting the bourgeois out of jail on bail. Apprised of this, the magistrates in Dunkirk complained to the council that the proper order of jurisdictions required that the appeal be heard instead at the Conseil Provincial of Artois. An *arrêt en commandement* adopted this reasoning, voiding all procedures in Paris and transferring the case to Arras.[114] But one is still left wondering why the Conseil Privé did not rule on this dispute: it had extensive expertise in addressing jurisdictional questions, and ones far more complicated than those posed in this case. In fact, the Conseil Privé possessed both the authority and the experience to have handled each of the 14 *cassations* under consideration here. It is even possible that some of these cases had begun before this council, but that the chancellor decided later that the issues at stake were important enough to warrant the king's personal attention.[115]

---

examples regarding the parlements (and not included by Bornier), see the *arrêts en commandement* of 4 June 1668 (Grenoble), 11 November 1669 (Paris), and 15 December 1670 (Bordeaux) in, respectively, E 1742 (*Répertoire*, 21: 98), E 1749 (ibid., 25: 320), and E 1758 (ibid., 28: 223).

[113] AN, E 1821; *Répertoire*, 54: 241 (9 November).

[114] AN, E 1822; *Répertoire*, 53: 324 (21 May).

[115] Antoine, *Le Conseil du roi sous le règne de Louis XV*, 297, discusses such transfers. Cases could be transferred from the Conseil Privé either by an oral order from the chancellor or by an *arrêt en commandement* (for an example of the latter, see the entry for 7 June 1674 in *Répertoire*, 35: 405). For their part, the high councils could send cases pending before them to the Conseil Privé (for an example, see the entry for 15 January 1703 in ibid., 92: 9). The fact that *arrêts en commandement* were sometimes reported by councillors of state or masters of requests also suggests the possibility that a case had originally begun at the Conseil Privé but was transferred later to a high council.

With this said, and bearing in mind that every case had its own unique characteristics, there nevertheless seem to have been several circumstances that increased the likelihood, but did not guarantee, that a high council would rule on requests for *cassation*. First, it certainly helped if the complaining parties had connections in high places. In 1683, for example, the Parlement of Paris rendered a judgment in litigation involving one Hélie du Fresnoy despite the fact that this individual held *lettres d'état* postponing the judgment of his case. This was a routine matter, the kind that the Conseil Privé dealt with on a regular basis. Perhaps Fresnoy's position as a chief clerk (*premier commis*) for the Marquis de Louvois, Secretary of State for War, accounts for the repeal of the parlement's sentence by an *arrêt en commandement*.[116] Indeed, six of the 14 *cassations* involved people whose status was sufficiently high to attract the attention of the high councils: prominent nobles of the sword like the Comte de L'Aubespine as well as high officials in the king's own administration, including councillors of state and judges in the sovereign courts.[117]

Second, a high council might pronounce *cassation* when it wished to clarify the intent of royal legislation or to encourage a parlement to apply consistently specific points of law. In 1707, one David Ancillon, a former Protestant who had recently returned to the Catholic fold, claimed that as a *nouveau converti* he was entitled to participate in the division of the estate of his grandfather, a Protestant minister who had left France. One of Ancillon's relatives challenged this pretension at the Parlement of Metz, arguing that a royal declaration of 1698, which confirmed the status of newly converted persons as legitimate heirs to the property of *émigrés*, had expired. When the judges disallowed Ancillon's claims, he turned to the king's council in 1708. In his request for *cassation*, he maintained not only that other, earlier legislation operated in his favor, but that even the declaration of 1698, which drew distinctions between adults and minors, still applied to him because he had reached his majority while residing in France. This was a complicated case, one involving questions of fact as well as the interpretation of several seemingly contradictory royal statutes. By using an *arrêt en commandement* to nullify the parlement's judgment and to allow Ancillon to pursue his rights of inheritance, the king informed the *parlementaires* that he personally wished them to interpret royal legislation on the property rights of former Protestants differently in the future.[118] In an equally complicated case, the Parlement of Paris in 1687 decided litigation in such a way that a 15-year-old girl, through the intercession of her adult fiancé, was able to set aside her father's will and to contract a marriage despite the opposition of her legal guardian and several blood relatives.

---

[116] *Répertoire*, 54: 94 (25 August). I was unable to consult the original *arrêt* in AN, E 1822.

[117] In addition to the *arrêt* cited in the previous note, see the following *arrêts* (with their location in AN, E and in the *Répertoire* noted in parentheses): 22 December 1687 (E 1843; 63: 341); 10 January 1695 (E 1894; 81: 21); 18 September 1695 (E 1894; 82: 207); 10 December 1708 (E 1944; 97: 458); and 8 May 1709 (E 1946; 98: 166).

[118] AN, E 1946; *Répertoire*, 97: 356 (17 September).

The *arrêt en commandement* that annulled the parlement's sentence stated explicitly that the judges had violated several ordinances of the realm and had improperly ignored the father's will, which stipulated that the girl could not marry without her guardian's permission. To underscore the king's displeasure, the *arrêt* was issued *de propre mouvement* rather than on the request of the guardian.[119]

Finally, the high councils could nullify a sentence if the allegations against the *parlementaires* were particularly serious. In 1683, for example, an *avocat* at the Parlement of Pau named Pierre de Place complained that this court had violated a number of procedural rules in judging a property dispute in which he was one of the litigants. It seems that the judges had appointed one of their colleagues, a Sieur de Salles, to serve as a *commissaire* in the case charged with collecting evidence. In his request to the council, De Place claimed not only that De Salles had completed several procedures without having heard all the parties in the case, but that he had failed to communicate crucial documents to the court at the time of judgment. De Salles apparently lacked the seniority even to act as a *commissaire*. What sets this case apart is that the *arrêt en commandement* nullifying the parlement's judgment also interdicted De Salles from his post until further notice.[120] The interdiction of a judge in a sovereign court was serious business, and to my knowledge it was always ordered by an *arrêt en commandement*; this no doubt explains why the Conseil Privé did not resolve this dispute.[121]

Whether they pronounced *cassation* on their own initiative or on the request of parties, and whether they dealt with public or private affairs, the high councils took steps to ensure that the cases coming before them received careful examination prior to a final decision. This is not to imply that these councils were obliged to follow the complex judicial procedures associated with the Conseil Privé. One must bear in mind that *arrêts en commandement* resulted not only from formal council sessions, but also from the meetings the king held on an individual basis with his highest officials. The very flexibility of their methods of work constituted the principal strength of the *conseils de gouvernement*, enabling them to respond swiftly to pressing problems. No *bureaux* of councillors of state were permanently attached to these councils to examine all the cases that came before them, and contact between the high councils and the assembly of

---

[119] AN, E 1841; *Répertoire*, 63: 227 (24 October).

[120] AN, E 1816; *Répertoire*, 53: 379 (5 June). For a similar case in which the allegations against a parlement were serious, see the *arrêt* of 20 November 1675 in E 1781 (ibid., 38: 310): the petitioners alleged that the Chambre de l'Edit at Castelnaudary had sought to protect a seigneur accused of violence by improperly evoking his case from a lesser tribunal.

[121] For the years 1661–1710, the *Répertoire* lists well over a hundred interdictions of judicial officials (at every level) by *arrêts en commandement*; in future work I will examine these in detail from the vantage point of the original *arrêts*. The sample of *arrêts* issued by the Conseil Privé examined earlier in this study contains only one interdiction, and this of a notary not a judge (27 February 1685: AN, V⁶ 686, no. 1). The sample of *arrêts simples* "en finance" discussed below contains no interdictions.

masters of requests was infrequent. Nevertheless, the principal members of the high councils—the controller general of finances, the chancellor, and the secretaries of state—all had their own "ministerial *bureaux*" to receive and sort correspondence, to coordinate investigations on the local level, and to prepare reports for their superiors in advance of council sessions and private meetings with the king.[122]

At their discretion, the high councils also could use procedures that the Conseil Privé followed as a matter of course. If a case was particularly complicated, a group of councillors of state might be called upon to serve as "commissaires d'avis," examining evidence and offering a collective opinion prior to a final decision.[123] Like the Conseil Privé, the high councils occasionally instructed the *procureurs généraux* of the parlements to submit written *motifs* explaining the judicial reasoning behind the judgments under attack. This allowed the judges to participate directly in at least some of the cases that concerned them.[124] While the high councils rarely called all the litigants involved in a disputed judgment to contest a complaint fully in writing—something that was common at the Conseil Privé—the *arrêts en commandement* do contain some references to the practice.[125] Certainly, private individuals whose requests for *cassation* came before the high councils were often required to follow the rules regarding the consultation with three *avocats aux conseils* and the payment of fines if their requests failed.[126] Finally, the fact that the *conseils de gouvernement* at times transferred cases pending before them to the Conseil Privé for final resolution according to all the procedural rules shows that the king and his principal advisers exercised discretion in choosing which cases to decide themselves.[127]

---

[122] For an overview of these *bureaux* in the eighteenth century, see Antoine, *Le Conseil du roi sous le règne de Louis XV*, 309–319, and for some valuable insights into this generally neglected subject for Louis XIV's reign, see McCollim, "The Formation of Fiscal Policy," 180–184, and two articles in the *Proceedings of the Annual Meeting of the Western Society for French History* 8 (1980): John Rule, "The Commis of the Department of Foreign Affairs Under the Administration of Colbert de Croissy and Colbert de Torcy, 1680–1715" (pp. 69–80); Douglas Clark Baxter, "Premier Commis in the War Department in the Latter Part of the Reign of Louis XIV" (pp. 81–89).

[123] For two examples drawn from the 23 *cassations* discussed above, see the *arrêts* of 10 December 1708 and 8 May 1709 cited above in this chapter, n. 117.

[124] For examples, see the *arrêts* of 10 January 1687 (AN, E 1839; *Répertoire*, 62: 22), 26 September 1690 (E 1859; ibid., 69: 205), and 18 June 1709 (E 1946; ibid., 98: 228). Moreover, as in the Conseil Privé, a *procureur général's motifs* could, if sound, save a judgment from *cassation*. For example, see Châteauneuf to Languet (Dijon), January 1679, AAE, *France* 949 ("mémoires des expéditions" of the secretaries of state, 1679), fol. 51v.

[125] Of the 23 *cassations* discussed above, one was "between parties," another was issued on *requêtes respectives*; either way, both indicate contests between litigants. See the *arrêts* of 6 April 1675 (AN, E 1781; *Répertoire*, 37: 254) and 23 November 1687 (E 1843; ibid., 63: 277).

[126] For an example of a fine, see the entry for 29 April 1675 in *Répertoire*, 37: 309. For examples of the participation of *avocats*, see the *arrêts en commandement* of 23 September and 25 June 1668 in Bornier, *Conférences des ordonnances de Louis XIV*, 1: clii–cliii, cciv–ccviii.

[127] For an example, see above this chapter, n. 115. For other examples from the year 1708 alone, see *Répertoire*, 97: 277, 279, 282, 315, etc.

The high councils also defined the grounds, or *ouvertures*, for *cassation* narrowly. The 23 *cassations* discussed above cite a total of 26 justifications for nullification, all of which correspond to the five grounds allowed by the Conseil Privé: questions of equity (1), and claimed violations of law (1), royal legislation (4), judicial procedure (6), and jurisdictional rules (14). If we isolate the 14 *cassations* involving the litigation of private individuals—the type of case in which the Conseil Privé specialized—the distribution of the 16 justifications mentioned in these *cassations* corresponds closely to the pattern observed earlier in the caseload of the Conseil Privé: most complaints concerned alleged violations of royal legislation (2), judicial procedure (6) and jurisdictional rules (6), while relatively few dealt with the judges' sense of equity (1) or their interpretation of the law (1). Like the Conseil Privé, then, the *conseils de gouvernement* adopted strict criteria for allowing parties to seek a redress of grievances at the very center of royal power.

When they decided cases involving *évocation* and *cassation*, therefore, Louis XIV's highest councils displayed the same spirit of restraint and moderation that characterized the conduct of the Conseil Privé. So long as the parlements abandoned their vocal and public opposition to royal programs, the king and his ministers were prepared to reciprocate by keeping their interference in the judges' judicial business to a minimum. As the high councils assumed primary responsibility for granting *évocations de grâce, de propre mouvement* and *générales*, the number of these *évocations* declined from the high levels typical in the era of the Fronde. Most parlements rarely experienced one of these *évocations*, and the councils were willing to review and to consider withdrawing those *évocations* that they did order. The decline in the number of *cassations* by *arrêts en commandement* was even more dramatic. When the high councils did nullify a judicial sentence or remove litigation from a parlement, they restricted their intervention to cases in which the assertion of the king's sovereign power was both reasonable and easily justified. The parlements themselves had long advocated the adoption of just such a policy.

This basic respect for the parlements' traditional judicial authority has also left traces in the third major collection of conciliar *arrêts*—the *arrêts simples* "en finance." As noted earlier, a number of council bodies prepared these *arrêts* during Louis XIV's reign: the Conseil d'Etat et des Finances; the Conseil royal des Finances; the ordinary *commissions* of Grande and Petite Direction; and most important as the reign progressed, the various *bureaux* that served the controller general of finances. Even these bodies, which did not normally concern themselves with the judicial activities of the parlements, proved to be sensitive to the judges' interests when they decided cases involving *évocation* and *cassation*.[128]

---

[128] For scholars wishing to explore these *arrêts*, it is worth recalling here the reasons why the judicial activities of the parlements do not figure prominently in these documents: (1) the

These cases were not numerous. A sample of 316 *arrêts* drawn from two years yields only one *évocation,* and this concerned a relatively simple question of jurisdiction. In 1713, the police judge in Chaumont-en-Bassigny, acting on a complaint filed by the master drapers of the town, fined several individuals for illegally engaging in the wool trade. One of these individuals, a hosier named Pierre Cornuot, appealed this sentence to the Parlement of Paris, which summoned both sides to contest the matter. In a formal request to the council, the drapers protested this summons, pointing out that a conciliar *arrêt* of 1699 had authorized the fines in question. The implication was that only a section of the king's council could act as the ultimate arbiter of disputes arising from these fines. An *arrêt* of 14 January 1714 adopted this reasoning, voiding all procedures at the parlement and instructing the parties to visit the provincial intendant of Champagne. After examining the evidence, this official would prepare a report that would serve as the basis for a conciliar resolution of this affair.[129]

The sample of *arrêts* also contains three cases involving requests for the nullification of parlementary judgments. In one, the tax farmer in charge of collecting levies on the delivery of mail contended that the Parlement of Rouen had exceeded its authority by investigating corruption in the king's postal service; royal legislation, he asserted, had awarded jurisdiction in this matter to the provincial intendants.[130] In another, a litigant claimed to have uncovered errors in a judgment the Parlement of Rennes had rendered in a suit pertaining to the inheritance of royal offices.[131] The third case concerned a Parisian banker named Jean Nicolas, who was a party in litigation pending before *commissaires* appointed by the council. He maintained that the Parlement of Paris had overstepped its authority when it ignored this prior arrangement and assumed jurisdiction over his legal disputes.[132] What is remarkable about these complaints is not the reasons for nullification that these parties offered: allegations that the parlements

---

fact that after 1661 these *arrêts* deal almost exclusively with financial affairs rather than with a broad range of domestic issues, a situation brought about by the emergence of the Conseil des Dépêches and the disappearance of the Conseil d'Etat et des Finances; (2) the limited competence of the parlements in financial affairs and the declining opposition of these courts to royal policies as the reign progressed; (3) the ability of the controller general of finances to use *arrêts en commandement* as well as *arrêts simples* "en finance" to express his decisions. Most *évocations* and *cassations* among the *arrêts simples* "en finance" pertain to courts that specialized in financial matters, such as the Parisian and provincial *cours des aides:* see, for example, the *arrêts* in AN, E 500, fols. 134, 505–507; E 859^A, fols. 81–83, 104–113v, 241–244, 315–317, etc.

[129] AN, E 859^A, fols. 253–256v (*arrêt sur requête*).

[130] *Arrêt sur requête* of 17 October 1676, AN, E 500, fol. 269. Two days later another *arrêt* (fols. 333–334) voided some procedures the Parlement of Paris had initiated in a criminal case over which the *lieutenant général de police* of Paris had jurisdiction; this was not, however, the *cassation* of a parlementary judgment (*arrêt*).

[131] *Arrêt* on *requêtes respectives* of 3 October 1676, ibid., fols. 148–153v.

[132] *Arrêt sur requête* of 2 January 1714, AN, E 859^A, fols. 23–24v. Note that on this date another *arrêt* (fols. 14–18) nullified just that portion of a judgment rendered by the Parlement of Dijon that failed to order a fine required by statute in convictions regarding contraband tobacco; the substantive portion of the sentence, however, remained in force.

had violated royal legislation or had exceeded their proper jurisdiction were legitimate and conventional grounds for *cassation*. What stands out instead is that the *arrêts* ruling on these requests displayed the same concern to avoid reaching hasty decisions that was evident in the Conseil Privé. Only in the case of the tax farmer did the *arrêt* nullify a parlement's sentence on the party's request without calling for additional procedures. The attempt to overturn the sentence of the Parlement of Rennes actually failed, and this only after both sides in the dispute had presented evidence. As for the banker's case, the *arrêt* did not give a final decision; it simply summoned his adversaries to contest his complaint fully in writing.

It may well be true, therefore, that during Louis XIV's reign the controller general and his collaborators became increasingly independent in administering the king's finances and made many decisions among themselves without consulting one of the councils—"par voie bureaucratique" in the words of Antoine.[133] But there is no reason to believe that these developments either posed an appreciable threat to the caseloads of the parlements or made the nullification of their judgments easier to achieve. *Evocations* and *cassations* by *arrêts simples* "en finance" were few in number and, it seems, awarded with care. These *arrêts* thus provide yet another indication that in matters pertaining to the administration of justice, the Conseil Privé was not alone in seeking an accommodation with the parlements.

---

[133] Antoine, *Le Conseil du roi sous le règne de Louis XV*, 319, 399.

VIII. CONCLUSION

Given the current state of historical scholarship on the French parlements, a comprehensive view of the relations between these courts and the monarchy of Louis XIV remains elusive. Only additional research on the local level will clarify the extent to which the *parlementaires* suffered an erosion of their wealth, power, and prestige in the aftermath of the Fronde. Lest it fail to detect subtle changes over time, this research should eventually encompass the entire period of Louis's reign. It certainly must take into account not only the fate of the political, social, and economic interests of the judges, but the evolution of their judicial and administrative activities as well; otherwise, historians will run the risk of judging a whole by the sum of only a few of its parts. On the national level, the contacts between the parlements and central institutions other than the Conseil Privé, whether formal council bodies or the principal domestic services of the state, also warrant full and methodical investigation.[1]

Despite this substantial agenda for future research, a study of the parlements' relations with a single council body can indeed illuminate larger issues relating to the exercise of state power in the second half of the seventeenth century. In the years before Louis XIV assumed personal rule, the conflicts between the Conseil Privé and the parlements over judicial issues formed a crucial dimension of the broader struggle between the monarchy and its traditional institutions. As a result, understanding how these conflicts were resolved in subsequent decades provides valuable insights into the nature of royal absolutism and its impact on the kingdom's highest courts of law. When viewed over the entire period of Louis's long reign, the history of the Conseil Privé also reveals important patterns in the crown's administrative conduct that emerged only gradually and beneath the swirl of notable events.

For historians accustomed to understanding the relations between the monarchy and its leading judicial institutions in terms of controversy and confrontation, the spirit of accommodation that guided the conduct of Louis XIV's Conseil Privé is perhaps the most significant theme that has emerged in this study. In all aspects of its work, this council attempted to bring order to its internal operation and to resolve in favor of the judges the

---

[1] Few modern studies focus exclusively on the history of Louis XIV's parlements after 1661, those by Hamscher, Hurt, and Paulhet being the most notable (see above, chap. I, nn. 2, 4, and chap. III, n. 41). Valuable insights into specific issues may also be found in the studies by Hanley, Beik, Gresset, and Kaiser (see above, chap. I, n. 4, chap. II, n. 13, and chap. III, nn. 41 and 42). Otherwise, the opportunities for research are unlimited.

grievances they had expressed at mid-century. On the issue of *cassation,* the chancellors and their colleagues not only defined narrowly the grounds for this legal action, but by their judgment of individual cases they served notice to litigants that the nullification of parlementary sentences would be difficult to achieve. The adjudication of *évocations de justice* and *règlements de juges* proceeded smoothly and according to well publicized rules. In the realm of judicial procedure, the council refined previous practices and established new ones in order to improve its efficiency and to smooth points of friction with the judges. These developments in the council's jurisprudence and procedures rested firmly on a solid foundation of carefully prepared and comprehensive *règlements,* the provisions of which often responded directly to the judges' complaints in the era of the Fronde. The entire enterprise was punctuated by a lively, informative, and frequently cordial correspondence between the chancellors and the law courts, a correspondence that provided the parlements with an avenue of recourse for the redress of grievances and enabled both sides to fulfill their legitimate functions in the daily administration of justice with a minimum of antagonism and mutual mistrust. Nor were efforts to reduce tensions with the parlements confined to the Conseil Privé. The *arrêts* issued by other council bodies reflected the same interest in infusing royal policy toward the parlements with a renewed respect for the judges' dignity and traditional judicial authority. *Cassations* and *évocations* issued by *arrêts en commandement* and *arrêts simples* "en finance" were few in number and awarded with a high degree of discretion.

These examples of cooperation and good will at the very heart of the central administration stand in sharp contrast to the traditional picture we have of the parlements' relations with the councils after 1661. Writing in 1947 (and reiterating his views in 1980), Mousnier reviewed the opposition of the parlements to the royal councils in the era of the Fronde and concluded: "But this was in vain. All these practices continued and gradually increased. *Evocations générales* and *de propre mouvement,* the sovereign judgment of individual cases in first and last resort, the suspension and *cassation* of [parlementary] sentences of all kinds, especially those concerning the observation of edicts and ordinances, multiplied."[2] Such a view, which is unsupported by the evidence, did not result simply from a failure to consult in a systematic way conciliar *arrêts* issued during Louis XIV's personal rule. It was also the logical consequence of two errors in interpretation that together continue to impede efforts to arrive at a balanced and nuanced assessment of the impact of royal absolutism on the judicial authority of the parlements. The first is the assumption, tacitly understood if not always explicitly expressed, that the crown's substantial attempts to curtail the political activities of the parlements must have been matched

---

[2] Mousnier, "Le Conseil du roi," 66; idem, *Les Institutions de la France,* 2: bk. 8, chaps. 2–4. But Mousnier is correct in his general view that the crown won a significant victory over the parlements during the Fronde, a point to which I shall return below.

by an equally aggressive policy on the part of the councils to make further inroads into the judges' judicial business. The second is the belief that the king's forceful assertion of conciliar supremacy over the sovereign courts in 1661 provided just such an opportunity for the councils to expand their review of parlementary judgments and to interfere with the caseloads of the parlements on a large scale. There were in fact sound reasons, both practical and theoretical, why such an approach had little appeal for the government of Louis XIV.

On the practical level, the king and his highest officials were sufficiently intelligent and politically astute to recognize not only that the parlements exercised useful, legitimate and important functions in the daily administration of the realm, but that it made little sense to antagonize them, especially in an age that witnessed a seemingly endless succession of pressing problems. From the vantage point of the parlements, the opening decades of Louis XIV's personal rule were marked by an ambitious program of judicial reform (the procedural codes of April 1667 and August 1670 being only the most notable examples) and by a declining political role for the high judiciary. While the later years of the reign remain largely *terra incognita* as regards the history of the parlements and other sovereign courts, it is likely that the judges experienced a number of serious difficulties, including a reduction of their official income and office prices, a decrease in the volume of litigation coming before them, and a host of financial expedients aimed at increasing their contribution to the war effort. In either period, an erosion of the parlements' judicial authority was not in the best interests of the crown. The enforcement of the king's reform legislation would have been inconceivable without the support of his highest judges, and continued conflict with the councils over judicial issues could easily have provided the parlements with a touchstone for a broader critique of royal policy, as had occurred in the years preceding the Fronde. There were thus both positive and negative incentives for the monarchy to respect rather than undermine the *parlementaires'* status as superior magistrates. Gambetta's famous dictum that "politics is the art of the possible" applies as much to the consolidation of royal absolutism in the seventeenth century as to the founding of the Third Republic in the nineteenth.

Renewed consideration for the parlements' judicial functions also accorded well with the king's conception of the state. In a revealing section of his memoirs, Louis reviewed each segment of society and its appropriate role in national life. The peasants supplied food, the artisans and merchants met material needs, the clergy taught morality and religion. "This is why," he continued, "far from slighting any of these conditions or favoring one at the expense of another, we ought . . . to bring to each . . . the perfection due to it."[3] Earlier in the memoirs, Louis elaborated this view as it applied to the parlements.

---

[3] *Mémoires de Louis XIV pour l'instruction du Dauphin,* ed. Charles Dreyss (2 vols.; Paris, 1860), 1: 250–251.

The elevation of the parlements . . . had been dangerous to the entire kingdom during my minority: it was necessary to humble them, less for the harm they had done than for what they might do in the future. As long as their authority seemed opposed to mine . . . , it produced some very bad effects in the state. . . . [It was necessary to reduce things] to their natural and legitimate order . . . , even if it had been necessary to take away from these bodies a part of what had been given to them in the past, just as the painter has no hesitation about softening what is most striking and most beautiful in his own work whenever he finds that it is bigger than it should be and clearly out of proportion with the rest of it.[4]

Such a view, which implied a reduction in the political influence of the parlements but not a repudiation of their judicial powers, also appears implicitly in the chancellors' correspondence with the judges and in the reform memoranda submitted by the councillors of state in 1665.

Important as these concessions to the parlements were, however, they were not a sign of royal weakness. There is perhaps irony in the fact that the quality of restraint that characterized the crown's relations with the judges was perfectly compatible with the resurgence of royal authority during Louis XIV's personal rule. For if the king tempered the discretionary power of his highest officials, he did so without relinquishing a single component of his sovereignty. While the councils certainly acted with moderation, their supremacy over the law courts after 1661 was assured. The Conseil Privé continued to adjudicate cases of *cassation, évocation de justice,* and *règlement de juges,* retaining complete freedom to determine its jurisprudence and judicial procedures. Other council bodies, especially the *conseils de gouvernement,* removed litigation from the parlements on important occasions and nullified parlementary judgments and administrative acts when these jeopardized the enforcement of crucial royal programs. One might even argue that Louis XIV as political artist painted the judges into a corner. The parlements had long called for reform within the councils, and by complying the king denied them a potentially explosive issue that they might have exploited in questioning other aspects of royal policy. In fact, the price the parlements paid for a successful settlement of their grievances with the councils was a high one: a reduction of their political influence and activities.

One must take care, then, not to exaggerate the extent to which the parlements had won a victory during the Fronde: the reappearance of the provincial intendants, the waning opposition of the sovereign courts to royal policies, and the monarchy's increased control over its own finances were only a few developments during Louis's reign that testify to the

---

[4] Ibid., 2: 443–444. Continued the king: "But I know, my son, and can sincerely assure you that I have neither aversion nor bitterness for my judicial officials. On the contrary, if age is venerable in men, it appears even more so to me in these ancient bodies." My translation of this and the previous passage differs only slightly from that provided by Sonnino in his edition of the *Mémoires,* 42–43, 155.

crown's success in overcoming judicial challenges to its policies.[5] If there was a retreat from the advanced positions of absolutism, it was an orderly and voluntary withdrawal rather than a rout spearheaded by the parlements. Nevertheless, the civil wars of mid-century had left an important legacy, one that ensured that the decline of the parlements, like the resurgence of royal authority itself, had significant limits. After 1661, there was a growing recognition in the highest circles of government that the monarchy's limited resources and bureaucratic apparatus should be directed toward controlling certain crucial sectors of the state's activities—war, financial policy, and a few areas of domestic administration. For the more "ordinary" aspects of governing the realm, the king's traditional officials should be left a free hand, unharassed by overzealous superior authorities. The spirit of innovation inherent in Louis XIV's absolutism was thus balanced by a conservative commitment to work through rather than to destroy traditional institutions.[6]

The history of the Conseil Privé permits yet another general observation about Louis XIV's reign. Scholars have traditionally divided the reign into two periods. The first, extending from 1661 until the late 1670s or 1680s, witnessed a talented generation of ministers promoting a broad range of reforms in many areas of national life. Thereafter, the personal abilities of Louis's ministers declined and reform foundered on the rocks of economic recession, military defeat, and the financial policies of expediency associated with an era of prolonged warfare.[7] One should not too hastily discard this interpretive device—it remains useful for assessing a number of important developments during Louis's reign. But it is equally true that not all aspects of the king's administration are clarified by punctuating the reign with turning points, watersheds, and clashes between constructive and destruc-

---

[5] Richard Bonney has been particularly critical of Moote's suggestion that *parlementaires* had salvaged a "victory-in-defeat" during the Fronde. See especially: *Political Change in France,* 444–446; "The French Civil War, 1649–53," *European Studies Review* 8 (1978): 71–100; and most recently, "La Fronde des officiers: Mouvement réformiste ou rébellion corporatiste?," *XVIIe Siècle* no. 145 (1984): 323–340. Like restrictions on the right of judicial remonstrance in 1667 and 1673, the waning of *lit de justice* assemblies at the Parlement of Paris provides yet another example of Louis XIV's intention to limit the judges' participation in affairs of state. For details, see Hanley, *The* Lit de Justice *of the Kings of France,* 321–328.

[6] In other contexts, several recent studies offer perceptive comments about the conservative aspects of Louis XIV's reign, whether in the king's own thinking or in the nature of his policies: Beik, *Absolutism and Society in Seventeenth-Century France,* 31, 279–281, 303, 333–334; Bonney, *Political Change in France,* 448–451; Dessert, *Argent, pouvoir et société au grand siècle,* chaps. 14–15; Lossky, "The Absolutism of Louis XIV," 11–12; Parker, *The Making of French Absolutism,* 136–145; and J. Russell Major, *Representative Government in Early Modern France* (New Haven, 1980), 634–636, 663–672.

[7] Notes a recent historian of absolutism, for example: "[By 1682] there were no new reforms in the offing, no new commercial foundations, no major changes even in the army, and barely a new idea to be heard. . . . the magic had gone." Parker, *The Making of French Absolutism,* 144. For literature on the historiographical debate concerning the division of Louis's reign into two periods as well as insightful comments about this debate, see Schaeper, *The French Council of Commerce,* chap. 1.

tive forces. Within the Conseil Privé, reform was gradual and steady, uninterrupted by the vicissitudes that undermined so many other royal efforts to improve the quality and efficiency of the principal services of the state. And the numerous references to the activity of Chancellor Pontchartrain in this study should caution against too easily portraying the king's later ministers as mediocre or incompetent. Political genius in seventeenth-century France did not consist solely of promoting ambitious reforms; it also entailed the ability, in difficult circumstances, to manage effectively and with a deft touch potentially recalcitrant institutions.[8]

Of course, the honeymoon was not destined to survive long after the Sun King's death in 1715. In fact, the reign of Louis XIV marked a hiatus between two periods of intense conflict between the councils and the parlements. A unique set of circumstances had facilitated an accommodation between these institutions: on the one hand, a central administration that was sufficiently self-confident about its authority to offer concessions to the judges and to resolve a number of grievances in their favor; on the other hand, a political quiescence on the part of the judges that enabled a compromise to take shape. In the eighteenth century, as the parlements renewed their vocal criticism of royal policies and attempted to expand their political role, the councils once again relied upon *évocations, cassations,* and *règlements de juges* to circumvent this opposition. The activities of the Conseil Privé, like those of the other council bodies, again became the subject of a spirited controversy with broad constitutional implications.[9] But the renewal of conflict should not obscure the progress this council had made since the mid-seventeenth century in ameliorating the conditions of its work and in refining its jurisprudence. "The life of the Conseil Privé during the reign of Louis XV," according to Antoine, "proceeded without caprice or arbitrariness. It functioned in an orderly fashion and worked with efficacy, conscientiousness, seriousness, and assiduity: conditions unlikely to attract much attention to this council."[10] The administrators who

---

[8] John Rule has long argued for a rehabilitation of Louis XIV's later ministers, for example in "Royal Ministers and Government Reform During the Last Decades of Louis XIV's Reign," in Claude C. Sturgill, ed., *The Consortium on Revolutionary Europe, 1750–1850: Proceedings, 1973* (Gainesville, 1975), 1–35. Historians should heed this reasonable call for revision. Two who have done so recently are Schaeper, *The French Council of Commerce,* and Patrice Berger, "Pontchartrain and the Grain Trade During the Famine of 1693," *Journal of Modern History,* Supplement 48 (1976): 37–86.

[9] For an introduction to this controversy, see: Antoine, *Le Conseil du roi sous le règne de Louis XV,* 411–423, 571–597; Bailey Stone, *The Parlement of Paris, 1774–1789* (Chapel Hill, 1981), 54–55, 71–74; and, for a general idea of the issues at stake in a published primary source, Jules Flammermont, ed., *Les Remonstrances du Parlement de Paris au XVIIIe siècle* (3 vols.; Paris, 1888–1898), 2: 714–808 (June 1767).

[10] Antoine, *Le Conseil du roi sous le règne de Louis XV,* 145. Concluding a rapid survey of Louis XIV's Conseil Privé (pp. 63–67), Antoine also anticipated some of the conclusions of this study: "Given the current state of our knowledge, the history [of Louis XIV's Conseil Privé] appears to be a slow and hesitant march accomplished by this council to rid itself gradually of annoying habits established in troubled times, to improve its procedure, and to develop more clearly certain juridical concepts, notably *cassation.*"

drafted the famous *règlement* of June 1738, whose provisions guided the conduct of the Conseil Privé for the remainder of the *ancien régime* and influenced French legal practice well into the twentieth century, especially on the matter of *cassation*, drew heavily on the practices and official regulations of Louis XIV's Conseil Privé.[11] The reign of Louis XIV thus made a positive contribution to the administration of justice in France and largely fulfilled the hope expressed in 1665 by Councillor of State Barillon de Morangis that reform within the king's councils would provide the courts of the realm with "a model, an example, and a law."

---

[11] For the *règlement* of 1738, see above chap. III, n. 10. For remarks about its legacy in French law, see the studies by Chénon and by Martinage-Baranger cited above in chap. IV, n. 8. For a full appreciation of how important developments at Louis XIV's Conseil Privé— both procedural (refinements in the system of *bureaux*, the participation of three *avocats aux conseils* in cases of *cassation*, the imposition of fines, and so on) and jurisprudential (such as the limited number of grounds for *cassation*)—survived into the eighteenth century, see Antoine, *Le Conseil du roi sous le règne de Louis XV*, bk. 1, chap. 1; bk. 2, chap. 1; and bk. 3, chap. 1.

BIBLIOGRAPHY

A. Archival Sources

The reader is referred to the footnotes for descriptions and full citations of manuscripts from central and regional repositories: in Paris, the Archives du Ministère des Affaires Etrangères, the Archives du Ministère de la Guerre, the Archives Nationales, the Bibliothèque de l'Institut de France, the Bibliothèque Nationale, and the Bibliothèque du Sénat; in the provinces, the Archives Municipales de Bordeaux, the Bibliothèque Méjanes (Aix-en-Provence), the Bibliothèque Municipale de Dijon, and the Archives Départementales of Bouches-du-Rhône (annexe: Aix-en-Provence), Ille-et-Vilaine (Rennes), and Isère (Grenoble); in London, the British Library.

B. Published Primary Sources

Almanach Royal. 1699, 1705, 1712.

Boislisle, Arthur Michel de, ed. *Correspondance des contrôleurs généraux des finances avec les intendants des provinces.* 3 vols. Paris, 1874–1897.

Boislisle, Jean de, ed. *Mémoriaux du conseil de 1661.* 3 vols. Paris, 1905–1907.

Catalogue général des livres imprimés de la Bibliothèque Nationale: Actes Royaux. 7 vols. Paris, 1910–1960.

Colbert, Jean-Baptiste. *Lettres, instructions et mémoires.* Edited by Pierre Clément. 7 vols. Paris, 1861–1882.

Dangeau, Philippe de Courcillon, marquis de. *Journal.* Edited by E. Soulié and L. Dussieux. 19 vols. Paris, 1854–1860.

Dumont, François, ed. *Inventaire des arrêts du conseil privé (règnes de Henri III et de Henri IV).* 2 vols. Paris, 1969–1971.

Etat de la France. 1656, 1658.

Flammermont, Jules, ed. *Les Remonstrances du Parlement de Paris au XVIIIe siècle.* 3 vols. Paris, 1888–1898.

Guillard, René. *Histoire du conseil du roy depuis le commencement de la monarchie jusqu'à la fin du règne de Louis le grand.* Paris, 1718.

Isambert, François-André, et al., eds. *Recueil général des anciennes lois françaises depuis l'an 400 jusqu'à la révolution de 1789.* 29 vols. Paris, 1822–1833.

Jousse, Daniel, ed. *Recueil chronologique des ordonnances, édits et arrêts de règlement cités dans les nouveaux commentaires sur les ordonnances des mois d'avril 1667, août 1669, août 1670, et mars 1673.* 3 vols. Paris, 1757.

Le Pesant, Michel, ed. *Arrêts du conseil du roi, règne de Louis XIV, inventaire analytique des arrêts en commandement, tome I (20 mai 1643–8 mars 1661).* Paris, 1976.

Louis XIV. *Mémoires for the Instruction of the Dauphin.* Edited by Paul Sonnino. New York, 1970.

Louis XIV. *Mémoires pour l'instruction du Dauphin.* Edited by Charles Dreyss. 2 vols. Paris, 1860.

Masson, Frédéric, ed. *Journal inédit de Jean-Baptiste Colbert, marquis de Torcy, ministre et secrétaire d'état des affaires étrangères pendant les années 1709, 1710 et 1711.* Paris, 1903.

Mousnier, Roland, ed. "Les Règlements du conseil du roi sous Louis XIII." *Annuaire-Bulletin de la Société de l'Histoire de France* (1946–1947): 93–211.

Ormesson, Olivier Lefèvre d'. *Journal.* Edited by Adolphe Chéruel. 2 vols. Paris, 1860–1861.

Rodier, Marc-Antoine, ed. *Recueil des édits, déclarations, arrêts du conseil et du Parlement de Toulouse.* 2 vols. Toulouse, 1756.

Valois, Noël, ed. *Inventaire des arrêts du conseil d'état (règne de Henri IV)*. 2 vols. Paris, 1886–1893.

C. Secondary Sources

André, Louis. *Michel Le Tellier et Louvois*. Paris, 1943.
Antoine, Michel. *Le Conseil du roi sous le règne de Louis XV*. Genève, 1970.
——. *Le Conseil royal des finances au XVIIIe siècle et le registre E 3659 des Archives Nationales.* Genève, 1973.
——. *Le Fonds du conseil d'état du roi aux Archives Nationales*. Paris, 1955.
——. "Le Mémoire de Gilbert de Voisins sur la cassation: Un Episode des querelles entre Louis XV et les parlements (1767)." *Revue Historique de Droit Français et Etranger* 36 (1958): 1–33.
Baxter, Douglas Clark. "Premier Commis in the War Department in the Latter Part of the Reign of Louis XIV." *Proceedings of the Annual Meeting of the Western Society for French History* 8 (1980): 81–89.
Beik, William. *Absolutism and Society in Seventeenth-Century France: State Power and Provincial Aristocracy in Languedoc*. Cambridge, 1985.
Berger, Patrice. "French Administration in the Famine of 1693." *European Studies Review* 8 (1978): 101–127.
——. "Pontchartrain and the Grain Trade During the Famine of 1693." *Journal of Modern History*, Supplement 48 (1976): 37–86.
Boislisle, Arthur Michel de. *Les Conseils du roi sous Louis XIV*. Paris, 1884.
Bonney, Richard. "The French Civil War, 1649–53." *European Studies Review* 8 (1978): 71–100.
——. "La Fronde des officiers: Mouvement réformiste ou rébellion corporatiste?" *XVIIe Siècle* no. 145 (1984): 323–340.
——. *The King's Debts: Finance and Politics in France, 1598–1661*. Oxford, 1981.
——. *Political Change in France Under Richelieu and Mazarin, 1624–1661*. Oxford, 1978.
Bornier, Philippe. *Conférences des ordonnances de Louis XIV*. 2 vols. Paris, 1729.
Bordes, Maurice. *L'Administration provinciale et municipale en France au XVIIIe siècle*. Paris, 1972.
Bos, Emile. *Les Avocats aux conseils du roi: Etude sur l'ancien régime judiciaire de la France*. Paris, 1881.
Boscheron Des Portes, C.-B.-F. *Histoire du Parlement de Bordeaux depuis sa création jusqu'à sa chute (1451–1790)*. 2 vols. Bordeaux, 1877.
Briggs, Robin. *Early Modern France, 1560–1715*. Oxford, 1977.
Chénon, Emile. *Origines, conditions et effets de la cassation*. Paris, 1882.
Cole, Charles W. *French Mercantilism, 1683–1700*. New York, 1943.
Coudy, Julien. *Les Moyens d'action de l'ordre du clergé au conseil du roi (1561–1715)*. Paris, 1955.
Coveney, P. J., ed. *France in Crisis, 1620–1675*. London, 1977.
Dent, Cynthia A. "The Council of State and the Clergy During the Reign of Louis XIV: An Aspect of the Growth of Royal Absolutism." *Journal of Ecclesiastical History* 24 (1973): 245–266.
Dessert, Daniel. *Argent, pouvoir et société au grand siècle*. Paris, 1984.
Dubédat, Jean-Baptiste. *Histoire du Parlement de Toulouse*. 2 vols. Paris, 1885.
Esmein, Adhémar. *Histoire de la procédure criminelle en France*. Paris, 1882.
Esmonin, Edmond. *Etudes sur la France des XVIIe et XVIIIe siècles*. Paris, 1964.
Floquet, Amable. *Histoire du Parlement de Normandie*. 7 vols. Rouen, 1840–1842.
Frostin, Charles. "Le Chancelier de France Louis de Pontchartrain, 'ses' premiers présidents, et la discipline des cours souveraines (1699–1714)." *Cahiers d'Histoire* 27 (1982): 9–34.
Glasson, Ernest-Désiré. *Le Parlement de Paris, son rôle politique depuis le règne de Charles VII jusqu'à la Révolution*. 2 vols. Paris, 1901.
Goubert, Pierre. *Louis XIV and Twenty Million Frenchmen*. Translated by Anne Carter. New York, 1966.
Gresset, Maurice. *Gens de justice à Besançon, de la conquête par Louis XIV à la Révolution française, 1674–1789*. 2 vols. Paris, 1978.
Hamscher, Albert N. "Ouvrages sur la Fronde parus en anglais depuis 1970." *XVIIe Siècle* no. 145 (1984): 380–383.
——. *The Parlement of Paris After the Fronde, 1653–1673*. Pittsburgh, 1976.

Hanley, Sarah. *The* Lit de Justice *of the Kings of France: Constitutional Ideology in Legend, Ritual, and Discourse.* Princeton, 1983.

Hurt, John J. "Forced Loans and the Wealth of the Magistrates of the Parlement of Brittany Under Louis XIV." Paper presented at the annual meeting of the American Historical Association, New York, December 1979.

———. "Les Offices au Parlement de Bretagne sous le règne de Louis XIV: Aspects financiers." *Revue d'Histoire Moderne et Contemporaine* 23 (1976): 3–31.

———. The Parlement of Brittany and the Crown, 1665–1675." *French Historical Studies* 4 (1966): 411–433.

———. "La Politique du Parlement de Bretagne (1661–1675)." *Annales de Bretagne* 81 (1974): 105–130.

Jouhaud, Christian. "Le Conseil du roi, Bordeaux et les Bordelais (1579–1610, 1630–1680)." *Annales du Midi* 93 (1981): 377–396.

Jousse, Daniel. *Commentaire sur l'ordonnance civile du mois d'avril 1667.* Paris, 1757.

Kaiser, C. R. E. "The Masters of Requests: An Extraordinary Judicial Company in an Age of Centralization (1589–1648)." Unpublished Ph.D. diss., University of London, 1977.

Kaiser, Colin. "The Deflation in the Volume of Litigation at Paris in the Eighteenth Century and the Waning of the Old Judicial Order." *European Studies Review* 10 (1980): 309–336.

Kan, Josef van. *Les Efforts de codification en France: Etude historique et psychologique.* Paris, 1929.

Kettering, Sharon. "The Causes of the Judicial Frondes." *Canadian Journal of History* 17 (1982): 275–306.

———. *Judicial Politics and Urban Revolt in Seventeenth-Century France: The Parlement of Aix, 1629–1659.* Princeton, 1978.

———. "A Provincial Parlement During the Fronde: The Reform Proposals of the Aix Magistrates." *European Studies Review* 11 (1981): 151–169.

Kleinman, Ruth. "Changing Interpretations of the Edict of Nantes: The Administrative Aspect, 1643–1661." *French Historical Studies* 10 (1978): 541–571.

Lacuisine, E.-F. de. *Le Parlement de Bourgogne depuis son origine jusqu'à sa chute.* 3 vols. Dijon, 1864.

Logié, Paul. *La Fronde en Normandie.* 3 vols. Amiens, 1951–1952.

Lossky, Andrew. "The Absolutism of Louis XIV: Reality or Myth?" *Canadian Journal of History* 19 (1984): 1–15.

Luçay, Hélion de. *Les Origines du pouvoir ministériel en France: Les Secrétaires d'état depuis leur institution jusqu'à la mort de Louis XV.* Paris, 1881.

Major, J. Russell. *Representative Government in Early Modern France.* New Haven, 1980.

Mandrou, Robert. *La France aux XVIIe et XVIIIe siècles.* Paris, 1970.

Martinage-Baranger, R. "Les Idées sur la cassation au XVIIIe siècle." *Revue Historique de Droit Français et Etranger* 47 (1969): 244–290.

McCollim, Gary Bruce. "Council Versus Minister: The Controller General of Finances, 1661–1715." *Proceedings of the Annual Meeting of the Western Society for French History* 6 (1978): 67–75.

———. "The Formation of Fiscal Policy in the Reign of Louis XIV: The Example of Nicolas Desmaretz, Controller General of Finances (1708–1715)." Unpublished Ph.D. diss., Ohio State University, 1979.

Michel, Emmanuel. *Histoire du Parlement de Metz.* Paris, 1845.

Monnier, Francis. *Guillaume de Lamoignon et Colbert: Essai sur la législation française au XVIIe siècle.* Paris, 1862.

Moote, A. Lloyd. *The Revolt of the Judges: The Parlement of Paris and the Fronde, 1643–1652.* Princeton, 1971.

Mousnier, Roland. "Le Conseil du roi de la mort de Henri IV au gouvernement personnel de Louis XIV." *Etudes d'Histoire Moderne et Contemporaine* 1 (1947): 29–67.

———. *Les Institutions de la France sous la monarchie absolue.* 2 vols. Paris, 1974–1980.

———. *La Plume, la faucille et le marteau.* Paris, 1970.

Mousnier, Roland, et al. *Le Conseil du roi de Louis XII à la Révolution.* Paris, 1970.

Pagès, Georges. *Etudes sur l'histoire administrative et sociale de l'ancien régime.* Paris, 1938.

Parker, David. *The Making of French Absolutism.* London, 1983.

Paulhet, Jean-Claude. "Les Parlementaires toulousains à la fin du dix-septième siècle." *Annales du Midi* 76 (1964): 189–204.

Phytilis, Jacques. *Justice administrative et justice déléguée au XVIIIe siècle: L'Exemple des commissions extraordinaires de jugement à la suite du conseil*. Paris, 1977.

Plassard, Jean. *Des Ouvertures communes à cassation et à requête civile*. Paris, 1924.

Ranum, Orest. *Richelieu and the Councillors of Louis XIII: A Study of the Secretaries of State and Superintendents of Finance in the Ministry of Richelieu, 1635–1642*. Oxford, 1963.

Rodier, Marc-Antoine. *Questions sur l'ordonnance de Louis XIV du mois d'avril 1667*. Toulouse, 1777.

Rule, John C. "The Commis of the Department of Foreign Affairs Under the Administration of Colbert de Croissy and Colbert de Torcy, 1680–1715." *Proceedings of the Annual Meeting of the Western Society for French History* 8 (1980): 69–80.

——. "Royal Ministers and Government Reform During the Last Decades of Louis XIV's Reign." In *The Consortium on Revolutionary Europe, 1750–1850: Proceedings, 1973*, ed. Claude C. Sturgill, 1–35. Gainesville, 1975.

——, ed. *Louis XIV and the Craft of Kingship*. Columbus, 1969.

Sauvel, Tony. "Les Demandes de motifs adressées par le conseil du roi aux cours souveraines." *Revue Historique de Droit Français et Etranger* 35 (1957): 529–548.

——. "Histoire du jugement motivé." *Revue du Droit Public et de la Science Politique en France et à l'Etranger* 71 (1955): 5–53.

Schaeper, Thomas J. *The French Council of Commerce, 1700–1715*. Columbus, 1983.

Serpillon, François. *Code civile, ou commentaire sur l'ordonnance du mois d'avril 1667*. Paris, 1776.

——. *Code criminel, ou commentaire sur l'ordonnance de 1670*. 2 vols. Lyon, 1767.

Shennan, J. H. *The Parlement of Paris*. Ithaca, 1968.

Stone, Bailey. *The Parlement of Paris, 1774–1789*. Chapel Hill, 1981.

Temple, Nora. "The Control and Exploitation of French Towns During the Ancien Régime." *History* 51 (1966): 16–34.

INDEX

Absolutism, character of, 1–2, 150–52
Aguesseau, Henri d' (intendant), correspondence of, 26n
Aligre, Etienne d' (Chancellor of France), 26n, 88; as councillor of state, 29, 30, 44
Amendes. See Fines
Arrêt of 8 July 1661, 21
Arrêts of king's councils, in general: archival location of, 8n, 11n; format and structure of, 35n, 41, 41n, 73n, 84, 84n, 85n, 86n, 87n, 92n, 94, 102, 102n, 103n, 111n, 112n; and supremacy over parlementary sentences, 21–22, 63, 149
Arrêts contradictoires ("between parties"): of Conseil d'Etat et des Finances, 112n; of Conseil Privé, 34–36, 41–42, 44, 46–48, 50, 61, 63, 67n, 73–74, 80, 85–87, 89, 94, 95n, 97, 101, 103; of *conseils de gouvernement,* 143n
Arrêts d'instruction, 35, 86n, 112n
Arrêts de propre mouvement, 35n, 111n, 112n, 138, 142
Arrêts de renvoi, 18, 120n
Arrêts en commandement (of *conseils de gouvernement*), 7–8, 10, 12, 35n, 75n, 78n, 83n, 108–44 passim, 148; *Répertoire* of, described and utilized, 8n, 111n, 111–44 passim. See also *Conseils de gouvernement, arrêts of*
Arrêts simples (of Conseil Privé), 8, 34–36, 72–73, 83n, 84–87, 89–90, 96, 100–2, 111n, 138n, 142n. See also *Conseil Privé, arrêts of*
Arrêts simples "en finance" (of Conseil d'Etat et des Finances, Conseil royal des Finances, and Grande and Petite Directions), 10–11, 12, 35n, 108–13, 116, 118, 133n, 135, 138n, 142n, 144–46, 148. See also *Conseil d'Etat et des Finances, arrêts of*
Arrêts sur requête: of Conseil d'Etat et des Finances, 112n; of Conseil Privé, 34–36, 40–42, 44–57 passim, 61–63, 66–68, 73–74, 85–87, 92, 94–95, 100, 103, 104–6; of *conseils de gouvernement,* 111n
Arrêts sur requêtes respectives, 41n, 42n
Assembly of masters of requests, 81–87, 89, 94, 107, 142–43
Avocats aux conseils, 24, 30, 91–93, 94, 102, 107, 143, 153n
Avocats généraux of the parlements. *See* Talon, Denis

Barillon de Morangis, Antoine (councillor of state), 30, 31, 153
Boucherat, Louis (Chancellor of France), 26–28, 58, 76, 89, 102, 129; as councillor of state, 29n; correspondence of, 26n
Bouchu, Claude (intendant), 121n
Brûlart, Nicolas (first president, Parlement of Dijon), correspondence of, 26n
Bureaux of the councils: in general, 11n, 35n, 81, 109, 133n, 142, 144; of Conseil Privé, 23, 25, 81–87, 89, 92n, 94, 102, 107, 153n; "ministerial," 143

Capitouls of Toulouse, 121–22
Cassation: in general, 9, 11, 12, 14, 17, 19, 35n, 36, 69, 79, 110n, 111, 152, 153; and Conseil d'Etat et des Finances, Conseil royal des Finances, and Grande and Petite Directions, 111–13, 145–46; and *conseils de gouvernement,* 109, 111–12, 135–46; and Conseil Privé, 30, 34, 37–40, 42–68, 83, 85, 87, 89, 91–98, 99–102, 104–7, 108, 148; grounds (*ouvertures*) for, 37–40, 42, 47–48, 73, 105, 144, 148, 153n; and jurists, 39n; and rules for initiating, 24, 40–41, 91–92, 96n, 99–102; on "simple request of parties," 14, 30, 39, 65–67; and suspension of parlementary sentences, 14, 20, 30, 39, 103–7. *See also* Parlements, in general, and *cassations*
Chambres de l'édit, 42n, 126n, 127, 136n, 137n, 142n
Chancellor of France, 3, 7, 31, 110, 137n; in Conseil Privé, 8, 22n, 25–26, 81–87, 140; in other councils, 6, 111n, 112n; and correspondence with parlements, 26–28, 36, 46, 58–61, 76–79, 80, 95–98, 130, 148, 150. *See also* Aligre, Etienne d'; Boucherat, Louis; Le Tellier, Michel; Pontchartrain, Louis Phélypeaux de; Séguier, Pierre; Voisin, Daniel
Châtelet of Paris, 77, 126, 127, 130
Clergy of France, 51, 53–54, 106, 124–25, 139n
Clerks (*greffiers*) of Conseil Privé, 88–89
Colbert, Jean-Baptiste (controller general of finances), 98–99; as intendant of Mazarin, 17
Commissions extraordinaires of the councils, 9n, 11n, 81, 124, 131, 133–35, 145

158

www.ingramcontent.com/pod-product-compliance
Lightning Source LLC
Chambersburg PA
CBHW080926100426
42812CB00007B/2386